Stars at War

Michael Munn

Robson Books

First published in Great Britain in 1995 by Robson
Books Ltd, Bolsover House, 5–6 Clipstone Street,
London W1P 8LE

British Library Cataloguing in Publication Data
A catalogue record for this title is available from the British
Library

ISBN 0 86051 954 6

Typeset in Plantin by Columns Design and Production
Services Ltd, Reading
Printed in Great Britain by WBC Book Manufacturers Ltd.
Bridgend, Mid-Glamorgan

For Betty and Karl
– with gratitude and affection

Contents

Foreword

The first thing for me to point out is that this book might not have been written if it were not for John Huston who first suggested the idea to me. I first met him in 1972, and in a series of meetings and interviews, he told me about his own World War Two experiences as well as that of others from Hollywood such as Clark Gable, William Wyler and John Ford.

Then came a series of interviews from 1976 with Lee Marvin, during which he told me of his experiences in the Pacific – 'Huston was shooting only with a goddam camera; I was shooting with a goddam rifle' – and I found myself collecting first-hand war stories from many of the hundreds of film actors, writers, directors and other film artistes I've met and interviewed over the last quarter of a century.

So, to them all, I am indebted; to John and Lee, both gone to give God or someone a little hell; to David Niven, who talked candidly and with less humour than usual on the set of *A Man Called Intrepid*, a TV film which was based on Sir William Stephenson for whom Niven had performed some duties during the war, and which sparked off many memories; to John Mills who recalled the days of the war on a cold, foggy day on location for *Quatermass*; to Kenneth More who I interviewed three times between 1976 and 1980; to John Sturges who I met at the Dorchester one day in 1975; to Anthony Quayle who I first saw when he was making *Great Expectations* in 1975 and last saw on a reconstruction of ancient Pompeii at Pinewood Studios in 1983; to Rex Harrison who was filming *The Kingfisher* in Hunsworth in 1982; and to all the others, some still with us, some sadly gone; Richard Todd, Frankie Howerd, Tony Curtis, Kirk Douglas, Dame Anna Neagle, Kenneth Connor, Trevor Howard, Bryan Forbes, Sir Harry Secombe, Sam Kydd, Denholm Elliott, Burt Lancaster, Walter Matthau, Mel Brooks and James Stewart.

A big thanks to Winston G Ramsey, editor of *After the Battle* magazine, for allowing me to delve into his picture archive. His publication, going now for more than twenty years, was also a valuable source of research material.

Thanks to Trevor Harvey and Roger Burden for their assistance with the research. I couldn't have done it without them.

And a very special thanks to my father – and to his generation.

1

Storm Clouds Over Europe

'If Hitler told Hans to walk on water, he would have drowned in the attempt.'

Anthony Quayle

'Had Lilli Palmer not managed to get out of Germany and arrive in England, then as a Jew she would not have escaped the Holocaust, which is a dreadful thing to consider,' said Rex Harrison who was to become Lilli Palmer's first husband when, as a working actress in war-torn England, she was treated by a cautious and at times paranoid British government as an enemy alien.

Yet if she found being a German living in wartime England difficult, it would have been nothing as compared with what would have awaited her had she returned to her homeland before 1945, or in fact had never left in the first place. For she was one of the lucky ones; a Jew who escaped the Nazis before it was too late and who found a tenuous welcome by a foreign country.

It could have been such a different story, for Lilli (or Lillie) Peiser was born into an ever-changing Germany, in Posen, on 24 May 1914. Her father, Dr Alfred Peiser, was a vastly important and highly respected surgeon at a major hospital in Berlin. During the First World War he had served in the army as a surgeon, running a field hospital at Verdun, and was awarded the Iron Cross. He hoped Lilli would follow his footsteps into medicine. But she was inspired by her Austrian

1

mother, Rosa, who had been an actress but had retired from the stage to devote herself to her husband and three daughters.

Lilli told her parents, 'I want to be an actress, like mama.'

The Peisers were a patriotic family, and a well-to-do one. During the difficult post-war years when Germany's inflation spiralled out of control, they fared better than most because of Dr Peiser's superior position and income.

He and Rosa were able to provide a warm, loving middle-class home life for the girls, all bound together in their strong Jewish faith. They were privileged at a time when more than six million Germans were out of work. The economy was in chaos, and the inflation that had been growing since the end of the Great War was out of control by 1923 when a single loaf of bread cost 201,000 million marks in Berlin.

Many of the hopelessly unemployed were attracted by the German Workers' Party which, under the leadership of Adolf Hitler, had become known as the National Socialist German Workers' Party – or the Nazi party.

Hitler's book, *Mein Kampf*, written in prison after he had tried to seize power in Munich in 1923, was a mixture of extreme German nationalism and abject anti-Semitism. Dr Peiser knew that his family would never be safe if the Nazis ever governed. So he was much relieved when, in the Reichstag elections of 1928, the Nazis won only twelve seats.

In America, the Wall Street Crash of 1929 sent the United States into a recession which reverberated throughout the world. For Germany's still fragile economy it was a disastrous blow. Unemployment, previously at around 1.3 million, suddenly shot to more than 6 million. The country's chancellor, Heinrich Brüning, faced growing opposition from Hitler who had consolidated his hold on the Nazi party and was touring the country, making impassioned speeches, stressing that the country's problems were due to the evil communists, socialists and Jews.

The party's popularity grew, and in the Reichstag elections of 1930, the Nazis gained 107 seats. Dr Peiser saw the writing on the wall. On 30 October, Jewish shops were attacked, windows smashed, and Jews everywhere were taunted.

When she was sixteen, Lilli, remaining adamant that she wanted only to be an actress, was permitted to take drama lessons. For the next two years she worked twice as hard, attending her normal school by day, and drama school by night.

She graduated in 1932 and was rewarded with a twelve-month contract with the Darmstadt State Theatre, one of the finest repertory companies in the whole of Germany, and she made her stage début in Berlin the same year. She was also in love for the first time, with Rolf Gerard, a medical student six years her senior.

Life should have been looking upbeat for the aspiring eighteen-year-old actress, but the family did not escape the surge of hatred welled up against the Jews of Germany. Although Hitler lost the 1932 presidential elections to eighty-five-year-old war hero Field Marshal Paul von Hindenburg, the Nazis won 230 seats in a Reichstag election of that year, making them the largest party in Germany and prompting the German president to invite Hitler to become his vice-president.

Hitler turned Hindenburg down; he wanted only the job of chancellor. Hindenburg rethought the matter and offered Hitler the chancellorship only to find Hitler wanted additional powers. Hindenburg refused his demands and chose General Kurt von Schleicher to be his new chancellor.

Alfred Peiser knew that it was only a matter of time before Hitler took control of the country. He and Rosa sent their eldest daughter, Irene, to Paris and, a month later, they decided to send Lilli as well, keeping Hilde, the youngest, at home.

Lilli protested. 'But my career! I have only just begun it.'

'You can still be an actress in Paris,' her mother told her.

'Terrible times are coming,' said her father, 'and you must be safe.'

'But what about you, and mother, and Hilde?'

'I have my work to do,' Alfred replied. 'We are safe for now. We will have to wait and see what happens.'

Lilli was put on a train to Paris to join Irene and was followed by Rolf; he and Lilli moved into an apartment together.

She immediately set about trying to find work as an actress. She decided to call herself Lilli Palmer because the French were unable to pronounce her surname. Then she and Irene decided to form a double-act as Les Soeurs Viennoises, which made them sound more Austrian than German; they began to get work in nightclubs.

Across the sea in Britain, few citizens felt particularly threatened by Nazism in 1933. To Anthony Quayle, a young English actor, Germany seemed to be 'a country regaining its self respect'.

The German chancellor resigned in January 1933, and Hindenburg had once more asked Hitler to take the position. This time he accepted.

In March, Quayle decided he wanted to visit Germany. 'I didn't know any Germans and had certainly never met a Nazi,' he told me, 'and when I did meet one he seemed a terribly nice young man.' He went on:

> His name was Hans Beckhoff and he worked at a German travel agency in Lower Regent Street [in London]. I went there after I'd just finished working at the Old Vic because I thought I'd like to see Germany. Hans seemed very courteous and, as canoeing was a great love of mine, I was interested to learn he had made the first crossing of the English Channel by canoe. I wanted to go canoeing down the Rhine but he said that it would be too cold in April for that and suggested I make for Cologne, and he gave me a list of country hostels.
>
> Then he invited me to his home so he could show off his canoeing trophies, and when I got to his flat which was in Notting Hill, the first thing I saw was a huge Swastika surrounded by photos of Hans and his canoeing partner. Above the Swastika was a telegram from Adolf Hitler congratulating Hans. He asked me what I thought of the telegram and all I could say was, 'Well, it's very nice.'
>
> He suddenly changed and became quite cold towards

me. He said, '*Nice?* Do you realize that telegram is from *Adolf Hitler?* Do you understand who he is? He is now the chancellor of the Third Reich.'

This, until now, very friendly, very warm young German held his chancellor in some kind of religious awe, and I became very uncomfortable. I'm sure if Hitler had told Hans to walk on water, he would have drowned in the attempt. All I wanted to do was get out of there, so I said, 'Well good luck to him and thank you for your help,' and I left.

Anthony Quayle was to meet Hans Beckhoff some years later. But Beckhoff was just one of millions to hold Hitler in what Quayle described as almost 'religious awe'. Under Hitler's chancellorship, Germany went through a series of reforms; trade unions were disbanded in May 1933, the Social Democrats were banned in June, and finally all other political parties were dissolved. On 14 July Hitler announced that the Nazi party was Germany's one and only political party.

It was the very thing Dr Peiser, and millions of Jews, had dreaded. Stress and worry led to a decline in Dr Peiser's health, and on 31 January 1934, he suffered a fatal heart attack. Lilli and Irene returned to Berlin for the funeral, and witnessed for themselves the growing hatred for Jews among ordinary Germans who were being urged to boycott Jewish shops and businesses. Jews were ejected from the civil service. The country had become dangerous for all Jews, and Lilli and Irene hastily returned to Paris.

Lilli had been seen by British-based, Hungarian-born film producer Alexander Korda (possibly when she appeared in an operetta at the Moulin Rouge). At his invitation, she crossed the Channel to England but unfortunately she was refused a work permit. She managed to make a 'quota quickie' for Warner Brothers, *Crime Unlimited*, and Gaumont British were impressed enough to offer her a contract. But she was still refused a labour permit and had to return to France.

President Hindenburg died in August 1934. Hitler announced that there would be no election for a new president; he would combine the offices of chancellor and president. He made the whole of the army swear allegiance to him as their Führer. The SS, now the government's official law enforcers, brought a reign of terror to all 'undesirables'. The Hitler Youth stirred up even greater anti-Semitism. The Nuremberg Laws of 1935 stripped all Jews of German citizenship, and they were forbidden to marry non-Jews so that the 'racial purity of the state' would be preserved.

Meanwhile Lilli Palmer, thinking she would be unable to return to Britain, received a sudden reprieve in 1934 when Gaumont British succeeded in securing her a work permit, renewable every three months. She went back to England and appeared with Will Hay in *Good Morning Boys*, and was directed by Alfred Hitchcock in *Secret Agent*. Her film career had begun well.

Conrad Veidt was another German actor who fled his country to escape the Nazis. He had been starring in films since 1917 and had first gone to Hollywood in 1927 to play Louis XI in *The Beloved Rogue*. Two years later he returned to Germany but in 1933 he took his Jewish wife to Britain to flee the Nazis and signed a contract with Gaumont British.

The following year he made a visit to Germany and was arrested. The German authorities claimed he was too ill to travel and were taking care of him, but his arrest caused an international incident. Gaumont British sent their own doctor over to Germany to examine him and ensure his release and return to Britain.

Billy Wilder also managed to escape the rise of Nazism. Born in Vienna to Jewish parents, he had begun writing screenplays for German films in 1929, collaborating with Robert Siodmak, the Jewish son of a Leipzig banker. Both Wilder and Siodmak fled Germany in 1933 to Paris. Siodmak remained there until 1939, while Wilder went on to America to begin his successful career as a Hollywood director. Many of his family he had to leave behind would later die in concentration camps.

Great talent in any field of the arts was no guarantee of

immunity from anti-Semitism in Germany. Composer Franz Waxman (who later won Oscars for his scores to *Sunset Boulevard* and *A Place in the Sun*) had been born in Königshutte in Germany, now Chorzow, Poland, and enrolled at the Berlin Music Conservatory. Aged only twenty-four, he began scoring German films in 1930, including *The Blue Angel*, but in 1934 he was beaten up in a Berlin street for being a Jew. He went to Paris and, in 1935, emigrated to America where he went on to become one of Hollywood's classic film composers.

In 1940 Robert Siodmak finally arrived on America's west coast where a considerable community of German actors, writers, directors and other film artistes had emerged. Among them was Marlene Dietrich, who had been born Maria Magdalene Dietrich in Berlin in December 1901. Her father, Louis Erich Otto Dietrich, was an officer in the Royal Prussian Police but died while Marlene was still a child. Her stepfather, Edouard von Losch, a cavalry lieutenant, was killed on the Russian front towards the close of the First World War.

Marlene Dietrich was an aspiring actress by 1921 and two years later she began playing small roles in German films. In 1924 she married a Czech production assistant, Rudolf Sieber; although the marriage fell apart, they never divorced and Dietrich remained Sieber's legal wife until his death in 1975.

After causing a sensation as Lola Lola in *The Blue Angel* in 1930, she went to Hollywood and signed with Paramount. She joined what became known as the 'Hollywood Committee' which was organized by Billy Wilder and German film director, Ernst Lubitsch, who had gone to America in 1921. The committee raised and sent sums of money to their contact in Switzerland, a man called Engel, for the purpose of liberating prisoners from the German concentration camps which were being set up. The first camps in 1933 were at Oranienburg, north of Berlin, and at Dachau near Munich.

Anyone who did not conform to the ideals of Nazi society – Jews, Jehovah Witnesses, communists, homosexuals, Catholic priests, pacifists – were sent to these camps. During the early days it was possible to help prisoners escape into Switzerland with the aid of secret organizations which Engel paid with the funds sent by the Hollywood Committee. These prisoners were brought to Los Angeles where members of the Hollywood Committee helped them to learn English and find jobs.

The American studios received their information about the developments in Germany direct from their European offices. Paul Kohner, the head of European production for Universal Studios, reported first-hand to studio head Carl Laemmle, himself a German Jew, that things were quickly changing in Berlin and that Hitler was spending much of his time at Berchtesgaden.

Carl Laemmle's nephew, director William Wyler, had been born in Mulhouse in Alsace in France, then annexed to Germany, in 1902. Early in 1935 he decided to take his new bride, actress Margaret Sullavan, on a belated honeymoon (they were married in November 1934) to Europe. From Paris they went skiing in Switzerland, on to Vienna and crossed into Germany to check into the Vier Jahreszeiten Hotel in Munich.

Wyler went walking while Margaret had her hair set, and ended up at the Odeonsplatz where he saw a monument that commemorated an early attempt on Hitler's life. A huge Swastika flew and two stormtroopers stood guard. Everyone who passed gave the Nazi salute. Wyler pushed his hands into his pockets as he read the plaque and knew he was being watched closely by the guards who noticed his failure to salute.

That evening, he and Margaret were having dinner in the hotel restaurant when a waiter announced that someone wanted to talk with him but had refused to come in. Wyler told the waiter he would not leave his dinner, and some minutes later a man sheepishly approached them. Wyler immediately saw that their surprise guest was wearing a Star of David on his coat. He was Walter Laemmle, one of Wyler's distant relatives; he was scared to death at being seen in the chic Vier Jahreszeiten.

Wyler had virtually to push him into a chair and make him order some food. Then he made Walter dance with Margaret. He saw how Laemmle was living in constant fear and tried to show him how to behave unafraid, but as Wyler noted, 'he was terrified the whole time'. Walter Laemmle managed to leave Germany a few months later and became a prominent Los Angeles antique dealer.

Another small group in Hollywood that emerged around that time was the Anti-Nazi League which included writers Lillian Hellman and Dorothy Parker, and actor Frederic March. They made speeches denouncing Nazism, but most Americans, including President Roosevelt, considered them as something of a lunatic fringe.

Douglas Fairbanks Junior was also concerned about the rise of Hitler. He spent much time in England where he was on first name terms with the younger members of the Royal Family. During the 1920s his famous father had formed a close friendship with the Mountbattens. Fairbanks Jr's standing in high society brought him into contact with Winston Churchill in 1936, and with Cordell Hull, the American Secretary of State.

His world travels made him aware of international affairs, and when he met with Austrian Chancellor Schuschnigg who confided his concerns over Hitler's intent to annex Austria, Fairbanks Jr filed a long report with the American State Department. He also met with Count Ciano, Mussolini's son-in-law, and German Ambassador Ribbentrop in London.

Hitler had vowed to his people that he would re-establish German supremacy in Europe and was creating an air force in defiance of the Versailles Treaty by which the Allied victors of the Great War had denied Germany the right to rearm itself. The more Fairbanks heard about the Axis, the more alarmed he became and continued to send reports of his findings. Convinced that America and Britain needed jointly to confront the growing threat of Germany's power, he made speeches promoting Anglo-American relations and wrote on the subject to newspapers. But most Americans accused him of carrying his pro-British attitude too far.

In March 1936, again in defiance of the Versailles Treaty, Hitler sent two divisions of German troops to the Rhineland. Had Britain and France intervened at that point, Hitler was prepared to back down and pull his troops out. But they did not, and Hitler had begun his move to take control of Europe.

On 11 March 1938, Germany closed its border with Austria, and massed its troops for invasion. The Austrian chancellor was given an ultimatum to stand down and submit to Nazi rule – or face violent invasion. The Austrian chancellor relented, and Austria became a part of Hitler's Greater Germany.

Life for the German Jews had become ever more intolerable. Lilli Palmer brought her mother and two sisters to live with her in her north-west London house in Parsifal Road, Hampstead; Rolf also came to live in London. The Peiser family fled just before Germany put such restrictions on emigration as to make the expected Jewish exodus virtually impossible.

In Britain, Winston Churchill told his friend Alexander Korda that war with Germany was inevitable.

Korda had begun his film career at the age of twenty-four in the year the First World War broke out, 1914. His poor eyesight made him exempt from conscription, and he had no desire anyway, in common with most Hungarians, to fight on behalf of the Austrians and Germans against the French and British.

Sharing in Germany's defeat in 1918, Hungary underwent a revolution in which the communists took control, but by August 1919, that government had collapsed following a counter-revolution under the command of Admiral Miklos Horthy, a blatant anti-Semite. There began systematic persecution of Hungary's Jews. Alexander Korda, although he hid the truth for most of his life, was a Jew.

He was arrested, and his actress wife, Maria, and his brother Zoli, a decorated soldier of the war, appealed directly to Brigadier Maurice of MI5 in Budapest. The British government had discreetly financed the right-wing coup, and

Maurice, not wishing to see the British regarded as supporters of brutality, especially where a popular film producer was concerned, had Korda released.

The brigadier told Korda, 'You and the beautiful Mrs Korda had best get out of Hungary while you can, and just to make sure, we'll provide you with a little discreet British protection.'

With Maurice's aid, the Kordas left Hungary in the autumn of 1919, settled for a time in Austria and Germany, and then, in 1926, in America. After a brief spell in France in 1930, Korda made the permanent move to Britain in 1931 and directed a series of historical films, often hiring Churchill as historical advisor. They became good friends and Korda even paid Churchill £10,000 for the rights to his book *The Life of Marlborough*, although he never did make a film of it.

Churchill had integrated Alex into his own private intelligence organization which consisted mainly of international businessmen with global connections. Churchill confided to Korda his doubts about Prime Minister Chamberlain's misplaced trust in Hitler.

When Hitler turned his attentions towards Czechoslovakia, a meeting was arranged in Munich on 29 September 1938, between Hitler, Mussolini, French Prime Minister Edouard Daladier and Neville Chamberlain. It was agreed that Hitler could have nearly 11,500 square miles of Czechoslovakia. On 1 October, Nazi troops marched into Czechoslovakia to claim their section of the country. Chamberlain returned to Britain and said, 'There has come back from Germany to Downing Street peace with honour. I believe it is peace for our time.'

In the House of Commons, Winston Churchill growled, 'England has been offered a choice between war and shame. She has chosen shame – and will get war.'

Korda had no reason to doubt Churchill's gloomy predictions, especially when Ernst Udet, a German pilot who produced special aerial photography for Korda, told him, 'I have to return to Germany. Fatty Göering and the *Luftwaffe* need me.'

'You think it will be war then?' asked Korda.

'The Führer is committed to it. It is a ludicrous situation.

Fatty tells me I am to be a general and that I am expected to get my pilots ready in such a short time. Hitler will not wait, whether my pilots are ready or not.'

Alex Korda, as a Jew, had good reason to share Churchill's opposition to appeasement. He did not hide his hatred for Nazism and learned, probably from Udet, that his name was on the Gestapo's *Sonderfahndungliste Grossbritannien* as an anti-Nazi. He was well aware that if he ever fell into Nazi hands, the Gestapo would be more thorough than Admiral Horthy's amateurs.

'If the worst does come,' he told friends and family, 'it will be dull, nasty and very German.'

The situation exploded in November 1938, when Ernst vom Rath, a German Embassy official in Paris, was shot dead by a teenaged Polish Jew. When news reached Germany, the Nazis used it as an excuse to begin an official campaign of anti-Semitic violence. Propaganda Minister Josef Goebbels sent orders to SA and SS squads, on alert throughout the country, to move against all Jewish communities.

Over the next twenty-four hours, almost 200 synagogues were burned, more than 7,000 Jewish businesses destroyed, 100 Jews killed and over 30,000 arrested and sent to concentration camps. That night became known as *Kristallnacht*, the 'Crystal Night,' or 'Night of the Broken Glass' because of the thousands of windows smashed in Jewish homes, shops and businesses.

Hitler's Final Solution had begun. What was left of Czechoslovakia began to disintegrate, and Hitler claimed areas that had not been agreed upon in Munich. Chamberlain protested but refused to take any action since Britain had no treaty with Czechoslovakia.

Poland became Germany's next target, but this time Chamberlain, on 31 March 1939, promised Poland military aid in the event of hostility. France also made a pact with Poland, and Hitler was dissuaded from invading. It seemed for a while that peace might be maintained.

In Rome, in March 1939, Benito Mussolini, Italy's Fascist

dictator, Il Duce, stood overlooking the Piazza d'Italia, delivering a stirring and flamboyant speech. Anthony Quayle stood in the crowd but did not join their excited chant, crying 'Duce! Duce! Duce!'.

They saw in their Duce something of the glory of the Caesars. He had begun to build his new Roman empire in May 1936, when he annexed Ethiopia. Then, in October, he had formed an alliance with Hitler.

'This Berlin–Rome connection,' Mussolini had promised his people, 'is not so much a diaphragm as an axis, around which can revolve all those states of Europe with a will towards collaboration and peace.'

Within a year Germany and Italy signed a pact with Japan, completing the Rome–Berlin–Tokyo Axis.

Mussolini was adept at delivering speeches that inspired and stirred his people. But Anthony Quayle, listening to him in that early spring of 1939, was neither inspired nor stirred. He said, 'What struck me most about it all was that I was watching a great performance.'

He said:

I was touring Europe in 1939 with the Old Vic playing *Henry V.* I went back to the theatre [after hearing Mussolini's speech] and overheard a chilling conversation between one of our own carpenters and the theatre's Italian carpenter. They were talking about the possibility of a war, and the Italian was saying with some regret, 'Yes, I think there will be a war between us.'

The English carpenter said, 'If there is a war, do you think you'll be fighting us?'

The Italian thought for a moment and said sadly, 'Yes, I think so.'

The Englishman said, 'By Christ, you'd bloody well better *not*.'

We toured the rest of Italy and when we boarded our ship at Genoa to take us to Alexandria, we saw a German ship in harbour which was carrying deserving German citizens on holiday at the expense of their State. They set

off fireworks which floated down to earth on little para-
chutes with Swastikas printed on them. It gave me such a
chill and I knew we were heading for war.

We went on to Cairo and it was there that I met up
again with Hans Beckhoff. We were performing at the
Opera House and he had heard I was performing there
and came to visit me. At first I thought this was a friendly
gesture, but he was so cold to me. I had the definite feeling I was being given a look over by German Intelligence.
I asked him what he was doing in Cairo and he said he
was the head of the *Reiseburo*.

He asked me what I was doing, and all I could say
was, 'I'm acting.'

He gave me a really condescending smile and said,
'Yes, so I see.' There wasn't much to say after that and
we shook hands and that was the last I ever saw of him.
[Quayle later wrote that there passed between them 'a
mutual, unmistakable declaration of war.']

We were in Malta when news came that Mussolini had
invaded Albania [on 7 April 1939]. The tension was really increasing.

There was an enormous armada of British ships in the
harbour of Valletta. I was told that Naval Intelligence had
discovered a pack of Italian submarines was hiding just
outside the harbour. So the commander of the British
fleet announced that there would be an anti-submarine
exercise using *live* depth charges. The news obviously
reached the ears of the Italian submarine captains
because a British destroyer captain told me, 'The buggers
came bobbing up like corks.'

Alexander Korda's marriage to Maria had fallen apart years
earlier and he had divorced her in California. Now in
England, he was living secretly with Merle Oberon. In June
1939, he decided it was time to make their union legal, and
took her to the south of France for a quiet, private wedding
ceremony. Plans for an extended honeymoon were suddenly
cancelled after Korda talked with an old friend of his,

Edouard Corniglion-Molinier, who had been a pilot and a colonel in the French Air Force and had later joined the Spanish Republican Air Force.

Korda asked him what brought him back to France.

'I am resuming my duties as a colonel of France. France will need all her sons when war comes.'

'Do you really think war is so imminent?'

'It is closer than anybody is willing to admit. The enemy will wait until the harvest is in, but not a moment longer.'

Alarmed, Korda returned to the hotel, booked passage on a train to Paris and to Calais, and a ship to Dover. They were not remaining in France one day longer.

They returned home to find Vincent, Alex's brother, deeply immersed in preparations for the filming of *The Thief of Baghdad*. As was their system, Alex produced the films and Vincent directed them. Vincent, at forty-two, was the youngest of the three Korda brothers; Zoltan, two years older than Vincent, was also a director.

Vincent Korda had previously made some useful royal connections when he was invited to stage *Peter Pan* at Windsor Castle in which the princesses Elizabeth and Margaret performed. After the show, King George VI and the Queen invited Vincent to tea, along with Cecil Beaton who had designed the costumes for the royal pantomime. During the evening Her Majesty noticed that Vincent looked in some discomfort. 'What is the matter?' she asked him.

'My feet hurt, Your Majesty,' he replied.

Her Majesty simply slipped off her shoes and said, 'Mine do too. Please feel free to take your shoes off if you wish.'

He did, with much relief. This royal connection was to prove vital to Vincent during the summer of 1939 when he went to Cornwall to film location scenes for *The Thief of Baghdad*. His camera crew largely consisted of Europeans, many of them exiles and refugees.

Somebody had obviously been keeping a watchful eye on these foreigners taking film down on the beach while ships moved to and fro out at sea. Hearing Vincent's strong accent convinced the observer that he was a German spy no doubt posing as one of the many Germans who had fled to England from the Nazis only to find themselves interned. It was often a difficult and lengthy process for these anti-Nazi Germans to prove to Scotland Yard's Special Branch that they were not enemies of England.

Before long, a car pulled up on the beach where Vincent was filming, and out jumped a number of police officers who promptly arrested him. Back at the police station he begged, in his very broken English, to be allowed to call the king's secretary. This, naturally, was met with jibes from the police who thought it a ruse. After some persuasion, a call was put through to the king's secretary, Vincent Korda's identity as a friend of the Royal Family was confirmed, and he was released.

2

War Declared

'I think another war will kill me.'

Alexander Korda

On 31 August 1939, Poland held its breath. Hitler's foreign minister Joachim von Ribbentrop and Joseph Stalin of the Soviet Union had agreed to divide Poland, and on 26 August 1939, Hitler had given orders to his generals to attack Poland. But he cancelled the order when Britain urged the Polish matter to be settled by negotiation.

Hitler asked Poland to send an emissary to Berlin to discuss the matter, and the Polish ambassador went to see von Ribbentrop. It was, however, merely a gesture. Hitler could not conceive that Britain would go to war for the sake of Poland.

None of this meant very much to little Roman Polanski. Aged six and in his first week at school, he lived with his parents in Cracow's Jewish quarter.

He had actually been born in Paris on 18 August 1933, where his Polish father, Riszard, was trying to make a living as an artist. Then Riszard met a Russian Jewess, Bula Katz, and in 1932 they were married. Bula had a daughter from a previous marriage, so when Roman was born he already had a sister. By this time, Riszard was having to work in a factory to make ends meet.

In 1936 Riszard was fired when the owner of the factory

17

decided that he no longer wanted Jews working for him.
Riszard did his best to work throughout the next year as a
freelance artist and carpenter. He was a man of great artistic
talent and intellect, and he manifested his frustrations in violent outbursts against Bula and Roman.

By mid-1937, with no prospects of any work, he decided
to move his family to Cracow near the border with
Czechoslovakia. It was a medieval city, set on the banks of
the Vistula River and flanked by the Carpathian Mountains.
The Polanskis settled in to a modest apartment. Roman was
a shy, slightly built child, terrorized by his sometimes brutal
father, and comforted by his protective mother. His earliest
memories were of sitting with her while she taught him to
read, write and draw. She was the most important person in
his life.

Riszard continued to struggle as an artist, presenting himself in public as a man of intellect, charm and talent, but his
continual failures to impress society and gain recognition
resulted in beatings for Bula and Roman.

In 1939, Riszard was invited by his brother, Raimund, to
join his small merchandising operation. It was only a few days
after Riszard began his new secure job that the Polish emissary went to see von Ribbentrop to tell him that Poland would
not yield to German demands. The next day, 1 September
1939, Hitler gave the signal for invasion.

A million men had been drawn up along the Polish border,
and at dawn they attacked from three directions. The *blitzkrieg*, or 'lightning war', had begun.

The world stood tense. An ultimatum was given to the
Germans to withdraw from Poland.

It was Saturday, 2 September, and John Mills and Anthony
Pelissier, who were both appearing at the Apollo Theatre in
Of Mice and Men, decided they would enlist that morning
before the matinée.

'I had the erroneous idea that if I volunteered before war
was declared,' Sir John Mills said, 'I would be given my
choice of unit and become an officer very quickly. So Anthony

Pelissier and I went out on the day before war was declared and found the naval recruiting offce and announced our intention to enlist. Unfortunately, they didn't want us.'

Sir John recalled:

The officer in charge told us there was no call for more men just then, so I said, 'But we will be needed if war is declared.'

Then he told me I was too old. 'Just how old do you think I am?' I asked. He said, 'You must be over thirty', and I said, 'I am *exactly* thirty.'

But I couldn't persuade him and he said that we ought to go back to doing our play and keep morale up by entertaining the people, and come back in a few months' time.

I told him, 'No thank you. Our intention is to join up now, and join up we bloody well will.' I was sure the army would take us, so off we went to enlist in the Rifle Brigade, but they thanked us and said there was a waiting list.

It was around noon and we really had to get back to the theatre by 2.30, so we'd more or less decided that we would give up when we saw a poster – 'Recruits Wanted for the Royal Engineers'. So off we went to join the Royal Engineers.

The recruiting sergeant swore us in and told us to report to 346 Company headquarters at Royston at 17.00 hours. So I told him that this was rather inconvenient as we had two shows to do today, and I appealed to his sense of humanity and explained how disappointed the audiences would be if the show didn't go on.

He just said, 'Well, I'll be buggered.'

I told him, 'No, it's *we* who'll be buggered if we let the audience down. Not to mention the fact that the management would probably sue us.' So I asked permission for us to report the next day at 14.30 which he agreed to. But he made it very clear that if we were one minute late, we'd be put on a charge.

Sappers Mills and Pelissier returned to the Apollo and did their final two performances. Then Mills went straight to the Comedy Theatre where his girlfriend, Mary Hayley Bell, was appearing in *Tony Draws a Horse*. Afterwards, in the deserted street outside the theatre, Mary told him, 'I'm going to say goodbye to you here, Johnny. If you have to leave tomorrow morning, I want you to know that I shall love you for ever.'

He wiped the tears from her face and proceeded to give a lengthy speech about his love for her, that 'not even that little bastard Hitler' would separate them and that they would spend the rest of their lives together 'in this world and hopefully the next'.

They got into his Lancia and drove to the flat she shared with her friend Janet who waited with Anthony Pelissier. They all drank champagne and a few hours later Mills and Pelissier climbed into the car and waved to the two girls leaning out of the top flat window.

John Mills was alone in his London flat when, at eleven o'clock, he turned on the radio for an announcement by the prime minister.

In Stratford-on-Avon, members of the Stratford Memorial Theatre Company, including an up and coming actor named Trevor Howard, were enjoying a drink at the Black Swan – or Dirty Duck, as they liked to call it – when the landlord called for hush. 'It's the prime minister.'

'Damn it,' said Trevor Howard. 'Here it comes.'

Alexander Korda was at home in Avenue Road with Merle at his side as they listened along with the rest of the British nation to the voice of the prime minister.

'This morning,' Chamberlain began, 'the British ambassador in Berlin handed the German government a final note, stating that unless the British government heard from them by eleven o'clock that they were prepared at once to withdraw their troops from Poland, a state of war would exist between us. I have to tell you now that no such undertaking has been received, and that consequently this country is at war with Germany.'

Korda felt a stab of doom. 'I think another war will kill me,' he said.

At the Black Swan in Stratford, Alec Clunes asked Trevor Howard, 'What are you going to do?'

'I'm going to finish this pint, then have another, and I suppose when Stratford has done with me, I'll go back to London and join the RAF.'

Anthony Quayle and his wife Hermione stood under the apple tree in their garden. For some time their marriage had been falling apart and Quayle would later write that she cried to him aloud that this catastrophe of war – like everything else – was his personal fault.

She asked him, 'What will you do? I suppose you'll go and join up?'

He didn't have to think it over. He had already decided. 'Yes,' he said, 'I will. Tomorrow.'

France had also issued an ultimatum to Germany, and was now at war too. Hitler could hardly believe it. He was so sure that neither country would go so far as to go to war for Poland.

John Mills and Anthony Pelissier had to get moving quickly or find themselves on a charge. Sir John recalled:

A friend from the *Sunday Express*, Stephen Watts, had joined the same unit as us, so after the broadcast I got in my car and picked up Anthony and Stephen, and set off through London. The streets were deserted – you could feel the city holding its breath – and we were just passing through Swiss Cottage when the first air-raid siren went off.

Apparently an unidentified aircraft had been spotted by radar and two flights of RAF fighters were scrambled. It turned out to be just a French civilian plane, but thinking the first bombs were about to fall on us, I pushed my foot to the floor and we broke all the speed limits. Then the all-clear sounded.

It was funny, because when we got to St Albans a man in a gas mask jumped out in front of us and began jumping up and down and trying to tell us something. I stopped but couldn't understand a single word he said in his mask, so I shouted at him that there was no air raid, that the all-clear had gone off half an hour ago. But he kept jumping up and down, waving at the sky, and Stephen said, 'He must be round the bloody bend,' and we left the man jumping up and down.

We arrived [at 346 Company HQ] and found the headquarters in a field surrounded by barbed wire, and it was really just a marquee for the mess hall, two large huts which were the offices, and around two dozen small huts where we all slept.

We went to the quartermaster who said that there was a shortage of everything, and issued us with one forage cap which Anthony got, a greatcoat for Stephen, I got a pair of working overalls, three gas masks for all of us, various eating utensils and three canvas palliasses. It was two weeks before our uniforms arrived.

We were put in a hut with about nine other men who all knew I was an actor – I suppose they had seen one or two of the few films I'd made – and they obviously thought we were a bit toffee-nosed.

But they changed their minds as we showed we were one of them and willing to be part of a team, and they all turned out to be great friends.

He recalled that on that first night as he lay on his uncomfortable straw bed, thinking of the girl he had left behind, he had never felt lonelier in his life, despite the fact that he was in a hut full of men.

The next day, 4 September 1939, Anthony Quayle volunteered. 'I decided I had to enlist when I heard the prime minister's radio broadcast. I wanted to be in the Field Artillery because my uncle had been a field gunner in the First World War. So the very next day I arrived at the depot of the Royal Horse Artillery near Regent's Park.'

The officer listened to Quayle's request and said, 'I am sure the Field Artillery will be glad to have you.' Then he said

Quayle would have to wait several weeks before being called.

He returned to his cottage where he told Hermione what he had done. She said only, 'You must do what you feel you have to do.'

That was the day the German 14th Army marched into Cracow, sweeping eastward along the northern edge of the Carpathian Mountains. Resistance was quickly put down.

For Roman Polanski, life at the age of six was suddenly to change beyond belief. The Jewish quarter where he lived was turned into an internment compound. He had only just begun school but the Germans were closing all the schools to Jews.

By 16 September 1939, Warsaw was surrounded and the population brought to its knees with saturation bombing. The next day the city capitulated. About 10,000 Poles had escaped in the hope of reaching France while resistance from the Poles who remained continued until October. Poland was divided between Germany and the Soviet Union. Stalin, determined that he would bring communism to the Poles, moved all the upper classes of Poland to camps deep inside Russia. In the eastern half of Poland the Gestapo and the SS began a six-year reign of terror for the Jews.

The declaration of war from Neville Chamberlain was heard on the wireless by a group of film stars holding a party on board a yacht just off Catalina on the west coast of America.

Douglas Fairbanks Jr and his wife Mary Lee had chartered the boat for the weekend. Their guests included Laurence Olivier and his future wife Vivien Leigh, and Nigel Bruce who was famous as Dr Watson in the Sherlock Holmes films. They had been joined by Ronald Colman and Benita Hume and were waiting for David Niven and fellow British actor Robert Coote, but before they arrived, the party heard that Britain was at war with Germany.

Vivien Leigh began to cry. 'Oh God. . . .'

American-born pro-British Fairbanks was as desolated as his British actor friends at the news. Olivier wrote that they 'felt blighted right through'.

In a small sloop moored at the Balboa Yacht Club, David
Niven and Robert Coote were awakened from their drunken
sleep by someone banging on the side of the boat. It was six in
the morning as Niven and Coote looked over the side at a
man in a dinghy. 'Are you guys English?' he asked.

'We are.'

'Then good luck to ya – you just declared war on
Germany.'

The man paddled away as Niven and Coote just stared
silently at each other. They were supposed to have joined
Douglas Fairbanks's party, but had drunk too much in the
Balboa Yacht Club to celebrate the end of filming.

They gave themeslves a quick toast with gin and set sail for
Catalina to join the party, but as Niven said, 'Nobody felt like
celebrating any more.'

Everyone went to their respective cabins. Fairbanks told his
wife, 'I suppose I'll join up right away, if they'll have an
American.'

Olivier told Vivien he would try to join the RAF, and if
they did not let him join up immediately, he would take flying
lessons.

Nigel Bruce tapped his leg which had been permanently
injured during the First World War, and told Robert Coote,
'Jolly unfair, Bobby. One war going to keep me out of
another.' Robert Coote had decided he would leave for
Canada to join the RCAF.

Fairbanks summoned his guests back on deck where he
opened the champagne. 'Well, here's to whatever it is,' he
said.

'To victory,' Olivier said solemnly.

On the Tuesday morning, the British consul in Los Angeles
was overwhelmed by British actors, old and young, stars and
bit-part actors, all volunteering for war service, including
Laurence Olivier.

The consul announced that the British government asked
that they all remain to fulfil their obligations to the studios
and theatres and continue to gain the friendship and
sympathy of the United States. That, it was said, would be a

greater service to their country than rushing to arms, unless they were already in the reserves.

Olivier was still filming. David Niven had served with the Highland Light Infantry until 1934 when he suddenly resigned his commission. He was not on reserve but he was under contract to Samuel Goldwyn. But both actors were determined to join up at the earliest opportunity.

Having been a regular soldier, Niven felt that as a patriot and an ex-regular he had no other alternative but to get into the war immediately.

A few days later he returned to his Hollywood home and got a call from an Austrian friend, Felix Schaffscotch, who had never made a secret of his admiration for Hitler. Nevertheless, Niven found him amiable.

'Hello, enemy,' Schaffscotch said jovially. 'What are you going to do?'

'Go back to England, I suppose.'

'Good. I'm leaving for Germany in two days. Why don't we meet up in Italy?'

But it was all easier said than done, as Niven recalled:

I was in Hollywood under contract to Samuel Goldwyn when we heard the news, and I wanted to get home and join up, but Goldwyn refused to release me. I told him that I'd been called up, which was a lie of course, and had to return to England immediately.

He said, 'I'll get back to you,' and half an hour later he called and said, 'David, I just checked with the British Embassy in Washington. They said nobody's been called up yet. They said the best thing for you to do is stay right here and carry on as normal.'

So I cabled my brother with instructions to send me a cable, saying 'Report regimental depot immediately Adjutant.' I went to Goldwyn with this cable. He knew very well that I had served with the Highland Light Infantry years before but didn't know that I had resigned my commission. So Goldwyn felt he had no choice but to release me.

The thing was, I didn't quite know what I was going
back to. I didn't want to go back into the British Army,
so I made enquiries about joining the Canadian Army
but was told they didn't need me.

Douglas Fairbanks Jr was also anxious to enlist, even
though his own country was not at war. He had been involved
in diplomatic activities for several years as an unofficial
ambassador for the American State Department. As the likeli-
hood of war had increased, he had been instrumental in
orchestrating the visit in May 1939 of King George VI and
Queen Elizabeth to America to strengthen Anglo-American
relations.

With the official outbreak of war, he applied to join the
Canadian Navy, but the US State Department scuppered his
enlistment by sending an unofficial message that in view of the
strong isolationist view in America, he would do better to stay
in America and continue publicizing Anglo-American relations.

British actor Kenneth More found that his attempt to volunteer was not welcomed with open arms. He had made a
couple of films and was in Birmingham doing rep when war
was declared. He was just coming up to the age of twenty-five.
In fact it was his birthday soon, on 20 September. He had
worked hard to make his way as an actor, but as soon as he
heard that war had been declared, he decided he wanted to do
more important things for his country:

> When I went to join up, I thought they would be wel-
> coming men into the services, but it wasn't that way at
> all. I just thought that defending my country was more
> important than being an actor, and I wanted to join the
> navy because my father had been in the navy.
>
> But the petty officer at the navy's recruitment office in
> Birmingham didn't seem overwhelmed to see me. He
> asked me my name and occupation and asked why I
> wanted to join the navy, and then he said, 'Thank you for
> coming, now please go home.'

I asked why, and he said, 'Because we don't want you yet. We've got all the men we need, and if we should need you, we'll let you know.' I left feeling very puzzled and very disappointed.

Men were being turned down every day. The forces lacked the administrative strength and necessary centres to deal with the number of eager young men ready to fight. There were lists of reservists who were already largely trained and would be the first to be called.

More arrived back at the theatre to see a 'CLOSED' sign going up. Then he read a poster about Air Raid Precautions. He suddenly had the idea that he would go to his nearest ARP centre and was delighted when they accepted him as an ambulance driver.

Lilli Palmer also volunteered to drive an ambulance, but she was turned down as an enemy alien. In fact, she was excluded from any kind of active service, even for the ARP. Furthermore, Gaumont British cancelled her contract, no doubt not wishing to be known for employing enemy aliens. Fortunately she had by now been granted a permanent work visa, and she set about trying to find work in London's theatres. But during those early days of the war – soon to be known as the Phoney War – theatres were being closed.

Her romance with Rolf ended, but, said Rex Harrison, 'Lilli wasn't entirely alone as she had her mother and sisters with her. She was acutely aware that she was safe, while in Germany the Jews were being rounded up and shipped off. She didn't complain of being regarded as an alien, although she wanted to be regarded as loyal to England.'

Trevor Howard was as good as his word. Upon returning to London, he attempted to enlist with the RAF. They turned him down. So did the army. He was told he would have to wait. But he was not too disappointed.

Years later he reflected:

It really didn't bother me that I had to wait. I had no great desire for Service life and I thought that after all my years struggling to become an actor I was going to waste those years by going into the Services and getting killed, which I also thought a waste. I really had no taste for war. I wasn't one of those eager types who thought it would be a great adventure. I knew it would be lousy, and I detested the very idea of having to kill another being. I sometimes think that, if I'd really had the courage, I'd have been a conscientious objector. Perhaps it took less courage to fight. Perhaps it was just that I didn't want Germans running my country.

In England all the excitement died down as the 'Phoney War' took root. But there was action, and tragedy, in the Atlantic Ocean on the very day war broke out when a German U-boat sunk the British liner *Athenia* which had left Liverpool bound for Canada. Of the 122 passengers who died, twenty-eight were American. Hopes were raised that this might bring America into the war but President Roosevelt knew the American people would not support any action.

It was the beginning of the U-boat terror. On 15 September the aircraft carrier HMS *Courageous* was sunk with the loss of 518 lives. The battleship *Royal Oak* was sunk in Scapa Flow on 14 October.

Anthony Quayle waited for his orders. They came through in October. 'My orders informed me I had been given the rank and pay of a gunner and was told to report to Officer Cadet Training Unit at the Training Depot of the Royal Regiment of Artillery CD. I had no idea what CD stood for, but I found out when I got to Plymouth – it stood for Coastal Defences, which wasn't what I'd wanted. I wanted to be at the front, wherever that was, but I was going to spend the war defending the ports of Britain.'

It was October 1939 before David Niven managed to arrive in England. He had travelled via Italy because he wanted to say goodbye to his Austrian friend who was on his way to join Hitler's army. Niven caught a train to Paris where he went to

see the air attaché, John Acheson, at the British Embassy, and
announced he wanted to join the RAF:

He said to me, 'Oh no, you can't do that, not here. You
must go back to England', and he secretly put me on a
mail plane that evening. So I flew back to Britain in a
plane full of mail bags and a few days later presented
myself to the Air Ministry.

I was ushered before a Group Captain who asked
me my name although it was obvious he knew who I
was.

'And what do you want?' 'I want to join the RAF,' I
told him.

He shook his head. 'Ever heard of Wilfred Lawson?'

'Of course. A wonderful actor,' I said.

'He's also a heavy drinker. We took him on and we've
had trouble with him ever since.'

I was pretty pissed off by now and I said, 'Look, I've
just come seven thousand miles at my own expense and
I'd like to join up.'

'We don't encourage actors to join this service.'

This made me so angry I said, 'Then fuck you.'

He herded me to the door, shouting, 'Get out! Get out
of my office *now*.'

I was on my way out when I passed an air commodore, and I said, 'And fuck you, too.'

I tried the Scots Guards, but they turned me down. It
was very depressing. It just seemed that, after I'd come
all the way back from Hollywood, every door was
slammed in my face. The problem was, nobody wanted
to see a film star in uniform at that time unless he was in
a film, being kept safe from the real action.

Goldwyn didn't help because he turned it into a publicity stunt; I had a couple of films opening in London,
and he wanted my arrival in London to reap all the publicity he could get. So he got his London office on to it
and I found myself giving a press conference explaining
why I hoped to get into the RAF.

The next day the papers came out with headlines like, RELAX, THE DAWN PATROL IS HERE and NIVEN SPURNS THE ARMY. There was one London film critic [Caroline Lejeune] who wrote an article that said, 'The British film fan does not want to see David Niven in the army, the navy or the air force. We want to see him him in his proper place, up there on the silver screen helping us to forget this war.'

This response, even criticism, depressed and distressed him. But it only spurred him on all the more to find himself a niche in the war.

3

The Phoney War

*'It didn't bother me that Lilli was German. She was just
very beautiful and very charming.'*

Rex Harrison

John Mills, Anthony Pelissier and Stephen Watts continued
training at 346 Company which was a searchlight battery.
They spent hours learning to recognize aircraft and how to
dismantle and assemble the Lewis guns. They marched by day
and trained with the searchlights by night. They also dug
trenches, filled sandbags and painted the huts to camouflage
them.

During the second week of training, Mary Hayley Bell
decided to pay John Mills a visit and got into the HQ by
climbing under the wire. She was immediately apprehended
by two MPs and told the sergeant that she had travelled there
in the ambulance she drove in London because she could not
bear to be parted from John any longer. She said that she had
not liked the look of the two MPs on the gate so she crawled
under the wire.

Sapper Mills was summoned. 'Is this the young lady whose
virtues you were extolling to me for over two hours in the pub
the other evening?' the sergeant asked.

'Yes, sergeant,' Mills replied, expecting a serious reprimand. But instead he was granted a pass to go to the
town's stores for turpentine with the strict order to return by
18.00 hours. He and Mary, at the sergeant's suggestion, took

31

the opportunity to spend a few precious hours at Banyer's Hotel.

Training finished at the end of October 1939 when Mills was posted to a country site that was situated between Royston and Cambridge. The nearest village was six miles away, and it did not even have a pub. His two friends were posted elsewhere. Each day he and the Lewis gun team stood from evening till morn.

That autumn turned cold early, and by the time November came it was freezing. Mills began to feel by this time that the only enemy he had was boredom. His day consisted of being on duty throughout the night, sleeping until noon, doing two hours maintenance and then back on duty again.

The only thing that kept him going was reading the letters from Mary. As far as being an actor was concerned, he had all but forgotten he'd had any life before the army. But then, shortly before Christmas, the CO at Battalion HQ in Cambridge asked him to organize a concert party, and he felt he had something else to brighten his life.

As November drew to a close, the snow came. Not just a light frosting but a howling blizzard. The road in both directions became blocked, cutting the unit off completely. They went without rations for three days, and John caught a dose of flu that had his temperature soaring.

When he staggered out of his bed and headed for the hut door, one of the crew, Jock, barred his way. 'Where do you think you're going?' Jock demanded.

'I have to have a pee.'

'Not out there you're not. It's like the Arctic.'

'What do you expect me to do then?'

Jock handed Mills one of his gum boots. 'Use this.'

It was an unusually generous gesture that formed a firm friendship.

'I was determined to become an officer,' Mills told me, 'so I wrote to the CO asking permission to be sent to Officer Cadet Training Unit. But I didn't hear back. So I figured that was that.'

★

Theatres had been closed at the outbreak of war. Everyone expected bombs to come raining down on the British Isles; bomb shelters were dug, windows blacked out and anti-aircraft guns emplaced. But the expected air raids did not happen. To many, the war seemed unreal, sham – the Phoney War was fought with a spirit of false optimism. The good humoured British sang 'We're gonna hang out the washing on the Siegfried Line', and theatres began to open towards the end of 1939.

Lilli Palmer landed a part in Leslie Banks's touring production of *You of All People* which opened successfully in Birmingham at the Alexandra Theatre. A few days after it opened audiences started to trail off as theatregoers chose to go and see Rex Harrison in Noël Coward's *Design for Living* which had opened at the Theatre Royal. Harrison had starred in the play in London when the outbreak of war forced theatres to close.

The casts of both plays were staying at the same hotel. That was where Rex Harrison first met Lilli Palmer.

'I walked into the hotel restaurant and saw Leslie Banks at a table with his cast, and I saw this beautiful girl which was Lilli – and I wanted Banks to introduce us, so a few evenings later I got Banks to do it.'

Soon they were seeing each other every day. 'It didn't bother me in the least that Lilli was German. To me she was just a very beautiful and very charming young woman.' Harrison was actually married at the time, but he and his wife Collette had separated.

Both plays moved to Liverpool but then went their separate ways. *Design for Living* was due to open in London on 23 December, so Rex and Lilli planned to meet up then. She was waiting the day he and the company arrived, and they spent the first Christmas of the war together.

The evacuation of Britain's children to safer parts of the country had begun on the eve of war. City-dwelling children, bewildered and tearful, were suddenly sent away. Vincent Korda sent his son Michael to the relative safety of the Isle of Wight, accompanied by his nanny. Alex rented a huge house in the country and persuaded his brothers and their families to move in with him and Merle.

It proved a disastrous combination as they all began to crowd one another and the expected immediate crisis didn't happen. After Michael was sent to the Isle of Wight, Merle Oberon was recalled to Hollywood by Warner Brothers. Zoltan, whose health was poor, left to recuperate in Arizona.

So much preparation for war had happened before the invasion of Poland – trench shelters were dug in parks, gas masks were issued, barrage balloons floated above skylines – that within a few months the whole population of Great Britain began to relax as life seemed to return to normal.

Vincent Korda moved back into his home in Hampstead. Alex moved back to his London home, lonely without Merle and reluctant to follow her across the Atlantic, knowing that his exit would be interpreted as cowardice. He busied himself, along with Vincent, with their plans to make *The Thief of Baghdad*. The war would yet intrude upon Alex Korda's life.

For thousands of children who had been evacuated to the country, it had seemed a needless exercise in view of the fact that no bombs had fallen on the cities, and many of them returned to their homes for Christmas. But in other countries, there was nothing phoney about the war. The USSR had invaded Finland at the end of November. The German pocket battleship *Graf Spee*, which had attacked and sunk British merchant vessels in the South Atlantic and Indian Oceans, was pursued towards South America by the British Navy and, following a ferocious sea battle, the German captain scuttled his ship in the River Plate on 17 December. This came as good news for Britain, just in time for Christmas.

David Niven had had no luck with finding a niche in the war by early 1940. He sat in the Café de Paris in London, gloomily watching the dancers on the floor and aware that many of the young men around him were in the Rifle Brigade. He was awakened from his dark thoughts by an announcement by the band leader: 'Ladies and gentlemen, if anyone is interested, the air-raid warning has just sounded.'

There were cheers and cat-calls and in a matter of seconds the music was playing and everyone was dancing again. Nobody was fooled any longer by the 'phoney war'.

Niven was suddenly struck by the sight of a beautiful WAAF and he found himself gazing blankly into her face. She did not seem to notice him, and he was about to go over and speak to her when someone said to him, 'Excuse me but my name is Jimmy Bosvile.' A young man in uniform was standing over him. 'I recognized you. I was with an air commodore this morning who was talking about a visit you paid to his office. I wish I'd been there.' Bosvile sat down and continued. 'Why don't you come to the Rifle Brigade?'

'You couldn't get me into the ladies' lavatory at Leicester Square,' Niven told him glumly.

He recalled:

Jimmy Bosvile was in the Rifle Brigade and in command of the 2nd Battalion. The Rifle Brigade was arguably the most famous of all the élite light infantry regiments, and three weeks later, with Bosvile's help, I was training at Tidworth as a second lieutenant.

I was an ex-regular and found that not too much had changed over the years and I quickly caught up with the much younger men.

Later I learned that I'd been earmarked for the 1st Battalion which was on the Belgian border. But at that time my job was to train the conscripts.

Around then I got to meet Winston Churchill. What happened was, I had a few days leave [in February 1940] and went to Ditchley for the weekend where Nancy and Ronnie Tree lived; Nancy was a cousin of Norah Flynn, one of Errol's ex-wives. Ronnie Tree was an MP who had voted with Winston Churchill against Chamberlain over Munich.

Churchill and his wife were among the guests, as well as Brendan Bracken and Anthony Eden, and when Churchill saw me sitting at the other end of the table, he got up and strode over and shook my hand.

He said, 'Young man, you did a very fine thing to give up a most promising career to fight for your country.'

The next day – it was Sunday – Churchill asked me to stroll in the garden with him, and he talked about the joys of gardening, and then got on to the subject of food rationing. He asked me about the problems a young officer in the army faced, and he was always most attentive to what I had to say. Ah! to have the ears of the mighty!

It has always frustrated me that I cannot remember much of what he said during this and subsequent strolls in the garden.

Ronnie Tree asked me to arrange a special screening of a Deanna Durbin film for Churchill, so I hired a private cinema in Soho, and invited the Edens and the Trees, but Churchill was late. [The date was 15 February 1940.] When he eventually arrived, he lit a cigar, drank a brandy and sat down to enjoy the film. Half way through he got up to leave. I saw him to the door and he thanked me but said that something important had come up and he had to return to the Admiralty.

What Niven did not know at the time was that Churchill's business for that evening was ordering HMS *Cossack* to chase *Altmark*, a supply ship, into the Jossing Fjord in Norway, board her and free 299 British merchant seamen whose ships were sunk by the *Graf Spee*. The mission was one of Britain's early successes. The war now seemed a lot less phoney.

4

The Dunkirk Miracle

*'We didn't really stand a chance and after about five days,
the Germans came in and rounded us up.'*

Sam Kydd

Around the time David Niven joined the Rifle Brigade,
Lieutenant Anthony Quayle was posted to the Hampshire
Heavy Regiment 'which consisted of three round towers stuck
out in the middle of Spithead between the Isle of Wight and
Portsmouth which could only be reached by open tender'.

He remained there, far from any of the action, while
German troops marched into Denmark and Norway in April
1940. He had no fond memories of Spithead. 'We had such
heavy seas that winter that I hardly set foot on the mainland.'

In fact, Lieutenant Quayle didn't have much to be happy
about in any aspect of his life at that time. 'I was married then
but it was falling apart quite frankly and I had little in my life
except the army and the war, so when I read a notice calling
for volunteers to go to Hong Kong, I put my name forward
[in April]. But that didn't work out, so I volunteered for
Gibraltar.'

The day before his posting came through, on 10 May 1940,
Chamberlain resigned and Churchill became prime minister,
and Hitler invaded Holland, Belgium, Luxembourg and
France, outwitting the British Expeditionary Force and
French Army which had prepared for an advance near the
coast. Instead, the German panzers thrust through Sedan and

overran northern France. The only route of escape for the retreating British troops was at Dunkirk.

A few days later a ship transporting Lieutenant Quayle crossed the Channel. The ship pulled into Cherbourg in the dark of night and Quayle watched as an infantry battalion disembarked. He knew that somewhere in the far distance a battle was being fought but as he stood on the deck and strained his ears, he could hear nothing of it.

He had expected the ship to pull out immediately, but it waited another hour, and then to Quayle's surprise, the battalion returned. He never knew why they had been sent back but guessed that the situation had been too bad to add further sacrifice.

'We were unescorted and we were afraid of getting picked off by U-boats, so we were all very relieved when we slipped through the Straits of Gibraltar and anchored. I will never forget the sight of the great Rock rising up out of the Mediterranean and all the town's lights blazing.'

He was put in command of a half-section of twin six-pounders on Detached Mole which lay between the North and South Moles; his job was to defend the entrance to the inner harbour. But the guns were only capable of dealing with fast torpedo boats that might try to break into the harbour, and that was never a distinct possibility.

Detached Mole could be reached only by boat, which meant that he was left to run his outfit without interference since it was too much effort for senior officers to go out and check on him.

It had been more than six months since Kenneth More had tried to enlist. Suddenly, in the spring of 1940, he received a letter asking if he would be interested in joining Defensively Equipped Merchant Ships. 'This seemed the next best thing to the Royal Navy,' he told me, 'so I accepted.'

He duly reported for basic training in Portsmouth and was then posted to Tiger Bay in Cardiff for two weeks to train on a four-inch gun. Then he was transferred to Liverpool to join the crew of the MV *Lobus* as a naval rating, gun layer (second class), in charge of a four-inch anti-submarine gun set above her stern.

My quarters were the former sick bay which was situated under the gun and above the ammunition store, which was a bit precarious. I inspected the gun and found I was totally unacquainted with this type so I asked a commander from the naval office to explain how it worked.

He told me, 'This is a 4.7 Japanese anti-submarine gun, made for His Imperial Japanese Majesty.'

I said, 'But how do I fire it, sir?'

'Well, I'll tell you,' he said. 'If I were you, *I* wouldn't fire the bloody thing at all.'

Three days later we sailed and I didn't know if I dared use the gun.

Trevor Howard was doing his best to join up, but he found his attempts thwarted. He was only twenty-four, so he was hardly considered too old. 'I wanted to join the RAF,' he told me, 'but for some reason they didn't want me, so I had a go at the army, and they turned me down too.'

While he was performing with the Harrogate White Rose Players, which was run by two ladies, Mrs Peacock and Miss Marie Blanche, call-up papers arrived for him at the ladies' house. They were so fond of him that, unable to bear the thought of losing him to the war, they neglected to mention that his call-up had arrived and saw to it that the papers met with an accident in the fire.

Consequently, the MPs turned up and arrested Howard. After the ladies explained the situation and prevented Howard from going to prison, he joined the Royal Corps of Signals. But they found it difficult to find him a job he was good at.

They tried him out on coastal artillery, but he spent three months proving to them that they had made a mistake. He tried to persuade them that he ought to be allowed to join the RAF, but since that was out of the question, he requested transfer to the infantry.

He was sent off to Officer Cadet Training Unit in Dunbar, Scotland.

'By a stroke of luck, the adjutant there was very keen on drama and thought he was a bit of an actor,' recalled Howard. 'So when I turned up I suppose he thought this was his chance and he got me to put on a play which I directed as well as acted in with him in it, too.'

This made army life more bearable and Howard settled down to make friends. But he found it all so monotonous, and he wondered if he would ever get to see any action.

David Niven, meanwhile, waited, not completely patiently, to be posted to the 1st Battalion in France. Then came the evacuation from Dunkirk in the last days of May and the first few days of June. The 1st Battalion was fighting in Calais with its back to the Channel, protecting the evacuation of the BEF from Dunkirk.

Thousands of Territorials, who only a week before had been at their daily jobs, were suddenly called up to be ferried across the Channel to help defend the retreat. Regulars were also shipped to Calais, including the Queen Victoria Rifles. Among them was Sam Kydd, a young man who would, after the war, become a popular character actor in films and on television.

He was put ashore in Calais on the Wednesday amid the confusion and disorganization of war; guns were being shipped over without ammunition, tanks without guns and transportation without the regiments for which they were intended.

David Niven received his orders to stand by along with 200 replacements. But the end came too quickly. By 4 June it was all over and the entire 1st Battalion had been killed or taken prisoner.

Machine-gun fire kept the QVRs pinned down on the beach. 'And there we were stuck,' Sam Kydd told me. 'We didn't really stand a chance and after about five days, the Germans came in and rounded us up. That's how I became a PoW. They carted us off to Poland, walking some of the way, going in cattle trucks. There was no food to speak of. We got to the camp and they cut off all our hair. I was behind the wire for the rest of the war.'

The camp most of the Dunkirk veterans were sent to was Stalag VIIIB at Lamsdorf, Upper Silesia in Poland. Stalag VIIIB also had a smaller compound for captured airmen, although most Allied airmen were sent to Stalag Luft III at Zagan in Lower Silesia.

There were about 25,000 PoWs in Stalag VIIIB who were divided into groups of about 3,000. 'It was terrible and demoralizing,' said Sam Kydd. 'We didn't get fed very well and we didn't get our mail from home, and to cheer ourselves up we started to put on shows. You had to adapt or you didn't make it. Some men became "wire happy"; they made desperate attempts to climb over the wire, and they were shot.'

The first six months following Dunkirk were, perhaps, the most grim for the PoWs of Stalag VIIIB. Then the food parcels from the Red Cross began to arrive, as well as musical instruments from the Swedish Red Cross for the shows which ranged from music hall and pantomimes to light comedy plays.

After Dunkirk, the Germans swept across France, and on 10 June 1940, the French government fled Paris, allowing German forces to enter the capital unopposed. Marshal Henri Pétain, the new French premier, signed an armistice with Germany which allowed him to govern southern France from Vichy, breaking a promise to Britain never to negotiate with Germany. Churchill agreed to forget France's promise if all French ships sailed immediately to British ports. Some ships did, but many, stationed off North Africa, remained loyal to the Vichy government which, by 1942, had become a government in collaboration with Germany.

For the thousands of Frenchmen who came under German occupation, their hopes lay in the efforts of tank commander Charles de Gaulle who flew to England to broadcast to the French, telling them that they had lost only a battle, not the war. The Vichy government sentenced him to death as a traitor.

The retreat from Dunkirk became something of a miracle to the British Isles. Despite the men, arms and equipment lost, almost 30,000 British troops were carried back home on destroyers, warships and, most famously, hundreds of small, private boats, manned by civilians, running the gauntlet, back and forth across the Channel.

The returning soldiers were welcomed home, not as a beaten army, but as heroes, and their defeat was turned into a celebration. Many of the young men who had not volunteered or had not yet been called up were so roused by what happened at Dunkirk that they virtually besieged the recruitment offices to get into uniform. Those who were not so young joined the Home Guard units that were being set up all over England in response to the now very real threat of invasion. Rex Harrison and director Carol Reed finished making *Night Train to Munich* in June and, as they both lived in Chelsea, they decided to join the Chelsea Home Guard.

It was commanded by General Sir Hubert Gough whose distinguished military career began when he joined the 16th Lancers in 1889 in India. He had risen to the position of first commander of the 5th Army in France during the Great War.

Harrison was soon made CO of a platoon which included a number of veterans. Since his only previous military experience was the Officers' Training Corps at Liverpool College, he did not take easily to this new role. He often hesitated when trying to enforce an order and had difficulty maintaining an authoritative tone. One old soldier, seeing Harrison was having difficulty, asked if he could be of assistance. Harrison gratefully replied, 'I'd love you to.'

He was still seeing Lilli who was still living in Hampstead with her family. 'As an enemy alien, Lilli was prohibited to leave her home after dark,' Harrison said, 'but I dreamed up ways of smuggling her out.'

The defence of the north bank of the Thames estuary stretching from Southend-on-Sea and up the Essex coast was entrusted to men of Shoeburyness Barracks.

Shoeburyness was not a particularly large garrison and the available manpower was limited. Among these troops was one Gunner Francis Howerd, a would-be actor who auditioned for RADA before the war and was turned down. He had decided to try his luck as a comedian and turned out a number of comedy revues for his local amateur dramatic society.

When war broke out he took another audition, for ENSA, the organization which supplied entertainment to the troops. He failed that too. The only audition he did pass in those early days of the war was for the army, and in 1940 he was posted to Shoeburyness Barracks and became Gunner Howerd of B Battery in the Royal Artillery.

Then he began putting on concert parties for the troops and the locals, and was introduced as Gunner *Frankie* Howerd, which became his stage name. His surname was actually Howard, but he later changed the spelling when he became a professional comedian.

When the men of his garrison were deployed along the Thames estuary, he was posted to Southend, an irony that was never lost on him, for as he told me, 'The entire population of Southend-on-Sea was entrusted to me and one other. Just the two of us.'

They made sandbags on the foreshore and lay spread-eagled behind them, with only the barbed wire between them and the invasion if it came.

'God knows what would have happened if the German High Command had chosen Southend as the point of their invasion,' he said. 'We had ten rounds of ammunition between us. I spent my time lying there thinking up sketches for my concert parties. The only thing that attacked was cramp!'

He was relieved to be posted to the small Essex village of Wakering, where he was ever ready, along with seven others, to repulse an 'invasion of German parachutists dressed as nuns'.

He enjoyed his time in Wakering. 'It was a pretty little village and it was a hot, dry summer. I loved being in the countryside; living in a tent in a cornfield was like being with the Boy Scouts after the regimentation of the barracks.'

They patrolled in twos, and while his young Welsh partner preferred to remain in their trench during their nights on watch, Howerd paced up and down the road scanning the skies for any sign of the expected invasion. 'I came to be regarded as extremely brave,' he said. 'I just think I was a bit dim.'

Actually, Howerd was not the cowardly man he came to personify in the TV series and film spin-offs of *Up Pompeii* which would make him one of Britain's best loved comedians during the 1970s. Nor was he hoping to become a hero. He enjoyed patrolling, mainly because it gave him time to work on his comedy routines. He would march up and down muttering to himself, working out his patter.

'I was never aware of danger,' he said. 'It simply didn't occur to me.'

Every now and again the young Welshman, unable to see Frankie in the darkness, anxiously called, 'Where are you, Frankie?'

'I'm here you idiot,' came Howerd's voice. 'Now shut up.' He was annoyed at having his dreams of comedy stardom disturbed.

He recalled, 'There was a farm nearby, and one day the farmer said to me, "We're so grateful to you. Just hearing your boots marching up and down gives us a feeling of security."

'I thought, *Poor bugger, if you knew the truth you'd move to London. You might be safer there.*'

Before the summer was over he was recalled back to Shoeburyness where he continued with his concert parties. Of one particular show, he said:

I decided I'd do a drag act with balloons as breasts and heavy make-up with lipstick that covered half my face, and I sang a song as an old ATS scrubber. Right in the middle of my song the air-raid siren went. The audience poured out and I rushed backstage to take off my dress and pop the balloons, but there was no time to get the make-up off. So I ended up taking up position on the parade ground with my rifle and pack and all this lipstick over my face.

An officer came round inspecting us and when he saw me he did a double take. I stood rigidly to attention trying not to tremble.He looked me over and gave an enquiring cough, and I stammered, 'Concert party, sir.'

'Concert party. Yes, right. Jolly good.' Then he walked away, turned to look back at me, and shook his head and carried on. He probably thought I was a candidate for a Section Eight.

The army church minister told Howerd that he could arrange for him to remain at the garrison and continue entertaining everyone, while others were sent off to the war. He decided to take the padre's advice who used his influence to have Howerd transferred to the quartermaster's office, and he became Bombardier Howerd.

'I really didn't think I'd make a good fighting soldier,' he told me, 'and I thought – if no one else did – I'd make a better comedian than soldier. It just seemed like common sense.'

In time he would surprise himself.

5

Children of War

'They were only taking women today – it had nothing to do with Roman.'

Raimund Polanski

On Gibraltar, on the morning of 10 June 1940, Anthony Quayle watched in amazement as a motor boat full of Royal Marines sped towards an Italian cargo ship which had anchored in the harbour for some weeks. The marines swarmed on board and, taking the crew by surprise, arrested them all. The men of another Italian ship just outside the harbour saw they were also about to be arrested, and raced for the shore, beaching their ship on Spanish soil.

'I didn't know what was going on at first,' said Quayle, 'until somebody explained to me that Italy had just declared war on us.'

After months of indecision, Mussolini sent his son-in-law, Count Galeazzo Ciano, to the British and French embassies in Rome to announce that Italy had declared war on the Allies. When asked why, he replied, 'Mussolini is only carrying out the plans he has made with Hitler.'

Il Duce himself appeared on the balcony of his residence to tell 250,000 flag-waving Italians, 'We will conquer. People of Italy, to arms! Show your tenacity, your courage, your worth.'

In Pozzuoli, a small, ancient Italian seaport town built on

46

volcanic ash from its still semi-active volcano and with its own superbly preserved amphitheatre, six-year-old Sofia Scicolone lived with her mother, Romilda Villani. Little Sofia would, as an international film star, be known as Sophia Loren.

Romilda was unmarried when she gave birth to Sophia in 1934. Sophia had the surname of her father, Riccardo Scicolone, although he refused to marry Romilda.

He lived with Romilda and Sophia at first, in a tiny room in a boarding house, but while Sophia was was still a a baby, he abandoned them. Romilda moved in with her parents who disapproved of their daughter being an unmarried mother. Their tiny apartment had a small lounge, a narrow dining room and two bedrooms. There was no bath. In these cramped conditions Sophia lived with her mother, her grandparents, two uncles and an aunt. They lived in abject poverty, starving for six days a week and eating on the seventh, as Loren would later write. Somehow, Grandma Luisa never failed to produce the 'miracle of the Sunday lunch'.

By 1940, Sophia had a two-year-old sister, Maria, also fathered by Riccardo; Romilda had secretly carried on with him in the hope of persuading him to marry her. He didn't.

Not long after Italy declared war on Britain, German tanks rolled into Pozzuoli. The inhabitants turned out to cheer and wave as the troops goose-stepped down the streets. It was a colourful spectacle; Sophia thought the soldiers were beautifully dressed in their handsome uniforms. Among them were the first blond blue-eyed men she had ever seen.

War, and the arrival of the Germans, brought a sense of excitement to Pozzuoli the people there had never known. Sophia watched the Germans playing war games in the back yards of the houses in her street. She found them friendly to talk to, and she waited eagerly for troop trains, *en route* from Naples to Rome, to stop at Pozzuoli where the soldiers disembarked to stretch their legs.

The excitement passed as war became a normal way of life. The town's facilities began to close – first the school, then the cinema, then the library.

Two days after Italy declared war, Britain launched bombing

raids on Milan and Genoa. RAF and South African bombers hit the Italian Air Force bases in Libya and East Africa, catching them by surprise. Italian striking power in the Middle East was severely crippled, but Italy retaliated, launching seven bombing raids on Malta.

Pozzuoli had a munitions factory which drew the attention of the RAF. Allied bombing raids drove the civilians into the railroad tunnel almost every night after the last train for Naples had left. At first Sophia was excited when the air-raid sirens sounded and everyone ran for the shelter of the tunnel. People dragged mattresses and blankets with them and lay in complete darkness. In the middle of the tunnel it stank of urine, faeces and rubbish, attracting rats and cockroaches. Everyone grew accustomed to it all.

One night Sophia stepped out of the tunnel to watch the raid. To her it had a magical quality as the sea became alive with flares that fell from the British bombers. Romilda, suddenly aware that Sophia was missing, ran through the tunnel in a desperate search for her. She found Sophia at the entrance gazing into the blazing sky and clapping her hands with excitement.

Romilda delivered a hefty slap to Sophia's face and, crying with relief, dragged her back inside. Sophia also began to cry; not, she later said, because of the slap, but because she had been torn away from the spellbinding spectacle.

There was a night when the air-raid siren failed to sound. Sophia awoke to the sudden thunder of bombs falling all around, shattering windows and rocking the building. Romilda shouted to Sophia to dress quickly, but as explosions shook the walls and lit up the room, the scared and confused girl got undressed and was standing naked and trembling when Romilda came back for her.

Romilda dragged the naked Sophia with one hand and Maria, who had lost her shoes, with the other towards the tunnel as explosions ripped the street apart. Shrapnel cut Sophia's face, covering it with blood.

The next morning the family returned to their apartment. Their street was covered in rubble and splattered with the blood of the dead and injured who lay in the road. Broken glass cut Maria's feet, and when they reached home, they found half of it blown away.

Winter came. Never-ending queues lined up for hours to collect water at the spring-fed fountain. Maria became constantly ill. Food became increasingly scarce. Sophia's mother went foraging each day while the uncles went to work at the munitions plant for meagre wages, usually spending each day repairing the damage caused by raids. There were many evenings when the family ate nothing. A crust of bread became a luxury.

Sophia took to creeping into the caretaker's garden and stealing fruit from the trees. The caretaker finally caught Sophia and yelled to all the neighbourhood, 'Look at her! Look at her eyes! They are the eyes of a thief!'

It was freezing in the tunnel each night. There was little clothing and bedding to go round. In the cold and dark, Sophia listened to hungry babies crying, couples screaming at each other, some making love to keep warm, women giving birth. Sophia tried to block out the sounds and grew afraid of the darkness; it was a phobia she never overcame.

One morning, Romilda took Sophia by the hand and, making sure they were not being followed, left the tunnel to go out into the countryside. They followed a narrow path to a series of caves where lived a goatherder who was a friend of one of Sophia's uncles. He filled a mug with fresh milk straight from one of his goats and gave it to Sophia.

They returned on numerous occasions, always in secret, so that Sophia could have what would often be her only food of the day. Fortunately, she remained healthy and was rarely ill, although she was so thin that the children took to calling her *stecchetta*, meaning 'stick'.

Poland had a history of anti-Semitism of which the occupying Germans took advantage. During the early days of occupation when the Jews were moved into the ghettos and were securely isolated, both the German and Polish authorities left them alone.

During 1940 Germany intensified its strict regulations on
the Jews in all Polish cities. Then they began constructing the
concentration camps. Young Roman Polanski, just seven years
old, ignored the strict curfew laws and, by perching on the
roof of a building on the edge of the ghetto, watched German
films projected on the walls of buildings outside.

The films attempted to persuade the Gentile citizens of the
wonders of Nazism, but Roman understood little of all that;
he was simply fascinated by the sights and sounds and wished
he could see them at close range.

Early in 1941 rumours spread through the Cracow ghetto
of the concentration camps while at the same time the
ghetto's rules were tightened. There were harsh penalties for
those who broke the laws. Curfew breakers were beaten by the
Polish squads hired by the Nazis to patrol the streets. Some
were executed on the spot for all manner of violations.

Roman heard his mother, Bula, talking bitterly about some
of the wealthier Jews who sought favours from the authorities
by informing on violators and offering money. Fear of being
sent to concentration camps set many Jews against one
another. But in the end no amount of bribery and information
saved any of them.

As the Polanskis' money and food ran out, Roman was sent
by his father, Riszard, out on to the streets to scrounge among
rubbish bins for any scraps of food and clothing. He met with
a couple of other boys who were also scrounging and who had
discovered a sewer that took them under the wire fence into
the main part of the city. They showed Roman the route and
each day he crept out of the ghetto to steal food from shops.

On one of these forays, he and a friend, a rather fat eight-
year-old, were filling their pockets with potatoes when they
were seen by the shopkeeper. He ran after them and others
joined in the chase. Roman was small and agile and managed
to escape through the city's alleys, but the other boy was
caught and taken to the police.

Roman arrived home, exhausted and shaking with fear that
his friend, who lived across the road, would give him away.
Some hours later, the boy, beaten and bloodied, was marched

by a squad of German soldiers back to his home. Petrified, Roman watched from behind curtains as his friend's grandmother came to the door. Roman could not hear what was being said but he saw that the officer seemed polite and was smiling. He saw the grandmother smile too. She turned to speak to the rest of the family who had come to the door. Then the officer drew his gun and shot the old woman in the head.

The Germans left and Roman felt hugely relieved that they didn't come knocking on his door. The next day he went through the sewer and continued his search for food. He didn't know that while he was gone the Germans had begun a round-up of Jews to transport to concentration camps.

They came to his house and banged on the door. Bula answered it while Riszard hid in a closet. The soldiers dragged Bula into the street to join a group of other women. Two soldiers searched the house but didn't find Riszard cowering in his hiding-place.

Roman returned to see his mother and the other women surrounded by soldiers. Men and children tried desperately to reach them and were brutally knocked away with the butts of guns.

Roman cried out and began to run towards his mother. She saw him and gave a sharp look that told him to stop. He halted only yards away. More women were being dragged out. A soldier looked at Roman who froze with fear. Bula shouted, 'Go, Roman! Hide!'

He turned and ran, making his way round to the back of the house by way of an alley, and running indoors to watch from the window. He was just in time to see his mother and the other women being dragged away.

He sat there for an hour or more, sobbing until, finally, his father emerged. He flew at Roman and began beating him, saying that the boy from across the road had informed the Germans that Roman had been with him. He told Roman it was all his fault his mother had been taken away.

Roman tried to explain through his tears that he only went into the city because his father had told him to steal food.

Riszard just kept on hitting him. At that moment Roman's
Uncle Raimund came in and pulled Riszard away.

'They were only taking women today, you fool,' Raimund
told Riszard. 'It had nothing to do with Roman.'

While the uncle and father argued, Roman fled to another
room and collapsed in tears. The argument subsided and
Roman heard his uncle and father discussing how they might
escape from the ghetto.

Roman hoped his mother would return, but the days went
by and she didn't come back. His father still blamed him and
treated him brutally until, two weeks later, Roman left his
home and took refuge at his uncle's.

The round-ups continued daily. The boundary of the
ghetto grew smaller. Raimund made arrangements with a
Catholic family by the name of Koslewski who lived in the
suburbs to take in his two children, Zbigniew and Josef, in
return for money. Raimund hoped they would also accept
Roman.

The night before the Nazis planned to make the final
round-up, Raimund gave Roman directions to the Koslewski
house and told him to take his two cousins there by way of the
sewer.

Roman reached the Koslewski home but the Catholics had
not expected Roman as well as the other two boys. They
decided it would be too dangerous to hide yet a third Jewish
child, although Mr Koslewski said they would do so if his
father gave them money.

Roman did not dare return to the ghetto and took to hiding
out for three days until, frightened and alone, he went back
home. He found the ghetto completely empty, with no sign of
either his uncle or his father. Everyone had gone to the camps.

He returned to the Koslewskis and begged them to take
him in. They dared not risk it, but they asked another family,
called Tomasialowicz, who lived on the outskirts of Cracow,
to take him in. The Tomasialowiczs agreed but they had to
have money which came out of the funds held by Roman's
cousins.

Mrs Tomasialowicz was an alcoholic who bought drink

with the money which she was supposed to spend on Roman. In her drunken state, she boasted to a neighbour that she was hiding a Jewish boy. The following day a German patrol came to the house.

Roman was in the backyard with the family children, and at the first sight of the troops, he climbed the garden wall and spent the night hiding in the basement of a granary.

In the morning he made his way to the Koslewskis where the matriarch took pity on him and persuaded her husband to let him stay. But he had to contribute to the family's finances, so at the age of eight he was sent out to work, as many of the boys of Cracow did, selling newspapers. He was assigned to a street corner, right next to the Gestapo headquarters, and was paid a small percentage from the daily profits which he handed over to the Koslewski family.

One autumn evening, Roman came across a recently reopened cinema and, remembering the films he used to watch projected on to the walls of buildings, he sneaked in. He had never been inside a cinema before, and he became engrossed in the film which was about German industrial progress and cultural superiority.

'After it was over,' he recalled, 'I couldn't wait to go again.' His fascination with those films would one day lead him to become a successful film director. But before then, he had to survive the Holocaust that was taking place.

Jews in other countries under German occupation were suffering the same fate. Czechoslovakian film director Milos Forman was the son of a Jewish professor of education and his Christian wife. Both of Forman's parents died in concentration camps – it was assumed if the husband was Jewish, the wife was also – and Forman, only six months older than Roman Polanski, was hidden and raised by relatives. The Final Solution was by no means exclusive to Poland.

6

The Battle of Britain

'As far as I could tell the only thing we were protecting was a goat.'

John Mills

Apart from a few ineffectual air raids by the Italian Air Force on Gibraltar during the summer of 1940, Anthony Quayle saw little action. Gibraltar had become more of a centre of operations, under the command of General Sir Noel Mason-MacFarlane; Mason-Mac to all who knew him. 'I really had a lot of affection and respect for Mason-Mac,' said Quayle.

Force H, the battle squadron based on Gibraltar, was under the command of Admiral Somerville. He offered the French fleet, harboured at Oran and Dakar, the chance either to join the British fleet, or to sail to the West Indies or any British port to be incarcerated. If they refused, they had six hours to scuttle their ships or be fired upon. The French refused all offers and on 3 July 1940, the British fleet opened fire.

It was a brief battle, from which only a few French ships escaped back to Toulon. A few days later the French sent bombers to attack Gibraltar.

Quayle recalled:

I remember the attack because I was having lunch with Mason-Mac in his house when the planes came. We quickly dived into a cupboard under the stairs as bombs fell all round the house. Mason-Mac took a cigarette from his case just as a bomb landed so close to the house that the whole building shook. It made him jump and he dropped the case and all the cigarettes spilled all over the floor. Those are the funny things you remember about the war.

In July 1940, a completely new undercover organization was set up; Special Operations Executive – SOE. Its task was to undertake unconventional warfare and propaganda projects in occupied Europe. Its major weapon was sabotage, and it used local Resistance fighters in conjunction with its own agents.

Winston Churchill called on his friend, Alexander Korda, for his help in SOE operations, asking him to transfer to America and set up his film company with two purposes in mind. One was to make films that would be patriotic but not propagandistic and would not appear to have any official backing from the British government. The other purpose had nothing to do with making films.

Korda was to set up offices in New York and Los Angeles that would be linked to a worldwide motion picture corporation. It had become difficult for British agents to work freely in the United States because of objections from American isolationalists. Churchill needed a base for British Intelligence that would be a perfect 'cover'. Korda's film offices would serve that purpose.

Korda himself was to act as a courier, and he often met with various members of SOE and MI5 who gave him instructions; they also warned him of the risks. He might be scrutinized by the FBI as a foreign agent, and worse, German agents might try to dispose of him.

Korda was willing to accept the risks, but he was reluctant to leave England at this time as he knew that to many his departure for America would be seen as an act of cowardice. He waited for as long as he could, and then made the move to the States, announcing that he and his brother Vincent needed Hollywood facilities to make *The Thief of Baghdad*.

Douglas Fairbanks Jr continued his efforts to fight what he

called 'the Battle of America' on behalf of Britain. From his
own pocket he set up three convalescent homes in England,
called The Douglas Voluntary Hospitals, and he took a leading role in founding the Franco–British War Relief Fund in
California.

He also hoped to formalize a mutual honorary citizenship
between Britain and America which President Roosevelt
promised would receive serious consideration. But the project
never came to fruition.

A number of Americans had set up the Committee to
Defend America by Aiding the Allies, and Douglas was
invited to become one of its three vice-chairmen. President
Roosevelt was campaigning for the 1940 presidential elections
and could not be seen to be helping Fairbanks, but he nevertheless invited Fairbanks to the White House many times to
hear of his efforts to aid the Allies.

The committee gradually helped to sway public opinion to
support Britain actively, enabling the president to sanction
supplies for Britain, neutrality patrols and the convoy system.

In August 1940, Fairbanks applied to join the US Naval
Reserve at San Diego and awaited the outcome.

Vincent Korda had his son Michael move with him to Los
Angeles but it took some 'adroit string pulling' by Alex to
organize Michael's evacuation. Gertrude, Michael's mother,
who was divorced from Vincent, went on ahead while Michael
and his nanny found themselves among a thousand crying,
excited, grief-stricken children on board the *Empress of
Canada*. The ship zig-zagged across the Atlantic to Montreal
where Gertrude waited for them. Then they caught the train
down to Los Angeles.

Alexander Korda had been right; he was criticized for leaving Britain. But he could not explain that he was acting as a
special agent for the British prime minister.

Clive Brook, the popular British character actor, was also
criticized for sending his seventeen-year-old daughter Faith to
the safety of California. Brook had made quite a name for
himself in Hollywood during the 1930s but he didn't remain

in America himself during the war years. He returned to Britain to make films. But there were still some who considered his decision to send Faith to America virtually a criminal act. Faith, who had trained as an actress at RADA, would later return to England to join the ATS and come in for further cruel and unwarranted criticism.

Among the evacuated children going to the United States that summer of 1940 were Laurence Olivier's son Tarquin who went over with his mother (and Olivier's previous wife) Jill, as well as Vivien Leigh's daughter Suzanne, accompanied by Vivien's mother. Olivier and Leigh had just married, and were now relieved that their children were safely across the Atlantic, especially as another ship, *City of Benares*, had been sunk by a U-boat, killing virtually all the children on board.

Although the children were now in America, Olivier and Leigh still wanted to return to Britain. In preparation for volunteering for the RAF, Olivier had been taking flying lessons at Clover Field. His instructor was Cecil Smallwood who taught most of the Hollywood stars who wanted to be pilots, including James Stewart. Managing to smash up three training planes, Olivier completed his training and qualified as a licensed pilot.

Whether children were evacuated to America or just to the safer areas of Britain depended on the class structure. Children from poor families in London went to the country. Children from wealthy families went to Canada or America.

Jack Hawkins, a star of British films since 1930 and also a respected stage actor, was relieved when his daughter Susan went with her mother, actress Jessica Tandy, to America. Jessica had been offered work there, and she and Hawkins had been gradually drifting apart as each put their respective careers before their marriage, so the move to America for wife and daughter seemed timely.

He had just said goodbye to them in the summer of 1940 and found himself in a London full of men and women in uniform. He noted, 'I felt lonely, unhappy and restless.'

Hawkins was twenty-nine years old and, for the first time in his career, felt that his work was no longer that important; it seemed the right thing to join up. So he and his friend, actor Andrew Cruickshank, went off to volunteer. They quickly discovered that the army was not looking for any more volunteers at this time.

Deciding to give the Royal Navy a try, Hawkins approached Lord Semphill whom he had met socially and whom he knew had 'something to do with the Royal Navy Air Force'.

'Why don't you come into the navy?' Lord Semphill asked him.

'I don't know anything about ships,' said Hawkins.

'That doesn't matter. I expect they'll ask you if you have ever been sailing. You just reply "Yes", and you'll be in.'

Hawkins decided that didn't sound satisfactory – 'especially as I suffered from sea sickness' – so he sought advice from a fellow member of the Savage Club who worked for the War Office, and was told he could sign on with a Guards regiment for seven years. That didn't suit Hawkins either.

The following week his friend called him and said, 'Don't tell anyone where you got this from, Jack, but if you go to the recruiting centre in Seven Sisters Road in Holloway, you can volunteer for the Royal Welch Fusiliers, the 23rd Foot. The order stopping recruitment hasn't got through to them yet.'

Hawkins collected Andrew Cruickshank and they drove off to the recruitment centre where a sergeant told them, 'There's no more volunteering.'

Hawkins said, 'But we want to volunteer for the Royal Welch Fusiliers.'

The astonished sergeant ushered them into another office where an equally astonished major demanded, 'How did you know about this?'

Hawkins explained that he had been told they could still volunteer for the 23rd Foot.

'That is correct,' said the major. 'I've had no order rescinding that. Very well, you had better have your medicals.'

Four minutes later, having been passed medically fit, they were back before the major taking the oath of allegiance and being presented with the king's shilling. 'I fancy,' Hawkins wrote, 'we were among the last soldiers in the war who went through this ceremony because men who were called up were not required to take the oath.'

A month later Hawkins and Cruickshank arrived at the gates of the regiment's barracks at Wrexham. They were very well dressed and had particularly smart luggage. The guards stamped to attention and shouted, 'Gentlemen 'ere!'

A sergeant marched up to them. 'Good, evening, gentlemen. Come to join us?'

The two actors smiled and confirmed they had indeed come to join them. A soldier was ordered to carry their cases and they were led to the guard room and given tea. The sergeant went to see the adjutant and returned to tell them the adjutant wanted to see them both.

The adjutant told them almost apologetically, 'There seems to have been a bit of a muddle as we don't appear to have your papers. When were you told to report?'

'We were told it was today because, as I understood it, this was when the regiment was expecting a new intake of recruits,' Hawkins explained.

There was a pause. Then the adjutant said, 'An intake of *what?*' Realizing the two men were not officer cadets but raw recruits, his manner darkened as he shouted at the sergeant to get them out of there and get them billeted.

The sergeant marched them across the parade ground and issued them with a denim uniform, a rifle each 'and that was about all'.

Secret military organizations were being set up around Britain, and David Niven decided to take advantage of the call for volunteers 'for a new commando unit under Colonel Dudley Clarke whose primary purpose was to make "cut and thrust" raids on the enemy coastline – so I put my name forward.'

Niven went before Colonel Clarke who revealed little about the unit except that he had some special ideas which would be disclosed at a later date. He ordered Niven to report to Lochailort Castle in the Western Highlands of Scotland for training.

Niven never boasted of any great aspirations to perform courageous acts. 'Most of the volunteers were made of much sterner stuff than I was made of,' he said. 'I was there out of boredom. I never was a hero.'

Among his instructors were Lord Lovat, demolition expert 'Mad Mike' Calvert, and numerous other highly decorated and important commando leaders. 'They taught us a variety of methods of silently killing.'

In July 1940, Niven and his fellow commandos were put to the test. Germany had bombed the Channel Islands of Jersey and Guernsey on 28 June 1940 and by 30 June Guernsey was under German occupation. It was decided that the commandos would execute a raid on Guernsey. To prepare for this they trained on the Isle of Wight.

Then, on 15 July, David Niven and his team landed on Guernsey. He later wrote in his memoirs that the operation was a success. But he told me, 'The truth was, it was generally considered a farce.'

The commanding officer slipped and fired his revolver, alerting the enemy. Three men said they couldn't swim to the pick-up boat. Those three were left behind.

'One team ended up on Sark due to compass failure, while another team landed on undefended points of the island to no purpose. We did manage to take a few bemused prisoners from their beds. But really, we were undertrained.'

The first large-scale bombing raid of the Battle of Britain came on 10 July 1940, with the raid on the docks in South Wales. By mid-August the Battle of Britain was intensifying and in September the *Luftwaffe* started its huge bombing missions on London, Southampton, Bristol, Cardiff, Liverpool and Manchester.

David Niven was promoted in September: 'I became a captain, and made liaison officer for MO9 which was the War Department responsible for commando operations.

'I was installed at the War Office where I shared a desk with Captain Quintin Hogg. But most of the time I was travelling around contacting the various commando units. Because of the very real and imminent threat of invasion, the commandos were switched from being offensive to defensive, and plans were drawn up for us to transform ourselves into an underground movement.'

He still spent occasional weekends at Ditchley and there was one conversation he had with Winston Churchill which he never forgot.

'He asked me what I was doing at the moment, so I told him about my part in commando operations.

'"You shouldn't be telling me this," he said. "Your security is very lax." I never knew for sure if he was genuinely angry, but he was probably right.'

By coincidence, Niven bumped into the mysterious WAAF from the Café de Paris at the National Gallery in London. She was Primula Rollo, a cipher clerk at the RAF Reconnaissance Squadron at Heston. It was love at first sight, as it was so often for couples meeting during the war years, and on 16 September *The Times* announced that a marriage would soon take place between David Niven and Primula 'Primmie' Rollo. In fact, it took place within a week, at the parish church of Huish on the Wiltshire Downs. Throughout the ceremony, the Battle of Britain raged above in a cloudless sky.

They bought a cottage near Slough and Primmie left the RAF. Determined to contribute to the war effort, she cycled each morning to Slough to help build Hurricanes at Hawker's factory.

It was a marriage that would last until her tragic death in 1946 and, according to all who knew Niven well, those six years of marriage were the happiest of his private life. It was a classic wartime love affair.

Shortly after the wedding, Niven volunteered for a new and highly secretive unit called 'Phantom':

It was one of the least known of the wartime special regiments, invented by Colonel Hopkinson who had realized during the retreat from Dunkirk that there was a dire need for reliable communication from the front line.

He came up with the simple idea of deploying highly mobile squadrons equipped with radios and dispatch

riders among forward units. We even used carrier
pigeons. 'Phantom's' commanding officer would remain
with the Army Commander, and when situations needed
clarifying, the 'Squadron' Commander checked his map
to find the 'Phantom' unit in the problem vicinity and
then sent a message directly to it.

I was made a major and took over 'A' Squadron. We
became involved in the preparations to form underground movements in the event of invasion. My own
special disguise was that of a parson.

A small part of Britain, a field in Royston, was being defended
by Sergeant John Mills and his crew. He said, 'As far as I
could tell the only thing we were protecting was a goat.'

It was now August and still Sergeant Mills and his crew
had not had the chance to fire in anger. Mills's request to be
sent to the Officer Cadet Training Unit had, so far, gone
unacknowledged.

One morning, just as dawn was breaking and we were
about to stand to, a plane shot out of the clouds. There
had been a raid on London and we knew German bombers were heading for home. I knew it was probably out of
range, but it seemed to be making a bee-line for the coast
so I ordered the crew to open fire on it anyway. We were
really all very excited.

A few minutes later the telephone rang. It was the CO.
'Sergeant Mills, did you open fire on an aircraft just a few
minutes ago?'

'Yes sir. We didn't hit it though.'

'Just as well. Congratulations, sergeant. That plane
was a Wellington.' It was one of ours! 'Report to me at
09.00 hours.'

The phone was slammed down. I reported and got a
real rocketing.

Two weeks later a brigadier turned up for an off-the-
record inspection of the gun sites, and I'm glad to say he
announced that he found our team in great shape. Then

he suddenly recognized me; I had produced a show at Cambridge. He asked me what I was still doing in the ranks, and hadn't I put my name down for an OCTU?

I said, 'Yes sir, the first week I joined the battalion.'

'You put on a damn good show. I'll look into it.'

The following week Mills was posted to the Officer Cadet Training Unit at Shrivenham, and reported to E Battery Watson Unit on 6 September 1940. A month later he was commissioned and posted to the 1st Rifle Battalion, Monmouthshire Regiment in Trowbridge, Wiltshire. He and Mary Hayley Bell made plans to get married.

He had been given command of a dozen sites scattered over a wide area of Trowbridge. But he was now niggled by a recurring pain in his stomach. He had tried taking various powders and tablets, but the pain was getting worse. Finally his sergeant persuaded him to report to the MO who sent him straight to the Forbes Fraser Hospital in Bath for an examination.

A week of tests confirmed that he had a duodenal ulcer. A board was called on 19 December to decide if he would be able to remain on active duty. After a year in the ranks and just a few weeks of having his own command, he was thoroughly depressed at the prospect of it all being for nothing. He was put on a special diet but when the board met it was decided he was permanently unfit for active service.

Mary collected him from the hospital. He was, he said, in a 'zombie-like state of acceptance'. The war was over for him. But now he and Mary could be together, and they set the date for their wedding – 16 January 1941.

On board the *Lobus*, sailing for Bermuda in late summer 1940, Kenneth More had formulated a whole new career 'as the author of countless love letters'.

He was writing them for the crew to send back to their girl-friends and wives. 'They seemed to think I was more expert at putting down words of love than I was with a gun.

'I used to write these wonderful love letters, very passionate.

I had a very vivid imagination and I promised all these sweet-hearts back home all sorts of things. I often wondered if the men were able to match up to all the promises I'd made on their behalf.'

They sailed to Bermuda, through the Panama Canal, down the west coast of South America, stopping at Ecuador, Peru and finally Chile. There they unloaded their cargo of Sheffield knives and forks and tinware, and took on hides and saltpetre among other stores needed in Britain.

It was a curious experience being in Chile as it was neutral and the bars there were frequented by German sailors whose ships had already been in port when war broke out and then were not permitted to leave.

At a bar called The Graf Zeppelin, we came across German sailors – pure Nazis they were, so it didn't take more than a few beers and a few choice words to get a fight started. It was like a scene out of a movie with fists flying and bodies being hurled through the air and bottles smashing on heads. I don't mind admitting I ducked under the nearest table to watch the brawl in relative safety.

Sometimes I was brave enough to pick up a bottle and hit a German over the head with it, but I always did my best not to get involved.

The Chilean Navy was pro-British, and the Army was pro-German, so during the fights, if the naval police arrived, the British sailors were given safe escort back to their ships and the Germans put behind bars for the night. But if the army police arrived, it was the Germans who went free while More and his shipmates were put in jail.

The *Lobus* pulled out of Chile and headed back for Liverpool, joining convoy HX84 in the Atlantic in November 1940. Only one ship protected the convoy, the armed merchant cruiser *Jervis* Bay.

Kenneth More recalled:

When we got to the Atlantic we came under attack from the *Admiral von Scheer* which was a pocket battleship and powered by diesel engines. It was so powerful we couldn't outrun it, so we didn't have much chance. But the captain of the *Jervis Bay* bravely turned towards the German ship and headed straight for her. *Jervis Bay* only had six-inch guns up against the German's eleven-inch guns and the *Jervis Bay* didn't stand a chance. But she kept on going, putting herself between us and the German, until the German sunk her. It was a brave sacrifice.

The rest of the convoy meanwhile scattered and the *Scheer* raced after us, but out of some thirty-five ships it only managed to sink five, which was not bad going considering.

After that we sailed into the worst storm I have ever experienced; a force 10 hurricane. The waves were double the size of our ship. God knows how we didn't go down. But we got through that.

What really worried most of us, I think, was wondering what we would find when we got home. We'd heard all sorts of reports that Liverpool had been completely wiped out and that London was in ruins. As it was, when we docked at Liverpool we found it virtually undamaged.

Later, I was ordered to report to Royal Navy Barracks in Portsmouth to go before an Officer Selection Board. I knew that Robert Newton, a fine actor and a renowned heavy drinker, had been an ordinary seaman, yet would hold officers of all ranks spellbound at The Goat pub in Portsmouth with his amusing stories. But the Officer Selection Board were not fans of his as he often returned to barracks so drunk that he climbed over the walls rather than try and get past the sentry. He had been caught several times and taken before the officer-of-the-night for punishment. He went before the Officer Selection Committee where he told the admiral that if they asked him to accept a commission, he would consider it. He would, he said, be doing the navy a great favour by accepting a commission.

Instead, they threw him out of the navy. So I expected that, as I was an actor, I could expect little favour. But the interview went well and to my surprise and delight I was commissioned as acting sub-lieutenant. I later learned that I was not to serve at sea after all, but had been chosen to train Merchant Navy officers in light anti-aircraft work. My delight quickly turned to depression as I wanted to see some real action.

Rex Harrison was still married, although separated. It was not considered the right thing for couples to live together in those days, especially when one of them was still married to someone else. So Harrison and Lilli Palmer had to be careful not to cause a scandal.

While he was filming *Major Barbara* at Denham Studios, he moved into a small cottage near the studio. Finally deciding to throw caution to the wind, Harrison had Lilli move in with him; she hoped to escape the daily onslaught London suffered from German bombers.

But not even Denham escaped the blitz. Hitler had allegedly ordered the studio to be bombed because it belonged to Alexander Korda. True or not, Denham certainly seemed to be a target.

'Filming began in June and was scheduled for a ten-week shoot,' explained Rex Harrison. But as the Battle of Britain raged on, filming was continually interrupted by air raids.

'We had spotters on the roof of the studio, so when enemy planes were sighted, our own alarm was raised and the whole cast and crew took shelter in the storage areas under the concrete studio floor. When the all clear sounded, we went back to filming.'

An estimated 125 bombs fell in the vicinity of the studio during the course of filming. On one occasion the skies above were filled with planes and the film unit only managed to get one single shot that day.

Some scenes were filmed on location in London. 'One day we arrived to find the street that we planned to film in had been completely flattened by the previous night's raid,' said Harrison.

Filming of *Major Barbara* was finally completed in December 1940. Rex Harrison noted that 'the air raids had caused the shooting schedule to stretch from six weeks to six months'.

Writer Harold French, a close friend of Rex Harrison, had moved out of London, but his wife, Phyl, had remained behind because she had a war job in the capital. One morning French telephoned home, as he did every day, but was unable to get through. He rushed back to London to discover that his house had received a direct hit and his wife was dead.

Distraught, French moved in with Harrison and Lilli who did their best to console him. French and Harrison began making plans to do *No Time for Comedy* as a tour and then open at the London Haymarket with French directing Harrison and Lilli.

No Time for Comedy was to begin its tour in December 1940, in Blackpool. Harrison recalled:

During rehearsals, two days before we opened, two detectives turned up at the Grand Theatre and asked for 'Peiser/Palmer'. Lilli presented herself and was led away. The law demanded that those like Lilli who were regarded as 'aliens' had to report to the police if they changed location and get their passport stamped by the police. This task had been the responsibility of the producer. Unfortunately, he had failed to notify the police that she was there.

The police refused to release Lilli and took her back to London. I was absolutely furious at the producer and it was three days after the play opened that they allowed her to return to Blackpool where her part had been understudied.

It was my responsibility, whenever we moved to a new town, to discover where the nearest air-raid shelter was. When the siren went during a performance, I would step up to the footlights and inform the audience where the

nearest shelter was. Usually, few people actually left the
theatre and we continued with the play.

On a wintry night in 1940 an Irish Fusilier was on his way to
his barracks in the North Wales University town of Bangor,
trudging through the thick snow. He was 'Cheerful' Charlie
Chester, a star of BBC radio whose promising career was
interrupted by the call-up. He was famous for his Cockney
style of humour, although he was actually born in Sussex.

As he made his way into Bangor, he suddenly noticed a
flashing light from the hill across the valley. He knew it was a
signal and, although he couldn't read Morse Code, he quickly
jotted down the dots and dashes on the back of a matchbox
and hurried to the officers' mess where he interrupted the
intelligence officer, Major Flint, who was having dinner.

Chester explained about the signal he had seen and
explained he couldn't read Morse Code.

'Then tap it out, man,' the impatient officer ordered.

Chester tapped the message while Major Flint wrote down
NWU, NWU.

'My God!' exclaimed the major. 'It's North Wales
University.'

A battery was put on the university and a patrol went out
searching for the source of the signal. Two men were rooted
out who had been sending a landmark to the German bombers on their way to bomb Liverpool.

The next day Chester's colonel summoned him and said,
'You're an actor, aren't you?'

'Yes, sir.'

'So you're used to disguises. How would you like to volunteer for special duties?'

Charlie Chester was only too pleased to end his days
marching with back-packs and standing guard duty, and was
posted to intelligence where he learned the art of counter-
espionage.

7

British Bulldogs

*'I think for the first time since the beginning of the war, I
felt I was doing something worthwhile.'*

Anthony Quayle

On the eve of the New Year of 1941, Laurence Olivier and
Vivien Leigh were finding it difficult to celebrate on board the
American ship *Exambion*; 'not what you would describe as a
queen among ocean liners,' noted Olivier. They were heading
for Lisbon in neutral Portugal from where they hoped to make
their way at last to England.

It was, said Olivier, 'the most apprehensive voyage I have
ever known'. Although the captain had American citizenship,
he was a German, and Olivier remained anxiously suspicious
of him.

As the captain asked his guests to raise their glasses in a
New Year's toast, he said, *'Deutschland über Alles!'*

Then most of the twenty-three passengers replied, *'Heil
Hitler!'*

Feeling desperately outnumbered, Olivier turned to a US
naval lieutenant who wore pilot's wings, and said confidently,
'To the American and the British naval air services.'

The pilot replied, 'I prefer to say, "To all pilots trying to get
home."' That is when Olivier realized this officer was not
planning to return to America.

The rest of the voyage was a nightmare for the Oliviers who
had personally known someone who had been removed from

a ship by Germans and taken to a prison camp. They nervously waited for the same thing to happen to them.

They reached Lisbon safely and called at the British Embassy to present a letter of introduction to the air commodore. He arranged for them to get on a plane bound for Bristol a few days later. The aircraft's windows were blacked out and, half way home, it caught fire when the pilot fired a recognition flare from the cockpit but forgot to open a window.

The passengers sat frozen in terror as they saw the co-pilot rush from the blazing cockpit to fetch a fire extinguisher. The fire was put out and they landed in Bristol in the middle of an air-raid.

Air-raids had become something the population of Britain had learned to live with. When *No Time for Comedy* moved to London in March 1941 at the newly opened Haymarket Theatre, its star Rex Harrison was put on firewatch duty, patrolling the building twice a week looking for incendiary bombs.

'We had a silent air-raid warning system,' he told me. 'If there was a raid during a performance, which was often at that time, a sign was illuminated at the very front of the stage, and anyone who wished to leave could do so while we on stage carried on with the performance. There was an instance when a bomb landed right on the hotel next door. The hotel was flattened and the theatre was hardly touched, but it definitely scared us.'

The Oliviers were living at their beloved Durham Cottage in London where they were visited by old friends – John Mills, Ralph Richardson and Jack Hawkins.

Jack Hawkins and Andrew Cruickshank had completed their three months' basic training for the Royal Welch Fusiliers and emerged as 'officer material'.

Hawkins had thereafter gone before the Officer Cadet Training selection board where 'as far as the board was concerned I was just one of those "actor chappies"'. But when he mentioned that he was fond of horse riding some of the officers became interested and asked if he ever went on the hunt. He replied that he used to go out with the Smith Bosanquet Hunt from Theobald's Park, and that seemed enough to satisfy them that he could go to Officer Training Corps at Pwllheli in North Wales. Cruickshank was also posted there where they found themselves 'guarding the Beddgelert Pass against all invaders'.

Because of the shortage of officers following Dunkirk, the training period was cut to ten weeks, and in 1941 Jack Hawkins emerged as a second lieutenant.

At Durham Cottage Hawkins kept grinning at Olivier and, knowing he had escaped the safety of America to come home and possibly get shot at, growled, 'You are a silly bugger!'

Not long after his visit to the Oliviers, Jack Hawkins was seconded to make a propaganda film, *Next of Kin*, which he found a welcome break from military life. After filming, he returned to his old regiment in late summer 1942, and a month later he received a letter from his wife, Jessica Tandy, who announced that she wanted a divorce.

Although he realized just how much he and Jessica had drifted apart even before the war, it nevertheless came as a shock. He said his sanity was saved when, shortly after receiving the letter, he was posted to India.

Ralph Richardson was happy to help Olivier to get into the Fleet Air Arm. Richardson was a naval commander working in the admiral's offce at Lee-on-Solent. He had joined the Royal Naval Reserve as an acting sub-lieutenant with the job of looking after secret files at Eastleigh. 'Secret books sounded exciting, romantic, perhaps they might even be a little naughty,' he said. In the event of invasion by the Germans, he was to destroy the files in the incinerator.

Although he had learned to fly in his own Gypsy Moth before the war, Richardson was, at thirty-nine, too old to fly in combat. He was, however, allowed to fly old sea planes to various airfields. His accident rate was alarmingly high and he became known as 'Pranger Richardson'.

'I was very lucky not to be killed,' he said. 'I had some narrow escapes. Old planes just kept falling to bits. One burst into flames just after I landed.'

With Richardson's direct help, Laurence Olivier entered the Fleet Air Arm, commissioned as a lieutenant and stationed at HMS *Kestrel* at Worthydown near Winchester in May, 1941. His job was to help train air-gunners by flying them about for an hour or so, giving them airborne practice.

Often, to cheer his fellow officers, he performed perfect imitations of the CO and the chaplain. He had a certain daredevil quality and was once heard while striding towards his aircraft loudly proclaiming, 'Those friends thou hast, bind them to thyself with thongs of steel.'

He decided one day to 'shoot up a friend', a practice forbidden by the Admiralty. He found the house of Jeanne de Casalis who lived near the coast of Folkestone and buzzed her as she stood in the garden, frantically waving her arms at him. He missed the house by a few feet, thoroughly enjoying himself, and as he climbed a Spitfire came alongside him. The pilot of the Spitfire was trying to warn him, as was Jeanne de Casalis, that there was a raid on Folkestone and he was not only in danger of getting himself shot down, but of having his friend's house completely destroyed too.

HMS *Kestrel* was also used by the army to train its artillery men. Soldiers were required, when on naval grounds, to treat naval officers as their superiors, a fact which was lost on Private George Munn and his companion who had been sent there to practice on ack-ack guns.

While returning to base one night, Olivier passed the soldiers who failed to salute him.

'You there,' Lieutenant Olivier called. The soldiers stopped. 'Don't you salute naval officers?'

'We're not sure if we're supposed to,' George Munn replied.

'When you're in naval barracks, you always salute officers.'

'Yes, sir.'

'Very well, let's not make a fuss about it. You'll know next time. Goodnight.' Olivier took his rank very seriously.

Richardson had appointed Olivier as parachute officer and came to see how he was getting on. Richardson noted that 'his manner was naval, was quiet, alert, businesslike, with the air of there being a joke around'.

He found Olivier's parachute section faultless and noted how he had got 'such a hand of the work' and was able to introduce Richardson to every Wren and seaman by name.

On his way back to the office it suddenly occurred to Richardson that Olivier had probably rehearsed it all. They remained firm friends and often went drinking together or to the theatre, and both became increasingly fed up because they were forbidden from taking a more active role in the war.

Their naval careers ended in 1944 when Tyrone Guthrie, who ran the Old Vic, asked the Sea Lords to release them to help him lead the Old Vic company. Lord Lytton, chairman of the Vic's Board of Governors, wrote to the Admiralty, pointing out the indispensability to the theatre of Richardson and Olivier, and how important they could be to the rehabilitation of the Old Vic which he hoped the Admiralty would consider as nationally important.

After the number of written-off and damaged planes for which the two actors had been responsible, Richardson noted how the navy seemed only too relieved to let them go.

The Café de Paris, where David Niven had met Jimmy Bosvile of the Rifle Brigade, was a popular haunt for servicemen, and early in 1941 a newly commissioned officer went there to celebrate having just passed out as a second lieutenant. His name was Richard Todd, a young actor aged twenty-one who, when he heard Chamberlain's broadcast declaring war on Germany, had gone straight to St Andrew's University in Dundee day to volunteer.

He was not at the university but he bluffed the selection unit into believing he was and convinced them that he had obtained a Cert A (which was a virtual guarantee of being accepted as officer material) in his school cadet corps – which was another bluff.

He had received his orders in June 1940 to report to Strensall in Yorkshire at the King's Own Yorkshire Light Infantry for basic training, and was then sent to officer training at Sandhurst. He narrowly escaped death there when, while on the second-floor corridor one night, he literally watched as a bomb came through the roof of the building.

The next thing he remembered was finding himself in the garden. He had stood up, feeling no pain, but because he was soaked he assumed he was covered in water from the radiators. In fact, when he got into the light, he found he was covered in his own blood; he had suffered numerous small wounds and was put into hospital to recover.

Now, as a new second lieutenant in London, he wanted to celebrate at the popular Café de Paris. It just so happened that when he arrived it was so packed he decided to go elsewhere. That very night a bomb made a direct hit on the Café de Paris, killing eighty-four people.

Second Lieutenant Richard Todd was put in charge of the infantry manning Dymchurch Redoubt, a Napoleonic moated fort on the Kent coast. His commander was General Bernard Montgomery who had decided that if the German invasion came, it would probably happen around this area. Todd's orders were that in the event of an invasion, his men would be on their own to fight to the last while the main defence lines would be formed on the high ground inland.

Montgomery put much emphasis on physical fitness and training, and formed the first battle schools to use live ammunition. Richard Todd was put on such a course at a mansion, known as the 'Rat's Castle' because of its ramshackle condition, near Folkestone. It was the first course held there for instructors and he later admitted that it was there he learned what war was really all about; learning how to live off the land and survive in realistic battle conditions.

In December 1941 he was posted to the Alabaster Force with the 1st/4th King's Own Light Infantry in Iceland, there to be trained in fighting in Arctic conditions by Canadian instructors and in mountain warfare by Norwegian instructors. Lieutenant Todd set up a battle school modelled on Montgomery's school in Kent, and personally selected and trained the instructors under his command. There he would remain until 1942.

In April 1941, Foreign Secretary Anthony Eden and General Sir John Dill, Chief of the Imperial General Staff, were on their way to London from Cairo and were forced to land in Gibraltar – 'either because of bad weather or a fault with the plane, I can't remember which,' said Anthony Quayle who had, in March, been made ADC to the Governor General of Gibraltar, Sir Clive Liddell. A few weeks later Mason-Mac had left the Rock to return to England and take command of the 44th Division at Canterbury which was one of the key positions if the invasion of Britain ever came.

Eden and Dill were very worried men, trying to sort out the situation in Greece where the Italians' invasion had failed and the Germans had come to their aid. Some 60,000 British troops were sent into Greece but now they and the Greeks were withdrawing and the situation was deteriorating rapidly.

There was no direct communication between Gibraltar and London, so Eden and Dill listened to the news on the radio each day in the billiard room of Government House. Quayle recalled, 'I remember seeing Anthony Eden leaning over a map laid across the billiard table listening to the gloomy news while Dill sat in silence.'

Eden asked Dill, 'What else could we have done, Johnny?'

Dill had no answer.

Quayle told me, 'I took Eden on a tour of the Rock because he wanted to speak to the troops. A sergeant said to him, "You must be very tired, sir." "Not so much tired," Eden replied with a faint smile, "as terribly, terribly worried."'

In June 1941, General Liddell was ordered back to England from Gibraltar and suggested to Quayle that he accompany him as his ADC. They sailed back aboard HMS *Argus*, an aircraft carrier.

Quayle recalled:

There were a couple of escaped PoWs on board who had been captured in Belgium during the first German attack. They told me they had been sent to a prison camp in Germany, were then moved to Poland where they had been put to work mending the roof of their hut. They escaped simply by jumping off the roof when the coast was clear and running for it. Some Poles helped them get to Spain where they were interned. There an underground movement helped them to escape and make it into Gibraltar.

The aircraft carrier arrived at Gourock and Quayle caught the train home. He had not had time to inform Hermione that he was returning. He had no key so he stood outside calling her name. After a while a bedroom window opened and Hermione looked out, half asleep. Then she was joined by a man – a close friend, Clifford Evans.

That was the end of Quayle's marriage, and it was a relief to him. He made plans to move out, and it helped him make up his mind what to do next:

General Liddell was now Inspector General of Training and with his commendation, I went to work for Auxiliary Units, a secret organization with the job of harassing the enemy should Britain be invaded.

My job was to organize the whole of Northumberland. Hide-outs had to be dug and camouflaged, men recruited and trained in secret. The reality was that these units would probably not last more than forty-eight hours following a German landing. I had about 200 men, all deadly shots with a .22 Winchester; they could handle plastic explosives and were expert in blowing up bridges, railway lines and anything else that would harass the Germans. I think for the first time since the beginning of the war, I felt I was doing something worthwhile.

Although men like David Niven and Anthony Quayle each found their own personal reasons for volunteering for more dangerous duties, and others like Laurence Olivier were prevented from taking a more active part, they all reflected the courage of Britain's countless unknown volunteers who defined the spirit of the British Bulldog.

In May 1941, the blitz on Liverpool began. Kenneth More, now Acting Sub-Lieutenant More, was stationed at HMS *Mersey*, a Royal Navy land barracks and former hospital.

More's quarters were in the cellars, offering some protection from the nightly raids. In a single week, the city was nearly razed. The docks and ships were ablaze, and More and other officers helped the ARP people each day, pulling bodies and survivors out of flattened buildings.

One night the barracks took a direct hit. More and the others sitting in petrified silence in their cellar heard only the crash. They waited for the explosion. It never came.

The commander asked for a volunteer to seek out the unexploded bomb. 'I didn't want to be stuck down there in what may well have been my tomb,' recalled More, 'so I volunteered.'

He made his way up the darkened stairs until he reached the top ward. There he discovered a huge hole in the roof and below him another hole going through the floor. 'At first I thought it was an aircraft engine from the glint of metal.'

He crawled down through the rubble and to his astonishment came across a land mine, still attached to its parachute. He reported back to the commander who decided someone needed to report to Headquarters which was situated under the Liver Building, some 600 yards down what was left of the road, and get instructions from the duty officer. It was likely that it could explode at any moment. Again, More volunteered:

I ran along the road, throwing myself to the ground every time I heard the whistle of falling bombs. There were fires all over the city and it seemed to take forever to reach HQ. I saw the duty officer who said that to evacuate the barracks in the raid might be more dangerous than staying put in the hope the mine didn't go off. He promised to get a disposal expert there in the morning, so I had to go back and tell everyone to stay put.

We didn't get any sleep that night, naturally, wondering if the mine would go off, but by morning nothing had happened and with the raid over, we cleared the barracks. The disposal expert arrived and went in alone. We waited outside in the street which was a real mess with buildings in rubble and gas and water pipes burst, overturned vehicles everywhere.

The disposal chap came out of the building and said he'd disarmed it and wanted to move the mine to the beach to examine it. Runways were set up and this mine, as big as a boiler, was rolled out and loaded on a truck.

Later that day we heard the mine had exploded on the beach while this disposal chap was examining it and he was killed.

The British-held coastal garrison of Tobruk in Libya had been under attack since 11 April 1941. Lt General Erwin Rommel, in command of the Deutsches Afrika Korps, had begun his sweep through Libya, pushing back the British, on 1 April. He needed to take Tobruk before pushing on into Egypt, but the British soldiers held off the ferocious assaults by Rommel's divisions of armoured tanks, artillery and Stukas. Rommel said that the British soldiers in the Tobruk garrison were 'rats in a trap'. The British soldiers took to calling themselves the Rats of Tobruk.

The battle for North Africa raged on and the Rats of Tobruk held out. On 4 May Rommel called off the assault but kept the garrison under siege.

The Iraqi Army, sponsored by the Nazis, attacked the British Embassy in Baghdad as well as the British air base at Habbaniyah. This was a vital link in the air route to India. The Iraqis were driven back, but in neighbouring French-ruled Syria, the Vichy presence threatened British-controlled Palestine and the Suez Canal. Churchill ordered a force of Australian, British, Indian and Free French troops into Lebanon on 8 June 1941. Damascus, the Syrian capital, fell on 21 June, and shortly afterwards the Allies also took Beirut.

In Sydney, Australia, actor Peter Finch read with interest the daily newspaper accounts of the Australian military confrontation with Rommel. He was particularly moved by the news that an old destroyer, the *Waterhen*, which had been recommissioned in 1939, had been sunk while just outside Tobruk harbour. It had been attacked by German aircraft while on the 'milk run', carrying ammunition and food from Alexandria to Tobruk.

Finch, at twenty-four, had made two films, appeared in plays and was something of a radio star, but after reading of the *Waterhen*'s fate, he went along to the Army Recruiting office in Martin Place on 2 June 1941, and enlisted in the 2nd AIF.

Gunner Finch of Specialist Group 2, attached to the 2/1 Light Anti-Aircraft Regiment, boarded the liner *Queen Mary*, bound for Port Tewfik, there to disembark for the Middle East campaign.

Shortly after Finch's arrival, the Middle East settled into an uneasy ceasefire when, on 14 July, the Vichy Governor and Commander-in-Chief of Syria allowed the Allies the right to occupy Syria and Lebanon. If there was little excitement for Peter Finch, he quickly learned to generate his own sense of adventure. While at Mersa Matruh, he decided to try out his acting skills by dressing up as a Bedouin Arab and wandering along the lines of an Aussie-manned machine-gun battalion.

He recalled, 'The outraged machine-gunners called me a fucking Wog and told me to bugger off and chased me into the sand-dunes with their bloody bayonets, and I had a hell of a job to find my way back through the barbed wire to my own gun-pit.'

His mad-cap antics, however, didn't always result in fun. He once stole a jeep and took some chums out to celebrate. Driving along a dusty desert road, he had to swerve to avoid an oncoming vehicle. The jeep overturned and Finch and his companions were seriously injured.

They ended up in hospital but Finch, who suffered amnesia as a result of the crash, could never remember the incident. But he felt guilty at having nearly killed his passengers, not least of all himself, and forever after he refused to take the wheel of a car, even in films. For years he suffered psychologically because of his near-fatal accident.

8

Isolationist America

'We're not at war with anybody.'

Louis B Mayer

President Roosevelt had warned that America might be forced into a war with Japan as far back as 1933 and had ordered the building of new warships. Roosevelt had been an isolationist, determined that America should not get into a war with Germany, but his opinion began to change when Japan launched open warfare on China in 1937.

For many years the US Navy had had a secret agent in their intelligence – John Ford. This legendary director of Westerns had always loved the navy and had, during the First World War, volunteered for naval duty only to be turned down because of bad eyesight. So he applied to become a photographer in the then new Naval Flying Corps which was experimenting with aerial surveillance. He was accepted because he knew how to operate a camera.

Because he always kept his secret naval career truly a secret, not even his wife, Mary, whom he married in 1920, knew the exact details of his activities, although she did become involved in some of them. When she met him he was in the uniform of the Naval Reserve and may well have been involved in secret operations by 1920.

During the 1920s and 1930s, Ford was as famous for his naval pictures as he would later be for his Westerns. He made his sea-going sagas as entertainment and propaganda. His biographer Andrew Sinclair wrote that he lived both as a film maker and as a navy spy. It fell to Mary Ford to entertain numerous admirals of the Pacific Fleet but Ford never told her exactly what he was doing for the navy.

Rear Admiral Sims, who believed that the future of the fleet depended on its air corps, recruited Ford for intelligence work. He went to work with Captain Ellis Zacharias who was to become commander of the 11th Navy District in San Diego and who was concerned over the rise of Japanese power in the Pacific. There was at that time no official intelligence unit, but Zacharias ran a semi-official unit using local naval reserve officers to collect information on Japanese and German influence in Mexico and the Far East. This information was passed to J Edgar Hoover and Vice Admiral T S Wilkinson.

Ford willingly conducted intelligence activities without pay and often on his own initiative. When he filmed *Salute* at Annapolis in 1929, he met with naval intelligence leaders and was given a mission to go to the Pacific. Officially he was to research and film sequences for his submarine film, *Men Without Women*, but he was also reporting on harbour access and defences.

In 1931 he took his wife to the Philippines for six months as the guests of the millitary commander there. Ford often disappeared on air-reconnaissance missions and used his Hollywood facilities for editing his intelligence films with the help of his editor Leon Sedlitz who told Andrew Sinclair, 'He was the perfect underground agent with a magnificent eye and an incredible memory.'

In his own two-masted sailing yacht, *The Araner*, Ford cruised from California to Acapulco in the mid-1930s after being briefed by Zacharias. American authorities were still allowing Japanese shrimpboats into San Pedro at Long Beach harbour. Ford kept a lookout for any shrimpboats commanded by disguised officers from the Japanese Navy. Aiding him in this were John Wayne, Ward Bond and even Mary. She managed to get on board a shrimpboat on the pretext of making a distress telephone call, and discovered in the captain's cabin a photograph of him in full naval uniform.

Another time she swam fully clothed near San Diego and emerged from the sea to ask if she could change her clothes at a house where Japanese businessmen were known to be staying. She discovered cameras and surveillance equipment.

By 1930 John Ford had risen to the rank of lieutenant commander in the naval reserve and received a commendation from the commander of the 11th Naval District for his initiative in securing information. He sailed for Hawaii where he secretly helped the air arm to develop its reconnaissance facilities at Pearl Harbor and reported on the lack of naval preparedness there.

While the rest of the world went to war in 1939, John Ford, convinced America would inevitably become involved, organized a private army of more than 200 Hollywood technicians in order to record actual combat. Officially, Washington wanted nothing to do with him. Meanwhile, Roosevelt was secretly and privately funding a foreign intelligence agency originally called the Co-ordinator of Information and later known as the Office of Strategic Services – OSS, the forerunner of the CIA.

Colonel 'Wild Bill' Donovan, who ran the agency, became aware of John Ford's activities but could not as yet recruit him as America was not at war. In 1940 and 1941, Ford made several attempts to find a financial backer for his army of film-makers in Washington, his objective being 'to record the history of the navy in World War Two and the role it played'. Eventually he was given permission to set up a historical unit in the Naval Reserve, comprising thirty-five officers and 175 enlisted men who met once a week to train on the back lot of Twentieth Century Fox.

Colonel Donovan, who was expanding his agency into the OSS, now recruited Ford and his unit and called them the Field Photographic Branch. The FPB began documenting naval strategy in Iceland against German U-boats as well as reporting on the defences of the Panama Canal.

Hollywood itself was split between those who wanted to

stay out of the war in Europe, and those who felt that America had held back long enough. Even MGM Studio boss Louis B Mayer was afraid of upsetting the Germans and in 1938 he screened *Three Comrades* for the German consul in Los Angeles to ensure that there was nothing in the film version of Erich Maria Remarque's anti-war novel that the Third Reich might find offensive.

In 1940 William Wyler filmed *Mrs Miniver*, the story of a British family caught up in the war. He wanted it to ram home a message to America, but as he said, 'Propaganda must not look like propaganda.'

Two weeks into the filming Mayer summoned Wyler and complained that the film was anti-German. Said Mayer, 'We're not at war with anybody. This picture just shows these people having a hard time and it's very sympathetic to them, but it's not directed against the Germans.'

Wyler replied, 'Mr Mayer, you know what's going on, don't you?'

Mayer replied that as far as he was concerned, they had theatres all over the world including some in Berlin and that they were not at war with Germany.

Wyler argued that since only one German featured in the film – a pilot shot down and discovered by Mrs Miniver – he was going to present the airman as 'one of Goering's little monsters'.

Mayer begged him not to 'overdo it'.

Douglas Fairbanks Jr had been waiting since August 1940 to find out if he had been accepted in the US Naval Reserve, and finally, on 10 April 1941 he was commissioned as a junior grade lieutenant in the US Navy. Earlier in the month he was asked by the State Department to visit a number of South American countries where Fascism had become a growing trend. The State Department hoped that his appeal as a film star might help to halt the trend spreading further.

In South America, as the president's personal but unofficial envoy – as far as the American public were concerned he was on a goodwill tour – he met with heads of government to touch on the subjects of naval and military bases for US forces and to investigate ways to counteract the flood of Axis propaganda into South America. When he returned after nine weeks, he was asked to go on nationwide radio to give his impressions.

The president wrote to him: 'Dear Douglas, From every source I have heard nothing but words of praise and commendation of the way you conducted yourself on your trip and I am sure it will do a great deal of good.'

In October 1941, shortly before Fairbanks began active service in the US Navy, he received a visit from his friend Captain Lord Louis Mountbatten who described his exploits on the destroyer *Kelly* off southern Crete.

The Germans had invaded Crete in May 1941, driving the British from the island following the invasion of mainland Greece in the previous month. During the battle for Crete, Mountbatten's ship *Kelly* was sunk (the story of which was made into the film *In Which We Serve*).

While staying at Fairbanks's home, Mountbatten received a telegram from Winston Churchill recalling him to take charge of Combined Operations.

As Mountbatten went off to take command of the brand new carrier *Illustrious*, Fairbanks reported to Charlestown Navy Yard in Boston where he met with wary hostility from some of the regular officers. They assumed that this Hollywood film star was merely seeking some kind of publicized glory.

During his first voyage on the destroyer *Ludlow* he was assigned extra watch duties and quartered in the petty officer's mess. In Iceland he joined the battleship *Mississippi*, an event which was reported in American newspapers. A sceptical captain asked Fairbanks if he had hired himself a press agent.

In Hollywood, Alexander Korda was secretly aiding Churchill by fronting for the SOE. His large offices in Los Angeles and New York were clearing houses for British intelligence and he had connections with film offices throughout the world through which vital intelligence information was passed.

Korda was also aiding Churchill in trying to rally American support against the Axis powers. But there were Americans who wanted nothing to do with the war. The America First Committee campaigned to keep the United States out of the war, and Churchill needed some forthright yet seemingly unofficial propaganda to make Americans aware of the danger that Nazism presented not just to Europe, but the whole world, including America.

He asked Korda to make a film about the battle of Trafalgar. The result was *That Hamilton Woman* (called *Lady Hamilton* in Britain), a blatantly pro-British film. In a sense it was disguised as a love story between Nelson and Lady Hamilton, providing a dual star vehicle for Laurence Olivier and Vivien Leigh. But more importantly it was the saga of Britain's fight for freedom against the Napoleonic Empire.

The film included a speech given by Nelson, reputedly written by Churchill, which, in part, said, 'Napoleon can never be master of the world until he has smashed us up – and believe me, gentlemen, he means to be master of the world. You cannot make peace with dictators, you have to destroy them.'

Korda was sure that German intelligence was suspicious of him and that Germany could possibly supply isolationist Senator Nye with information that could prove dangerous to Korda and, ultimately, the whole of Churchill's secret operations.

Korda came under attack in America for 'inciting the American public to war', and he received a subpoena to appear before the Senate Committee on 12 December 1941. He knew he could be deported.

In England, Churchill was depressed by the continual advance of Germany throughout Europe, although it looked less likely by this time that Britain would be invaded. He confided his glum thoughts to David Niven during one of their garden strolls. Niven asked him if he thought the Americans would ever enter the war.

'Mark my words,' Churchill replied, 'something cataclysmic will occur.'

Back in America, five days before Alexander Korda was due to appear before the Senate Committee, the Japanese attacked the US naval base of Pearl Harbor on the Hawaiian island of Oahu. It was 7 December 1941. John Ford complained that his findings about naval readiness at Pearl Harbor were ignored. The Japanese effectively crippled the US Pacific Fleet. President Franklin D Roosevelt had no choice but to declare war on Japan, and because Japan had signed the Tripartite Pact with Germany and Italy, this effectively brought America into the Second World War.

Roosevelt had done all he could to prepare America for war and, by 1941, the US Navy was prepared for action at sea. But efforts from the isolationists had prevented the US Army from being prepared. Consequently, Japan concentrated its efforts on the Pacific Fleet.

On board *Mississippi* in Icelandic waters, Douglas Fairbanks Jr, acting as assistant communications officer, received a message from Lord Mountbatten – 'Welcome to the party'.

The subpoena against Alexander Korda was cancelled. A few weeks later he returned to England where, at Churchill's recommendation, he received a knighthood. He was the first person in the film industry to receive such an honour.

Many months after Pearl Harbor, David Niven reminded Churchill of his prediction about America and asked him what had made him say it.

'Because, young man, I study history.'

He had known, as did President Roosevelt, that America would probably one day be forced into a war with Japan. Now that Britain and America were fighting a common enemy, Roosevelt established a warm relationship with Churchill and opened the way for complete cooperation between the two Allied nations.

9
America Goes to War

*'There are ordinary corpses, and there are Marine corpses. I
figured on being a first class corpse.'*

Lee Marvin

Now that the United States was in the war, there was at last
unity within the nation which had been so divided. Only a
minority had ever favoured entering the war, but by dusk of
7 December 1941 – 'a date that will live in infamy,' as
President Roosevelt described it – all the arguments between
the majority who urged neutrality and the minority who
pressed for war had ceased.

Strikes that were in progress were called off by labour
leaders and union members began working round the clock to
further the war effort. Young Americans began volunteering in
their thousands, and recruiting offices had to call in extra help
to process the overwhelming numbers of eager recruits.

On 8 December 1941, Britain declared war on Japan.
Three days later Germany and Italy, honouring treaties with
Japan, declared war on America.

William Wyler had finished filming *Mrs Miniver* but after
Pearl Harbor he decided to go back into the studio and
reshoot the end scene in which a vicar gives a sermon in a
bombed-out church. The final version of the sermon
impressed Roosevelt so much that he had the text printed in
leaflets to be dropped over German-held countries and broadcast over Voice of America.

The text read:

We, in this quiet corner of England, have suffered the loss
of friends very dear to us. Some close to this church –
George West, choirboy; James Ballard, stationmaster and
bellringer and the proud winner, only an hour before his
death, of the Beldon Cup for his beautiful Miniver Rose.
And our hearts go out in sympathy to the families who
share the cruel loss of a young girl who was married at
this altar only two weeks ago. The homes of many of us
have been destroyed and the lives of young and old have
been taken. There is scarcely a household that hasn't
been struck to the heart. And why? Surely you must have
asked yourselves this question. Why, in all conscience,
should these be the ones to suffer? Children, old people,
a young girl at the height of her loveliness. Why these?
Are these our soldiers? Are these our fighters? Why
should they be sacrificed? I shall tell you why. Because
this is not only a war of soldiers in uniform, it is a war of
the people - of all the people - and it must be fought, not
only on the battlefields, but in the cities and in the villages, in the factories and on the farms, in the home and
in the heart of every young man, woman and child who
loves freedom. Instead, they will inspire us with an
unbreakable determination to free ourselves and those
who come after us from the tyranny and terror that
threaten to strike us down. Fight it, then! Fight it with all
that is in us. And may God defend the right.

In America, endless queues formed at the recruitment centres. Among them was a young man who would become the
most decorated GI of the war and, later, the star of countless
Western films. His name was Audie Murphy, a slightly built
seventeen-year-old lad who worked in a radio repair shop in
Greenville, Texas. When he tried to enlist in the Marines he
was turned down because he was underweight. He tried the
Paratroopers and was rejected for the same reason.
He didn't give up and finally made it into the Infantry. He

was sent to Fort Meade where he became known as 'baby face' because of his extreme boyish looks. He was determined that as soon as he finished basic training he would request a transfer as a glider pilot. But he seemed destined for a desk job after he fainted during his first drill parade. He was assigned to be a post office clerk, and that is where he remained throughout 1942. It was hardly an impressive beginning for America's most famous recruit.

The Marines accepted only the toughest young men. Few came tougher than Lee Marvin. He had been sent by his father, Lamont Marvin, to St Leo's, a Benedictine-run prep school which Lamont hoped would pull his wayward son into line. Lee Marvin was, he said, 'a pain in the ass to my father'.

He was also a pain in the ass to the monks. 'I was the scourge of St Leo's,' he said. 'They lost patience with me and kicked me out. I was eighteen and war had been declared, so I thought, what the hell, I'd give the Marines what for.'

When he told his dad he was going to enlist, Lamont said, 'I think you've made the right decision, son.' Lee told me, 'I think that meant he hoped the generals might do the job the monks failed to do.'

His choice to join the Marines – and only the Marines – was a strange one for someone who rebelled against discipline at every turn. But he had his reasons. 'I knew I was going to be killed and I just wanted to be killed in the best outfit. There are ordinary corpses, and there are Marine corpses. I figured on being a first class corpse.'

He enlisted – 'and then waited, and waited. I figured maybe the generals had been tipped off by the monks and had changed their minds.'

They hadn't. It just took some time to find a niche for the man who, after the war, would become the cinema's booziest hellraiser. Finally, in August, he received his orders to report to the Marine base at Parris Island, South Carolina. There he collected his rifle and uniform and began boot-camp training.

It didn't take him long to get all the sergeants hating him. As they roared commands at him, he would just stare blankly ahead, his eyes betraying his insolence and contempt:

They'd threaten to put me in the stockade, have me shot, and I'd look up and see a bird and say, 'Isn't that a finch?' Then I'd watch as the sergeant's blood vessels nearly burst out of his neck.

They just wanted to dehumanize you. One sergeant said to me, 'Why don't you just shoot yourself?'

So I asked, 'Why don't you fuck yourself, sergeant?'

I thought for sure they'd put me in the stockade. A sergeant stood with his face an inch from mine, balling me out, and I looked dumb and said, 'Could you speak up a little.' But that was all in the first few days, and I quickly learned the best way to survive that hell camp was to take the shit and button the lip.

A couple of weeks in boot-camp was as much as I, or the sergeants, wanted to take, and I was told to report to Camp Pendleton.

I decided I'd just hitch a lift, and outside the camp there I saw my old man. I thought he'd come to give me a pat on the back and wish me luck, but he had a kit bag and said he had joined up too. He was going to help out the British on their anti-aircraft detachments. So we hitched a ride south together. I guess I felt really proud of him and he did of me. When we arrived, we shook hands and said not much, but I never felt closer to him than I did then. And then we went our separate ways.

Another who stood in line to enlist was seventeen-year-old Bernard Schwartz. He was the son of Hungarian Jews who lived in the New York Bronx which was an area segregated into ghettos. Bernie Schwartz decided that one way of escaping these areas and to ensure that they never became like the ghettos of Poland, was to fight the Nazis.

Bernie Schwartz was the real name of the young man who would go to Hollywood a few years after the war and become Tony Curtis.

He joined the navy and became a third class signalman on board sub-tender USS *Proteus*. There he was confronted by anti-Semitism among his own comrades. He thought they were all in this war together to stop Hitler rounding up the Jews in order to put them into ghettos far more horrendous than the one in which he had lived.

Another young Jew who joined the navy in 1942 was Issur Danielovitch. His parents had escaped the anti-Semitic pogroms in Russia at the beginning of the century to settle in America. He grew up wanting to be an actor, and at the American Academy of Dramatic Arts in New York he decided to change his name in the hope that it would help his career. He stole Douglas Fairbanks's Christian name, made it his surname, and then thought up Kirk.

Kirk Douglas graduated from the academy in 1941 and was carving out a promising career in a small way – he played a singing messenger boy on Broadway in *Spring Again* – when at the age of twenty five he got his call-up papers. He left Broadway behind and spent the few months at the midshipman school at Notre Dame University where he learned navigation, gunnery and damage control. He found the courses hard going and was particularly poor at aircraft identification.

'I hated it all,' he said, 'the classes, the drilling, and everything had to be done at the double.'

No one was more surprised than he when he graduated as a naval ensign assigned as a communications officer on an anti-submarine patrol craft in the Pacific.

Charlton Heston was also intent on making a career for himself as an actor but had had little time, at the age of nineteen, to make any headway after majoring in Northwestern's Fine Drama Department's School of Speech before he enlisted in the Army Air Force in 1942. Instead of learning how to be an actor, he had to learn how to operate radios aboard B-25 bombers at Greenboro in North Carolina.

Burt Lancaster had just arrived in New York to take up a $6,000-a-year contract with the Concert Bureau of the Columbia Broadcasting System in July 1942 when he was drafted into the army.

As well as being an actor, he had also been a circus performer. To add to his variety of talents, while he was waiting for his orders, he worked as a singing waiter in a nightclub near Union City, New Jersey.

Four months later he was sent to Fort Riley in Kansas and was assigned to the Special Services Branch of the 5th Army. 'I wanted to get in the Engineers because I thought my experience in rigging in the circus would qualify me,' he told me, 'but I guess I didn't make the grade. Instead, because I was an actor, they decided I'd be better qualified to produce shows for the troops. I thought I'd be a hero – they made me an entertainer.'

Actually, although he never liked to reflect on it, Lancaster saw plenty of action in the war.

Other recruits later to become big names in Hollywood included Ernest Borgnine who joined the navy in 1935 and was discharged at the end of the war. Lee Van Cleef was also in the navy, as was Rod Steiger who joined up at the age of sixteen and served on a destroyer in the Pacific. Glenn Ford was a Marine, so was Robert Webber and future director Richard Brooks who was just getting started as a screenwriter. The Army Air Force included Dick Van Dyke, Robert Altman who was a teenage pilot, and Charles Bronson who was a tail gunner aboard a B-29 bomber. Telly Savalas was a GI who was injured in action and awarded the Purple Heart.

These men were among the thousands of nobodies from the United States who made the difference in the Second World War.

10

Hollywood's Heroes

'I waved goodbye to Bogie and told Jack Warner, head of the studio, "Goodbye, Jack, I'm in the army now."'

John Huston

As army camps were set up all over America, Hollywood stars were sent on tours to entertain the troops who were yet to see action. Among those who toured the camps was Marlene Dietrich. She also visited factories asking workers to give a percentage of their earnings to the government in return for war bonds. She raised a million dollars and was awarded with a medal for her efforts by the Secretary of the Treasury.

Dietrich had previously been approached by Nazi agents while she was filming *Knight Without Armour* in England in 1937, trying to persuade her to return to Germany and make films there. It was said that she was visited by the German ambassador in England, Joachim von Ribbentrop, with a personal and generous offer direct from Hitler. She rejected the offer and as a consequence all her films were banned in Germany. America accepted her as a citizen in 1939. By the time war broke out she was still involved with the Hollywood Committee, helping to raise money to aid European refugees escape to America.

Among those who made it to California was French film star Jean Gabin. Dietrich was given the job of helping him to adjust and to teach him English. It was the beginning of a romantic relationship that lasted throughout the war.

In Hollywood, news of the war had some famous folk wondering whether or not to give up their lucrative careers to get
shot at. Marlene Dietrich was later outspoken about
Hollywood people who volunteered for service and who
immediately received officer's rank without any training, calling them 'ninety-day wonders'. Most actors, she noted, did
not fight. 'Some did, but not many,' she later said. 'We often
wondered what they would tell their children.'

Dietrich would later join the US Army and be sent to the
front to experience virtually all aspects of being at war apart
from having to kill.

A man who was certainly no ninety-day wonder was
Douglas Fairbanks Jr, although in his early days in the war he
was constantly criticized and maligned. He had been transferred from the *Mississippi* to the Office of Naval Intelligence
and War Plans. He now only wanted to fight in the war as
anonymously as possible without creating publicity. Yet even
this move brought criticism from a congressman who asked
the Secretary of the Navy if Fairbanks was being shown
favouritism by being given a 'safe' job. Finally the Bureau of
Naval Personnel told him his presence ashore was an embar-
rassment and he was immediately ordered back to sea.

He spent the next three weeks minesweeping and chasing
submarines out of Staten Island in New York harbour. He was
then transferred to Task Force 99, serving aboard the flagship
USS *Washington* at Scapa Flow, guarding the northern sea-
lanes off Iceland and Norway. He volunteered for extra duties
to prove his worth when he found that even there he was
resented by some officers.

In early 1942 the 'King' of Hollywood, Clark Gable, considered joining the Army Air Force. This was unthinkable for
a man who was the biggest male star at Metro-Goldwyn-
Mayer. According to David Niven, Gable's wife, Carole
Lombard, hated everything that Hitler stood for and even
before Pearl Harbor she had argued that America should get
into the war. But, according to Niven, to Clark Gable the war
'seemed like a famine in China, something one read about in
papers and then turned hurriedly to the sporting page'.

The day after Pearl Harbor Lombard wired the president, offering her and Gable's services in any way they could. Some time later the Gables were asked to go on a bond-selling tour. Gable was filming at the time and had to stay behind while Lombard started her tour in Salt Lake City, going down through to Texas and on to Fort Wayne, Indiana. She had originally planned to return to Los Angeles by train, but eager to get home, she managed to get a flight on a milk-run plane. She phoned Gable and delighted him with the news of her early return. Her plane stopped off at Las Vegas and then took off again for the home run. It flew into a storm and crashed into Table Top Mountain. There were no survivors.

Gable was about to get into his car to go to the airport and meet his wife when he got a call from MGM telling him that something had gone wrong with Carole's flight. Eddie Mannix, a studio executive and close friend of Gable's, was on his way over and a plane had been chartered to fly to them to Las Vegas.

In the car, Mannix told Gable that an explosion had been spotted in the sky some thirty miles from Las Vegas and that a fire had been seen on Table Top Mountain. They caught their plane and, arriving by car at the foot of Table Top, Gable insisted he wanted to join the search. But Mannix persuaded him to stay behind, stressing it could be a false alarm. Mannix himself went up the mountain with the search party and some hours later, after searching through the debris of the plane scattered in the deep snow, he identified Carole Lombard.

On hearing the news, Gable locked himself in a hotel room for twenty-four hours. He held back the tears until finally a friend persuaded him to go home. There he read the last of a series of notes Carole had left for him – one for each day she was away – and that was the thing that made him break down and sob for hours.

He took himself off to the Rogue River, his favourite fishing camp, and drank solidly for three weeks. Then he went to Washington to see General H H Arnold, commander of the American Army Air Force, asking for advice about enlisting. He didn't want an easy commission, and applied for admission to the Officers Candidate School. He passed a physical at Bolling Field, and then went back to Hollywood to continue his film. When he reported for work at the MGM studio, he appeared unchanged. On the last day of filming, 12 August 1942, he became Private 1912507. That same day MGM cameraman Andrew J McIntyre also joined the AAF and together they started a three-month course at Officer Cadet School in Miami, Florida.

One of Gable's first instructions was to shave off his moustache and get a regulation haircut. At forty-one, he was considerably older than the majority of cadets but he coped with every physical demand. He found the written examinations the toughest part of the course, but his actor's memory helped him through, and on 29 October he was commissioned as a second lieutenant.

As an officer, he was able to grow back his moustache. He was sent to the Flexible Gunnery School at Tynall Field near Panama City, Florida, and at the end of 1942 was sent to Seven Miles Gunnery School, Fort George Wright at Spokane, Washington.

The AAF made use of Gable's 'one of us' attitude for publicity and he was commissioned to make a film about recruitment and gunnery training. He arrived in Texas to begin training his film unit, known as the 'Little Hollywood Group' because it included men such as Andrew McIntyre and screenwriter John Lee Mahin, at 508th Bomb Squadron at Biggs Field. He was now a first lieutenant, and on 16 April 1943, he and his 'Little Hollywood Group' were flown to Britain to begin their work, filming under combat conditions, at Polebrook in Northamptonshire.

Mickey Rooney joined the army to entertain troops, Robert Stack was in the navy, Robert Ryan entertained as a Marine, and William Holden was a lieutenant in the army who also spent most of his time entertaining the troops. Robert Taylor, a lieutenant in the navy, served as a flight instructor with the Navy's Air Transport. Few Hollywood actors were put in the front line. James Stewart was: as a bomber pilot in the United States Army Air Force he flew twenty bombing missions over Germany.

Lew Ayres, the star of *All Quiet on the Western Front*, declared himself a conscientious objector and refused to fight. Narrow-minded studios who saw this as cowardice shunned him, and theatres refused to show his films. Later he joined the army to take up non-combatant service as a medic, and distinguished himself under fire.

The army knew it was important to have the war recorded, not just for posterity or for training, but also for propaganda, so professional film makers were welcomed into the Signal Corps of the Army Pictorial Service under the command of Colonel Schlossberg. Screenwriter Sy Bartlett had been commissioned as a captain, and he took Colonel Schlossberg to Hollywood to find suitable recruits. Bartlett recommended Frank Capra, Anatole Litvak, William Wyler and John Huston. Frank Capra was the first to arrive in Washington as all the others were still in the middle of productions.

Major Capra and Colonel Schlossberg quickly clashed over how to film documentaries. When William Wyler finished *Mrs Miniver* he called Schlossberg and announced he was ready to come to Washington. The colonel told him to wait a little longer while he sorted out his problems with Capra.

John Huston was thirty-five and, having established himself as a respectable screenwriter since 1931, had made his directorial début for Warner Brothers in 1941 with *The Maltese Falcon*, starring Humphrey Bogart. He followed this with *In This Our Life*, starring Bette Davis and Olivia de Havilland, and looked all set to establish himself at the studio as a leading director. But on little more than a thoughtless impulse, he decided to risk it all for a commission with the Signal Corps.

I had a friend, Sy Bartlett, the writer, who was in the Reserve. After Pearl Harbor he was called up and commissioned as a captain in the Signal Corps. He came to visit me on the set of *Across the Pacific* with Humphrey Bogart and Mary Astor, at the Warner Brothers studio, and he asked me if I'd like to accept a commission in the Signal Corps, and I said yes and signed a piece of paper.

A few weeks later a small package came to me in the mail. I didn't look at it too closely; it had a list of names of military personnel and various army posts, and I just put it aside. I hadn't realized this was my order to get into uniform. My name was on the list somewhere, but I hadn't seen it, or been looking for it.

I went back to making the picture and was at the studio when I got a call from some major in Washington asking me why the hell I hadn't reported for duty. I told him I was in the middle of making a film, and he said, 'Lieutenant Huston, do you wish to resign your commission?' and I said, 'No, sir.'

'In that case, get your ass over to Washington.'

I said 'Yes, sir.'

Huston hadn't finished the film, but he rewrote a scene which had Bogart trapped in a room in Panama, his hands tied behind him and surrounded by Japanese soldiers armed with machine guns. Huston spent the night shooting the scene, knowing there was no logical way for Bogart to escape. And he left Warner Brothers to figure out what to do next.

Then I waved goodbye to Bogie and told Jack Warner, head of the studio, 'Goodbye, Jack, I'm in the army now.' And the next day I was in Washington while Vincent Sherman, who took over direction, tried to figure out a way of getting Bogie out of an impossible situation. It was just my way of saying goodbye and thanks to Warners.

I reported to US Army Signal Corps Headquarters in Washington [in April 1942] for active duty, and then spent weeks and weeks doing nothing. I begged them to send me to China or India or anywhere the action was, I pulled every string I could, but all I ever saw of the war was from behind a desk in Washington. I actually burst into tears once with frustration.

In May, William Wyler, having heard nothing more from

Schlossberg, went to Washington and was met by Major Frank Capra who had won his battle with the colonel. Schlossberg told Capra, 'You Hollywood bigshots are all alike – a pain in the ass.' Capra had been given the go-ahead to commission his own film personnel and Wyler came under his command. Before long he was a major in the United States Army Air Force having had 'no training, nothing', and knowing only that his duty would be to make a film about the 8th Army Air Force.

Back on the Warners lot, Vincent Sherman had solved the predicament in which John Huston had left Bogart by having one of the Japanese soldiers suddenly go berserk, allowing Bogart to escape in the confusion, proclaiming, 'I'm not easily trapped'. In Washington, Huston needed a similar radical solution to his entrapment.

Finally, in August, he was ordered to report to the Aleutian Islands to take documentary film in that particular theatre of combat. The Japanese had attacked the chain of islands, which stretched between Alaska and Siberia, on 3 June 1942, as a diversion before their massive assault on the mid-Pacific atoll of Midway which occurred the following day.

Veteran director John Ford was on Midway when the Japanese struck. He had been appointed by the navy as chief of the Field Photographic Branch with the rank of lieutenant although he was not exactly a 'by the rules' man; he resented the State Department's directive that the OSS could not operate within the United States. Ignoring the directive, he sent his editor Robert Parrish and a petty officer to make a photographic report on the State Department building. With long-focus lenses, they shot film of Marine guards playing cards. Parrish and the petty officer were spotted and arrested and brought before Ford and a Marine captain for court martial.

Ford argued that the film showed how poorly the Marines were guarding one of America's most important buildings, and the Marine captain agreed that the charges should be dropped. Ford then used the film to urge the president to allow the OSS to operate within the United States, but Roosevelt maintained that Ford and his men could work only overseas.

When naval intelligence discovered that the American-held Midway Islands were to be attacked by the Japanese fleet in June 1942, Ford flew to Midway with a cameraman. Flying Fortreses arrived on Midway in the night. The following morning the island's radar picked up a strike force of 108 Japanese Zeros heading right for them.

The American bombers now had to get off Midway to avoid being wiped out in the raid. Ford was out by the runway filming them taking off when suddenly, from behind the clouds, Japanese Zeros came in for the attack. Ford put himself and his cameraman out in the line of attack to film the take-off of American fighters, sitting right next to machine-gunners as Zeros zoomed in on them. A bomb blast wounded him in the left arm, but still he kept filming even as debris covered him and his cameraman. Another Zero zoomed over their heads, dropping its bomb close by. All around buildings and planes were in flames but Ford and his cameraman continued filming from behind sandbags.

Rear Admiral Bagley awarded Ford a citation 'for distinguished service in the line of your profession when on June 4, 1942 the Naval Air Station, Midway Island, was bombed and strafed by Japanese aircraft. Despite your exposed position you remained at your station and reported an accurate account of the attack, thereby aiding the Commanding Officer in determining his employment of the defending forces. Your courage and devotion to duty were in keeping with the highest tradition of the naval service.' Ford received the Purple Heart and the Air Medal and, later, a special Oscar for his completed documentary film, *The Battle of Midway*.

The battle for Midway became a conflict between Japanese and US aircraft carriers. By 5 June the Japanese had lost four aircraft carriers and suffered a massive defeat. But by 6 June Japanese troops had occupied the two westernmost Aleutian islands, Attu and Kiska. Four days later the Americans discovered the Japanese presence and a campaign began to drive them from the Aleutians.

John Huston arrived on Umnak Island that summer of 1942 and met his five-man camera crew.

We flew out to Adak which was at the tip of the
Aleutians. It was nearer to Japanese-held territory than
any other American-held territory in the world. We were
only 250 miles from Kiska which the Japs held, and less
than 500 miles from Attu, also Jap-held.

We lived in tents; all the personnel did. The Seabees
had made an airstrip made out of sheets of metal and the
only huts there were the hospital and Bomber and
Fighter Commands.

The Aleutians have a strange beauty about them.
There are undulating hills of moss and not a single tree.
But there were rivers of salmon – and mountains, some
of which were volcanic topped with snow and puffing
smoke. Then there was the fog – you're flying in brilliant
sunshine, the next moment you're lost in thick fog
thrown up by the warm currents from Japan running into
Arctic flows.

The Japanese didn't know we were there but they
found us two weeks after I arrived. I was crossing the airstrip when I heard a plane which didn't sound like one of
ours. You get to know the sounds of your own planes. I
looked up and there was a Japanese Zero. He obviously
saw us and got the hell out fast before we could even
man an anti-aircraft gun. Now the Japs knew we were
there and we knew we could face an invasion. We set
about digging trenches, but the main job was to run
bombing raids.

We stepped up the bombing missions against Kiska
and Attu and my crew and I flew with them.

In charge of Bomber Command on Adak was Colonel
William O Eareckson. 'He lived like his men, taking no privileges and personally leading the most dangerous missions,'
said Huston. 'He invented low level bombing, bringing his
planes in to Kiska no more than ten feet above the ocean's
surface before zooming up to drop delayed-action bombs on
targets.'

Huston found that 'although the operations there were not

of the same magnitude of the African or European campaigns,
the Aleutian campaign was very, very costly in terms of
casualties'. Many American planes were claimed by the severe
flying conditions. 'There was no radar at that time and the
pilots had only compasses and the seats of their pants to guide
them.'

Planes going to the islands from the States piloted by
young men who had no previous experience of such conditions also suffered considerable losses; they often found
themselves flying blindly through fog into mountains. 'On one
occasion only three B-26 bombers out of twelve flying from
the States actually made it to Adak, and the surviving three
planes broke up on landing,' said Huston.

His job was to take film in combat, and his first mission
was on a B-24 which was late taking off because the tail gunner was missing. By the time the plane was in the air the rest
of the command were a hundred miles ahead on their way to
Kiska, so Huston's plane was ordered to turn back.

On returning, the crew discovered that during the short
time they had been in the air a violent rainstorm had hit Adak,
leaving the airstrip flooded. As they came in to land, the
brakes froze and the aircraft careered forward uncontrollably,
smashing into two other B-24s, shearing off its wings and finally sliding to a halt. The pilot and co-pilot were slumped
unconscious in the cockpit.

Huston heard someone yell, 'Christ! We've got to get off
before the bombs go off.'

The crew scrambled towards one of the exits but it was
jammed. They hurried to another exit and tumbled out:

> I was one of the last to get out. But instead of running for
> cover I decided this was an excellent opportunity to film
> some action. I ran round to the nose of the plane and
> began filming the rescue team of four or five men work-
> ing frantically to get the pilot and co-pilot out before the
> bombs went off. I was on my knees, filming, telling
> myself, 'Good man, Huston! You've got nerves of steel!'
>   Suddenly I just began to shake uncontrollably. I put

the camera down and ran like hell. I expected the plane to blow all to hell, but the bombs didn't go off.

During his next mission to Kiska, Huston's plane was attacked by Japanese Zeros. He had nothing to aim at the enemy other than his camera, and he sat behind the waist gunner filming over his shoulder. Finally he lowered the camera, having seen nothing but what was on view through the lens, and was shocked to find that the waist gunner was lying dead at his feet.

The belly gunner beckoned Huston over to assume control of his gun so that he could take over the waist gun. The gunner had to stand with one foot on the dead man as there was no time or room to move the corpse out of the way. Huston took the belly gun and opened fire. Machine-gun fire from Zeros blasted all around him. 'You could hear nothing but the racket of battle,' he remembered. 'We were badly cut up, but we made it back to Adak.'

Among his camera crew was Sergeant Herman Crabtree, standing six feet four inches and 'strong as an ox. We'd load him up with all the camera equipment to carry out to the planes, but he pleaded with me to let him go on a mission because he was the one member of my team who always had to stay behind. He wasn't a cameraman and there was no reason for him to fly with us.'

Crabtree persevered. 'If I learn to use a camera,' he pleaded, 'can I go?'

Huston simply said, 'Sure, Herman, sure,' thinking that Crabtree would probably not take the time to learn how to film. But Crabtree pestered the other cameramen to train him, and finally he came back to Huston and said, 'I can operate an Eyemo, Lieutenant Huston, so now can I go?'

Huston relented and put him on a flight. It turned out to be one of the most disastrous missions, losing two of their twelve bombers. The ten that returned were badly shot up and there were casualties on each plane. Huston's plane was among the first to return to Adak and he waited for Crabtree's plane which had had a severe beating. When it touched down,

Huston ran to see if his sergeant was OK. Crabtree climbed out.

'Did you get anything?' Huston asked him.

'Yes, sir, I think I got a Zero.'

No one had yet managed to get a good shot of a Zero. 'What? Are you sure?'

'Yes, sir. The Zero came at us and I could see it through the finder and the camera was running.'

They began walking across the airfield. 'How did you like it, Herman?'

'I don't know yet, sir.'

'Do you want to go again?'

'I think so, sir.'

Huston wasn't convinced. He said. 'When?'

'Well,' said Crabtree, 'about next Tuesday when I get over being scared.'

Crabtree rose high in Huston's estimation. Another of his team he considered particularly outstanding was Lieutenant Rey Scott:

Rey had no regard for authority and I thought him to be a lovely rogue. He was rather fatalistic and thought if it was his time, then it was his time, so he risked his neck at every opportunity. He wasn't happy unless he was being shot at, and during missions, if he ran out of film, he whipped out his .45 and shot back.

He also drank quite a bit and one night, after getting through an entire bottle of rum, he went out to the airstrip and commandeered a crew, telling them that there were orders for a midnight raid on Kiska. There had never been a midnight raid on Kiska, but he somehow convinced them and he had them on board the plane when someone in Bomber Command heard what was going on, and the raid was immediately cancelled.

There were countless funerals. Huston decided it was important to film at least one. The rain was pelting down through the fog out of which appeared the pallbearers who, he remembered, were in black 'looking like the Aleutian ravens that always hung in the air above our heads'.

The padre began the service. 'In my house there are many mansions.' Suddenly the fog lifted and in the distance Huston saw a smoking volcano, widely scattered thunderstorms and at least six separate rainbows.

In the event of an invasion by the Japanese, a simple alarm system was set up. Three cannon shots meant that the Japanese were about to land. One cannon shot indicated all clear. One night explosions were heard in the distance. Then came the three cannon shots. Every man ran from his tent to the trenches. 'We cocked our .45's,' said Huston, 'and nervously awaited the invasion.'

Nothing happened for an hour and a half. Then came the single cannon shot. Everyone returned to his tent. Then they heard further explosions and the three cannon shots. They ran back to the trenches. But nothing happened.

'This continued for the next few days and nights and everyone was getting very jumpy. It turned out the explosions were not the Japanese guns but our own mines outside the harbour going off spontaneously. They had been planted by a guy called Brown who earned the nickname "Blow'em up Brown".'

Four months after arriving, Huston decided they had all the footage they needed. A hurricane was reported heading for Adak, making flying impossible, so Huston and his crew boarded a troop transport ship, USS *Ulysses S Grant*. The hurricane struck, blowing the tents all over the island and causing the *Grant* nearly to collide with two other ships while trying to clear the harbour.

The *Grant* rode out the storm for three days, by which time the ship's orders had been changed and Huston and his crew were transferred to a destroyer which was heading for Kodiak. The heavy seas caused mass seasickness, although Huston escaped this malady. On board he met a man who seemed reluctant to discuss his job. The man finally admitted he was a mine engineer.

Huston asked his name and the man replied, 'Brown.'

'Not Blow'em up Brown?'

'I'm afraid so,' Brown replied. He was on his way to Washington to explain why his mines were faulty.

Two days later the destroyer was ordered back to Adak, having been assigned a more important mission. It seemed Huston would never get back to America. They were put aboard an oil tanker and this time they made it to Kodiak. Then it was a flight to Anchorage in Alaska and on to Whitehorse in the Yukon. Then the weather closed in once more. A pilot managed to land and announced that all was clear over land to Prince George in British Columbia. Huston and his crew boarded the plane:

> The clouds were low, the rain was pelting down and we were flying through canyons and valleys, and dodging mountains; it was more terrifying than any bombing mission. The pilot didn't dare fly above the clouds because we would lose radio communication. We'd be heading through blinding rain and then suddenly, as a mountain would rear up before us, the pilot would pull back with all his strength and we'd be desperately climbing to avoid crashing. I was soaked in perspiration when we finally landed at Prince George to refuel.
>
> Then we went on to Vancouver, landed again, then headed for Seattle, and would you know it, Seattle was closed in so we had to turn out to sea and circle. But we finally made it, and I lived to tell the tale.

11

Stars in Battledress

*'I was one of a number of "key actors" which the govern-
ment had classified as exempt from war duty.'*

Rex Harrison

The Entertainments National Service Association – ENSA –
became vital to maintaining the morale of troops, and the task
of organizing entertainment, not just at home but overseas,
fell to British film producer Basil Dean. He had been involved
in Expeditionary Forces Canteen – EFC – during the First
World War. That became the NAAFI (Navy, Army and Air
Force Institutes) which had organized canteens with low
priced food and some entertainment for service men and
women and at the same time make a profit.

When ENSA was born in 1939, Basil Dean sought cooperation from the NAAFI which helped Dean financially,
allowing ENSA to pay its performers £10 a week. Because
theatres had to close at the outbreak of war, there were many
entertainers, from top-name professionals to talented amateurs, eager to volunteer. ENSA's headquarters was at the
Drury Lane Theatre from where Dean pestered the War
Office into providing accommodation and venues for its performers, whether at home or overseas.

ENSA organized parties in all sorts of places, such as at
Greenock in Scotland where British film star Gracie Fields
performed from the back of a lorry at John Brown's shipyard.
Some 6,000 men crammed around, many unable to see her,

so she climbed on top of an upright piano and continued her act in a virtual crouching position for more than half an hour.

Her husband, Italian-born film director Monty Banks, was threatened with internment, and when the British authorities couldn't be persuaded to allow him to remain free, he and Gracie left for America. She was immediately criticized for deserting her country. To prove them wrong, she and Banks embarked on a tour of America and Britain raising war bonds for Britain. She was bitterly hurt by the criticism and, later, returned to England to tour service bases and the Far East.

British film idol George Formby entertained the forces in France and only just got out before the Dunkirk evacuation. He later toured the Middle East and caused a storm when he criticized some of the British entertainers who remained at home.

Hollywood stars Bebe Daniels and her husband Ben Lyon spent much of the war in London entertaining throughout Britain. On a number of occasions when Lyon returned to America, he always brought back luxury foods for their neighbours in London. Lyon eventually enlisted in the US Army and became a colonel while Bebe Daniels was among a number of stars who crossed to Normandy following D-Day to entertain the exhausted Allied troops.

In the Middle East Joyce Grenfell and her pianist were prepared to go anywhere, singing and performing monologues from jeeps and trucks, in hospitals and on mountains.

Because it was too dangerous to send these civilian stars to the very front lines, Army Welfare suggested to the War Office that professional entertainers who were serving in the forces be enlisted in what became the 'Stars in Battledress'. Among the recruits were actor (and later director) Bryan Forbes, who had been involved in intelligence, Sergeant Harry Secombe, Sergeant Charlie Chester, Terry-Thomas and *Carry On* actor Kenneth Connor who had been trained in signalling and machine-gunnery and was one of the lucky ones who escaped at Dunkirk.

Harry Secombe, when being given his pay, would fall out of line, blow kisses, collect his packet, trip on the way back into line and blow a raspberry. Some stars were moonlighting in cabaret spots. Terry-Thomas was found out and ordered back to headquarters. The unit was looked down on by the War Office for its unruly behaviour and all were quickly pulled into line.

The Stars in Battledress may have been first and foremost entertainers, but the War Office would not let them forget that they were also regular soldiers, and there was a war to be won.

Because Rex Harrison was under contract to do the play *No Time for Comedy*, he was unable to devote himself to ENSA. He also had thoughts of joining the RAF. During the run of the play, in January 1942, one of the cast, Arthur Macrae, suddenly left to join up. Following Macrae's example, Harrison made up his mind to do likewise, and went before an RAF board.

'I was very sure that I was one of a number of "key actors" which the government had classified as exempt from war duty,' Harrison told me, 'but I was determined that would not stop me. In the end it was only my bad eyesight which kept me from active duty.'

He was sent to the RAF depot at Uxbridge for a six-week Officers Training Course. His departure from the play brought it to a close on 24 January 1942. Lilli Palmer remained at the house in Denham while Harrison was away at Uxbridge.

'It became almost impossible for us to meet. Lilli was not permitted to go more than thirty miles from her police station without special permission, and she had to be home by midnight. I think that during the six weeks I was at Uxbridge I only managed to see Lilli twice.'

He was unaccustomed to sleeping in the same room as forty other men, having been used to the luxury of hotel rooms, and he found it difficult to sleep at first. Nor did he take to having his hair cut to regulation length. Much of his training outside in the bitter cold was more exerting than anything he had ever experienced.

'Actually it made me more physically fit than I'd ever been

before, or have been since, and I felt rather proud of myself. I was, after all, thirty-three, just coming up to thirty four, and all the other men were much younger than I. Then I was posted to RAF Benson as a Flying Control Officer with the Photographic Reconnaissance Unit. My commanding officer was none other than actor Hugh Wakefield.'

It was now impossible for him to meet Lilli at all.

In the Middle East, Gunner Peter Finch was serving in Syria. One night he and his unit went to the Australian Army Camp in the Sinai desert at Beitjera to see a show featuring Lieutenant-Colonel Jim Davidson, the band leader who had been put in charge of the Amenity Services which organized entertainment for the Australian troops.

After the show, Finch introduced himself to Davidson who thought that the actor ought to be entertaining the troops as well. Finch would have loved to stay on with Davidson but he had to go back to Syria.

Not long after, Finch received orders to return to Australia. He boarded an ammunition ship and sailed for Adelaide. From there he was posted to Darwin to man a Bofors anti-aircraft gun.

He arrived in time for the first Japanese attack on Australia which occurred on 19 February 1942. Four Japanese aircraft carriers had anchored within 200 miles of Darwin which was a key staging post in Allied supply routes to the East Indies. Now 188 Japanese aircraft rained bombs down on Darwin.

'The first time the Japanese came over,' Finch remembered, 'we all dug trenches for people to get into as a sort of hopeful protection from the bomb blast.'

The first wave of bombs sent a covering of earth over one of the trenches in which Finch saw a soldier buried up to his chin. As soon as the first planes had gone, he and a couple of other men ran to pull the buried soldier out with nothing to use but their bare hands. But before they could get him, a second wave of planes shot out of the sky. All Finch had time to do was put a cigarette in the soldier's mouth, light it for him and tell him, 'You'll be okay, sport. I'll be right back.' He dashed for cover, but as soon as it was clear, he and others ran back to the trapped soldier and managed to dig him out.

The attack lasted half an hour, sinking eight ships and nearly destroying the harbour and parts of the town. Some 240 people were killed and over 300 injured.

'There had never been greater loss of life in a single day in Australia,' wrote journalist Douglas Lockwood, 'nor, in some respects, a day of greater ignominy.'

The attacks continued over the next twenty-one months. But Finch, it seems, was needed more by the Department of Information than by Darwin, and he was posted to Sydney to make propaganda films to promote war bonds. His commanding officer, Major Mader-Jones, told him, 'I'm sorry you're leaving us, Gunner Finch. You weren't the army's greatest gunner, but you've been bloody funny.'

For Britain, the war with Japan had begun with a series of crushing blows. The Japanese had captured Malaya and Singapore shortly after the attack on Pearl Harbor, providing Britain with perhaps the gravest humiliation ever suffered by the British Army. The Japanese pushed into Burma in January 1942, forcing back the British forces stationed there into India. The British withdrawal through Burma was the longest in the history of Britain's army.

In March 1942 William Joseph Slim took charge of Burcorps – the Burma Corps – and faced the task of covering the continuing retreat from Rangoon in Burma into India. Lieutenant Jack Hawkins found himself deep in the Indian jungle as second-in-command of a Bren-gun carrier platoon.

There, in the summer of 1942, he received a letter from America which summoned him to appear at a divorce court in Las Vegas. The date set for the divorce had passed three months earlier.

He was enjoying his service but he and his CO did not get on. Suddenly Hawkins was ordered to attend a course which consisted of a sixty-mile march, mostly through cotton soil which Hawkins described as being 'like fine powder when it is dry, and adhesive cotton-wool when it is wet'. His group's supplies included a goat which they had to slaughter, skin and butcher to teach them how to 'live off the land'.

Hawkins complained bitterly and constantly until the officer in charge summoned him and said, 'Hawkins, you're making a bloody nuisance of yourself.'

Hawkins explained that he never kept his thoughts and feelings to himself, and always said outright what he thought.

The officer told him, 'That's why I want you to join the staff and run the shows for the visiting top brass.'

These 'shows' were not the usual camp entertainment but exhibitions of the men's discipline and training. Nevertheless, Hawkins saw it as an opportunity to indulge in something that wasn't too far removed from show business, and he found a natural amphitheatre just outside of Poona (Pune).

He took care of the visiting brass and directed the troops as they displayed their skills at digging trenches and advancing under cover. Throughout, Hawkins gave his own scripted commentary which he liberally laced with rude remarks about the top brass. The top-ranking audience thoroughly enjoyed it all and, eager to maintain a theatrical flavour, Hawkins ended the shows with a cocktail party for his guests.

General John Grover, the general officer commanding the 2nd British Division in India, congratulated him on the show he had seen and began reminiscing about the First World War. He told Hawkins about a concert party called the Cross Keys that had entertained the troops, and said, 'That's just what we need here.'

Hawkins agreed and General Grover immediately commissioned Hawkins to organize entertainment for the troops.

By early autumn, Jack Hawkins had found himself actors and musicians to form a large dance band from the ranks, and with access to divisional funds, he organized all the scenery and costumes.

His show premièred at the local garrison theatre. The musicians played by ear and Hawkins did an impersonation of Carmen Miranda. It was a huge success and he was able to acquire the services of army engineers to construct a folding stage which followed the new Cross Keys company from camp to camp throughout India.

He admitted later that he regretted not being an active, fighting soldier, but he said that since he was not a regular, he had a 'pretty well developed ambition to remain alive'. Nevertheless, he went with the Cross Keys to the front to entertain the troops who were defending the Indian borders against Japanese attempts to invade from Burma.

12

Disaster at Dieppe

'You wonder if the cost of the operation in human lives was worth it all.'

David Niven

On 9 May 1942, the American carrier *Wasp* arrived off Malta with sixty Spitfires. On board the *Wasp* was Douglas Fairbanks Jr who had been transferred there as a 'special observer' on detached duty from USS *Washington*.

The island of Malta had been under attack since June 1940. It held a vital strategic place in the narrows of the Mediterranean for the British with three airfields and a great naval dockyard. Being only fifty-five miles south of Sicily, it was an ideal launch pad for air and sea strikes against ships carrying food and arms for the Italians and, later, German forces in North Africa.

In December 1940 Hitler increased the German air offensive on Malta and the air-raids intensified. The attacks increased in savagery throughout the next year as the island struggled to survive, losing many of its badly needed aircraft.

The Spitfires from *Wasp* landed on Malta and the Germans immediately launched a bombing raid. The Spitfires were scrambled into action and foiled the *Luftwaffe*'s attempt to destroy the aircraft on the ground.

These reinforcements alone were not enough to save Malta. Rommel, who managed finally to capture Tobruk in June 1942, believed that Malta was no longer a threat.

Meanwhile, Fairbanks was promoted to lieutenant in June and transferred to the US cruiser *Wichita* on the PQ17 convoy carrying planes, tanks, guns and other much needed supplies to Murmansk, Russia.

Since the first convoy to Russia in August 1941, Hitler had stepped up attacks on convoys by U-boats, aircraft and lighter surface forces. Convoy PQ17 gathered in Hvalfjord in Iceland in late June 1942. The huge fleet of merchantmen, rescue ships, fleet carriers, destroyers, corvettes, minesweepers, armed trawlers, anti-aircraft ships, submarines and cruisers, including *Wichita*, sailed on 27 June. Six days later the convoy was attacked by air but suffered no losses. But after a succession of intensifying attacks over the next several days, the convoy lost twenty-four of its thirty-four ships, including hundreds of tanks and planes, and 153 sailors. On 4 July the convoy was ordered to scatter.

The mission was a disaster and subsequent cover for PQ convoys was strengthened even more with greater success, due in part to Douglas Fairbanks who returned to USS *Washington* to file his reports on the Malta and PQ17 operations. Someone in Washington read the reports and wrote that 'the best thing that could happen was for some celebrity like Fairbanks to be either severely wounded or killed, because it would show that there was no favouritism in the naval service'.

By the spring of 1942 the threat of Germany's invasion of Great Britain had virtually passed. Bombardier Frankie Howerd was transferred from Shoeburyness, where he had been manning defence posts, to an Experimental Station in South Wales at Penclawwd, a fishing village on the Gower coast near Swansea. The so-called Experimental Station was little more than a smattering of Nissen huts. He grew bored and, belying his image as a comical coward which he developed in his post-war career, wanted only to do something positive for the war effort.

Anthony Quayle had also become restless once more. He came under the command of Colonel The Lord Glanusk for whom Quayle had little respect. He found the colonel condescending and patronizing, and in June 1942, Glanusk summoned Quayle to his office and informed him that he took a dim view of him.

Quayle replied that his feelings were reciprocated. For this insubordination, he expected to be court-martialled. He went to Brown's Hotel in London to see Mason-Mac who had just returned from Moscow. Mason-MacFarlane told Quayle he was to be sent back to Gibraltar as Governor and Commander in Chief. 'Do you want to come with me, Tony?'

'I'd love to, sir. But I can't. I had a quarrel with my colonel and I think I'm going to be court-martialled.'

'Balls! Come and be my military assistant. Leave your colonel to me. Be back here in forty-eight hours. That's all.'

Mason-MacFarlane resolved Quayle's dilemma and in forty-eight hours they were flying from Plymouth back to Gibraltar.

Mason-MacFarlane wasted no time in informing his staff that the reason for his return was Operation 'Torch'. This was the code name for a vast amphibious invasion of North Africa in which landings would take place simultaneously at Algeria and Morocco. The Combined Fleet would be under the command of British Admiral Sir Andrew Cunningham. General Eisenhower, the Supreme Allied Commander, would make his headquarters in Gibraltar which would be the springboard for the whole operation.

Defences on the Rock had to be strengthened and new operation headquarters tunnelled out. Mason-MacFarlane told his staff that he didn't know the exact date of the landings, 'And I wouldn't tell you if I did.' They could take no chance of the slightest leak in security.

Quayle witnessed some of the most important of the Allied leaders arriving in and departing from Gibraltar. In August General Montgomery arrived, staying only one night before flying on to take command of the 8th Army in Egypt where he would soon be attacking the Afrika Korps at El Alamein. At dinner Monty dropped his voice so low that the entire table had to fall silent in order to hear him. Yet despite his quiet voice, Quayle found him an enormously impressive man.

Since his posting to HMS *Mersey* in Liverpool, Acting Sub-Lieutenant Kenneth More had become impatient to go to sea. He'd been stuck in those barracks for almost a year. 'I wanted action, you see,' he told me, 'so I asked my CO for a transfer, but he just said I was too valuable where I was. Then I asked the advice of an old chief gunner's mate, a retired petty officer who always had good advice, and he told me to have a sudden attack of appendicitis and have them whipped out because after being on sick leave they would inevitably post me somewhere else.'

He read up on the symptoms in a medical book and, putting on an award-winning performance, was suddenly stricken during a lecture with what appeared to be acute appendicitis. After the operation to remove his appendix, the doctor told him, 'There was nothing wrong with your appendix, but since you're obviously going back to sea, it's just as well you got them out now rather than later.'

When his sick leave was over, he was sent to HMS *Excellent*, the gunnery school on Whale Island off Portsmouth. One night in the mess he saw a young lieutenant who, it turned out, was Prince Philip Mountbatten. More decided he'd go over and introduce himself, but he was stopped in mid-stride by a commander.

'Where do you think you're going?' the commander asked.

'To talk to Lieutenant Mountbatten.'

'Over my dead body.'

'Why?'

'Because you just don't do that, that's why. If you do, I'll have you doubling round the parade ground for two days solidly.'

More continued his training and, in May 1942, received his orders to report to HMS *Aurora* as additional watch keeping officer. 'I was absolutely delighted,' he told me. 'She was one of the navy's crack light-cruisers who made quite a name for herself during the siege of Malta.'

He reported to the ship that very morning. 'I looked up at her, lying alongside a dock, and thought how sleek she looked. She had six six-inch and eight four-inch guns, short range and anti-aircraft weapons; I couldn't believe my luck.'

On a morning in July 1942, *Aurora* sailed down the Mersey and up past Northern Ireland to escort a fleet of mine-layers. Kenneth More, standing duty as watch keeping officer, stood on the bridge straining his eyes to peer through the thick fog on lookout for icebergs. Every now and then one of the mines being laid exploded prematurely, breaking the eerie silence of the sea.

The job done, *Aurora* turned south to escort a convoy carrying troops to North Africa via the Cape, although *Aurora* itself was only going as far as Freetown on the west coast of Africa.

More was on the bridge as officer of the watch when orders came through from the commodore of the convoy; 'Follow Zig-zag 11', which was one of several patterns of movement designed to confuse U-boats. The ships were to follow the bearing for ten minutes, when another course would be given.

Captain 'Bill' Agnew of the *Aurora* was having a nap in his chair, so More decided he would cope with the situation and gave what he considered were the necessary orders. *Aurora* altered course.

> I felt like I was completely in command of the situation, when I suddenly heard a frantic shout, 'The wheel's to port instead of starboard!'
>
> The captain leapt from his seat, saw what was happening and roared at me, 'You're heading for the commodore's ship, you idiot!'
>
> I didn't know what to do and just stared at him, and ahead I could see the bulk of the troop carrier as we headed towards her. Captain Agnew shouted orders down the voice pipe, we went into a 45 degree turn and he averted the almost certain loss of two Royal Navy ships.
>
> Signal flags were run up the mast of the commodore's

Portrait of a wartime fairytale: RAF Flight Lieutenant Rex Harrison and his wife, 'enemy alien' Lilli Palmer, produced son Rex Carey, who was born during a terrifying air raid.

The familiar screen face of Kenneth More, portraying Captain Shepherd in *Sink the Bismarck*. As a lieutenant in the Royal Navy, More saw active service off North Africa, Sicily and in the Pacific.

Lieutenant John Mills served with the 1st Rifle Battalion, Monmouthshire Regiment, and served with distinction until he was discharged through ill health.

The battlefield face of David Niven (*left*). During the invasion of Europe and advance through Germany, Lieutenant-Colonel Niven's job was to help keep the peace between the Allied leaders.

Acting Sub-Lieutenant Laurence Olivier took his rank and duties seriously when stationed at HMS Kestrel at Worthydown, where he gently reprimanded soldier George Munn (the author's father, inset) for not saluting him.

In the film *A Bridge Too Far*, Dirk Bogarde portrayed Lieutenant-General Frederick Browning, a role that brought back memories of Dirk's part in the actual battle for Arnhem.

Major William Wyler on board the *Bad Penny* of the 91st Bomb Group of the 8th Air Force.

Lieutenant Douglas Fairbanks Jr meets King George VI on board the
USS *Washington* while on duty at Scapa Flow in June 1942.

Sophia Loren relived many of her own war experiences in the film *Two Women*, the story of a mother and daughter trying to escape the war in Italy. Loren, playing the mother, saw her real self in the younger actress, Eleanora Brown, who played the daughter.

A scene from the film *Battle of the Bulge*. Mel Brooks recalled the real battle: 'We're in the Ardennes. We get out of the trucks, we start walking. Suddenly all around us are Tiger tanks. It's the Battle of the Bulge. And it ain't like the film, believe me.'

Lieutenant-Commander John Ford *(left)* of the American naval secret service agency, OSS, spied on the Japanese, was wounded during the battle of Midway and emerged from the war as a Rear-Admiral.

Top: John Huston *(far right)* and the men from the American Army Air Force stationed on the Aleutians in 1942. *Bottom, from left*: William Wyler, writer Sy Bartlett, John Huston and Anatole Litvak congratulate each other on receiving the Legion of Merit.

ship; 'Name of officer-on-the-watch' which of course was me. Captain Agnew was flushed with anger but very relieved we hadn't sliced the commodore's ship in two, and he decided that as captain he took responsibility for all that happened on his ship. He sent a return signal; 'My responsibility. Officer-of-the-watch under training.'

I kept a very low profile after that until we arrived at Freetown.

Lord Louis Mountbatten had been building up the Combined Operations and, in July 1942, was told by the United States Chief of Staff that he could have an American officer of his choosing. He asked for Douglas Fairbanks Jr.

Fairbanks was given a cover appointment in the London Headquarters of the US Naval Forces where Mountbatten informed him that he wanted him to help create the Chemical Warfare and Deception department. Fairbanks's job was to pass on the department's information to the American Forces, but more specifically to devise means of decoying the enemy, especially in regard to the exact point at which the eventual invasion of Europe would take place. Fairbanks was to use his special knowledge of sound effects combined with camouflage and illusion techniques.

While Operation 'Torch' was on stand-by, Churchill and the Allied commanders prepared for Operation 'Jubilee', a joint Canadian and British amphibious attack on the French port of Dieppe.

The plan was to seize the port, occupy France for about twelve hours, capture enemy documents and prisoners, and generally test the Germans for what would eventually be a complete Allied invasion of France. It had originally been scheduled for July 1942, but the weather conditions had been too bad. So it was finally decided to launch 'Jubilee' in the early hours of 19 August 1942.

Fairbanks led a series of small raids along the French coast by commandos under his command on HMS *Tormentor* from which his landing craft was launched. The real attack was against Dieppe itself with Canadian infantry going in first, supported by tanks. But first the enemy strongpoints on the high cliffs had to be knocked out.

David Niven, leading 'A' Section of 'Phantom', accompanied Lord Lovat's No 4 Commandos in an attack on 'Hess' battery about one and a half miles west of Dieppe. They landed on the shore at 4.50 am. Half the unit of 250 men followed Major Derek Mills-Roberts up a narrow gulley to the clifftop while Lovat took the rest of the unit in a wide arc to attack the battery from the rear. Niven was probably with Lovat's attack force.

At 6.28 am exactly Spitfires zoomed down on the battery and two minutes later the commandos of Lord Lovat fixed bayonets and charged. They successfully seized the battery and returned to the beach. They lost forty-five men, some of them from Niven's 'A' Section.

The rest of the assault met with disaster. The surprise attack was discovered when landing craft ran into a German merchant convoy. The landing craft in the main attack were half an hour late and the Germans, alerted by the convoy, were ready.

Other Allied prongs suffered massive losses due to inaccurate landings and the readiness of the Germans. It was a disaster on a huge scale; the Allies lost 1,027 men, and another 2,340 were captured.

Captain Niven had the dreadful task of writing letters to the wives and girlfriends of the men lost from 'A' Squadron. He said it reminded him of a scene from his film *Dawn Patrol* when the CO had to write letters of regret. The adjutant told him, 'It doesn't matter how you word it, sir, it'll break her heart just the same.'

Said Niven, 'You wonder if the cost of the operation in human lives was worth it all. You could say that the mistakes at Dieppe taught us invaluable lessons that ultimately saved lives later during the Normandy invasion.'

The British had captured some German prisoners during the raid on Dieppe who were put in handcuffs. The story reached Hitler that the Germans had been thrown into irons, and he ordered that British POWs be treated the same.

Denholm Elliott, a sergeant pilot with the RAF, remembered how, as a PoW, he was shackled from dawn till night in the small compound for captured Allied airmen within the huge PoW camp at Lamsdorf in Upper Silesia, Poland.

A keen amateur actor who became a leading star of postwar films, he took part in PoW shows, even though Hitler had banned all entertainment. The RAF PoWs had a better time of it than many other captured Allies because their guards were usually the more civilized *Luftwaffe*; they turned a blind eye to Elliott and his cast erecting their portable theatre and putting on shows. The guards even obliged by taking off the actors' chains when they had to go on stage, putting them back in irons after the show.

Entertainment played a huge part in keeping up the morale of PoWs. Those servicemen who were also actors found themselves behind the wire with a vital job simply by putting on plays and shows.

In Stalag Luft III there was a considerable pool of acting talent, including Roy Dotrice who apparently excelled playing female leads, *Carry On* star Peter Butterworth and Rupert Davies, who was an officer in the Fleet Air Arm.

British soldiers who were taken prisoner were not so lucky. Their guards were generally Nazis. Sam Kydd, who was in the Lamsdorf camp, told me:

> The guards were really quite harsh, especially the younger ones; the older guards often turned a blind eye if you bent the rules a little bit. But the young Nazi guards really came down hard on us. There were days when we went outside the camp to do various bits of work and the guards kept a lookout for anyone trying to exchange food with the Polish civilians. Chocolate was very popular among them because it wasn't something they ever got, and we never got many real eggs. So I had three bars of chocolate I was going to exchange. You had to put the chocolate in a hole in the ground, but I was seen by the guards and put into solitary confinement for a month; just darkness, no chance to wash, no fresh air, not much

food, freezing at night. I came out sick and had to report to the doctor.

At best, the food was bad! We used the same tea leaves over and over and then when they were well beyond their sell-by date we put them back into the packets, sealed them up and sold them to the guards.

After I got better I got interested in the entertainment programme and took part in a Christmas pantomime which was a mixture of all the traditional pantomimes. We had a scene in which *There'll Always Be An England* was played very quietly and the audience began singing it, and it just got louder, swelling into a mighty chorus. There were grown-up men standing with tears running down their faces; it was beautiful, because all the frustration and humiliation we had all felt was being thrust aside, and we had our pride once more.

Another PoW who was to become a well-loved actor was Clive Dunn, Corporal Jones of the British Home Guard in the TV series, and film of, *Dad's Army*. He was with the 4th Hussars and was captured in Greece and put in Stalag XVIIA, a well-organized camp with a fine entertainment programme. He appeared in numerous plays including Ivor Novello's *Glamorous Night* complete with lavish costumes, a full orchestra and a talented chorus. But somebody had to play the gypsy princess, and so Clive Dunn took the role.

In September 1942, Lieutenant Richard Todd and the entire British contingent were relieved in Iceland by the Americans. Todd was sent on yet another course at Catterick for Battalion Signals Officers. His talent as an actor was put to full use when he discovered he was supposed to have a basic knowledge of Morse Code. He didn't, and after a furious dressing down by his commanding officer, he decided to impress his superiors by using his actor's memory to learn and present an entire lecture on 'The atomic theory of Electricity'. This was all the more impressive since no other officer on the course dared to attempt this particular subject. He had earlier bluffed his way into the army, and he did it again, this time to gain a mark of 'Catterick D' which was one of the top two marks out of the 200 personnel taking part.

Unfortunately, his success was rewarded by a posting as a signals instructor to the Regimental Depot at Berwick-on-Tweed which he considered a backwater from which he wanted desperately to escape.

Trevor Howard was given an emergency commission of second lieutenant in the Airborne Division to become one of the Red Berets. An intensive year-long training course ensued and he wondered if he would ever get into the war proper.

During 1942 Faith Brook returned to England after filming *The Jungle Book* to appear on stage in *Aren't Men Beasts?* at the Brixton Theatre in London. A newspaper reported, 'Faith Brook deserted the country in 1940 and has now come back into the good life of the theatre without first paying her dues.' It neglected to mention that she had tried to join the Wrens.

Even the House of Commons debated the matter. But Faith kept calm and when the play reached the end of its run she applied to join ENSA. On the day she was accepted, her call-up papers arrived. She had been rejected by the Wrens and her sudden call-up into the Auxiliary Territorial Service seemed suspiciously like a calculated act by her critics in high places.

The War Office asked her to take part in a publicity drive for more recruits into the ATS, and she was sent to train at a motorized unit, learning to drive heavy vehicles and passing every course. Then to her delight she was enlisted by Stars in Battledress. No one criticized her again.

13
Into Africa

*'Patton walked in with his pearl-handled revolvers strapped
to him, so I politely reminded him he didn't need to be
armed. I thought he would probably shoot me.'*

Anthony Quayle

In Gibraltar, in October 1942, Anthony Quayle received word
that Churchill would be passing through and stopping off;
absolute secrecy had to be maintained. He would be arriving
in disguise, but Quayle had no idea what kind of disguise.
When Churchill's black Liberator with an escort of
Beaufighters landed, its American pilot jumped out and told
Quayle, 'The first passenger to alight will be Air Commodore
Frankland.'

Quayle said, 'I beg your pardon?'

The pilot repeated himself and then climbed back into the
plane. A few moments later Churchill, dressed in the uniform
of an Air Commodore, climbed out, removed his cigar from
his mouth and gave his famous 'V' sign.

I drove Churchill and his detective to Government
House, and all the while Churchill asked questions. He
said, 'Young man, are you prepared to sell your life
dearly?'

I said, 'I hope so, sir.'

He said, 'Because this old fortress is soon to be the
centre of historic events.'

He became a frequent visitor during those weeks

leading up to 'Torch' and we had masses of troops arriving and the runway was extended for use by Flying Fortresses.

As a prelude to 'Torch,' General Montgomery and his 8th Army began his attack on the Afrika Korps at El Alamein in Egypt on 23 October 1943. Hitler quickly returned Rommel, the 'Desert Fox', to take command of the hard-pressed German forces.

Toward the end of October a courier from London went down in his plane off Cadiz. His body was washed up on the beach and recovered by Spanish coastguards. The Spanish Navy allowed the body to be brought to Gibraltar. General Mason-MacFarlane and Anthony Quayle searched the body and discovered a note that read:

Dear Mason-Mac,
Just to tell you that the date for 'Torch' is finally set. It will be 8 November.
Look forward to seeing you very soon.
All the best – Ike.

They now had to decide if it was possible that Spanish intelligence had discovered this note, consequently putting the whole operation into jeopardy. British intelligence decided that it was unlikely that the letter had been previously removed from the body, and Mason-MacFarlane reassured Eisenhower and the War Cabinet that it was safe to proceed with Operation 'Torch'.

Eisenhower arrived on 4 November, the day that, under attack by the 8th Army, the Axis powers began to retreat from El Alamein. SOE quietly spirited General Henri Giraud, opposed to the Vichy government and living in retreat in the south of France, to Gibraltar. He was needed to persuade the French troops in Algeria and Morocco to join with the Allies when the invasion of North Africa took place. But he was under the impression that he would in fact command the entire operation.

Recalled Quayle, 'When Mason-Mac heard this, we ran down the HQ tunnel hoping to clear the matter before Giraud met with Eisenhower. We were too late. Out of his room burst Giraud, furious and refusing to have anything to do with the operation.'

On 7 November, a massive amphibious invasion force assembled off the coast of North Africa. There were more than 500 ships, among them the *Aurora*. 'It was,' said Kenneth More, 'the largest convoy I had ever seen. Ships for as far as the eye could see.'

More, control officer in charge of the four-inch anti-aircraft guns, was surprised to hear a brief announcement over the tannoy; 'Ship's company will see to it that they wear clean underclothes.'

More asked the ship's surgeon, Lieutenant Sam Balfour, who was passing by, what that meant. 'If you're wounded,' the surgeon explained, 'clean clothes give you a better chance of escaping infection.'

The *Aurora*'s primary job was to prevent any French warship leaving the port of Oran in Algeria. More recalled: 'I felt like I was living the classic nightmare all actors have; when you're about to go on for Act II and you don't even know what happened in Act I. I didn't know what to expect. I was on the after control platform with the anti-aircraft guns and could hear only the throb of the engines.'

A searchlight from the coast suddenly lit up the *Aurora*. The ship's six-inch guns opened up, knocking the searchlight out. Other lights came on. Guns began firing down on the ship from the hilltops, exploding in green blasts; the French used green dye in their shells so they could check where their shells landed.

A huge French destroyer suddenly steamed out of the harbour and the *Aurora* gave chase, firing on her and setting her on fire. She continued to fight back but after twenty minutes she was beached in flames.

Two more ships tried to dash for freedom. Captain Agnew swung his ship around, heading for the French ships which were trying to escape. The *Aurora* fired on them and with another British destroyer, *Boadicea*, they managed to get one of the French ships, but the other escaped.

In the morning of 8 November 1942, the invasion of North Africa began. Algiers was the first objective to fall to the Eastern Task Force, a combination of British and American troops, led by Major General Charles M Ryder.

John Ford turned up in Algiers, sent there as a punishment for daring to make a film, *December 7th*, which criticized the glaring mistakes that resulted in the Japanese attack on Pearl Harbor. The film was shelved.

He was also unpopular with the Atlantic fleet commanders who despised his disrespect for authority. The Washington generals and admirals in charge of European operations decided to send him to cover the invasion of North Africa. There he met up with Colonel Darryl Zanuck, filming for the Signal Corps. They decided to form an advance outfit for the next stage of the invasion and, in a blue Chevrolet which Zanuck had commandeered in Algeria, they drove ahead of the front line.

Coming across a beautiful old church, they decided it would make a great background shot if the Germans didn't destroy it before the Allies arrived. Ford had run out of cigars and demanded that Zanuck share his last one with him. Ford began walking towards the church with a camera, just as a shell from the German artillery landed dangerously close. Ford and Zanuck were thrown into the air. When they picked themselves up, they realized they were unhurt although the camera had been destroyed.

All Ford said to Zanuck was, 'Did it hurt the cigar?'

At Oran the Central Task Force under Major General Lloyd Fredendall met stiff oposition from the French. It took two days for Fredendall to reach and take Oran.

General George S Patton led the Western Task Force on to the beaches near Casablanca in Morocco, but not before a tremendous naval battle took place during which the French ships were annihilated. On the beach there was total confusion brought about by inexperience of large amphibious landings. Patton, furious, strode up and down the beach, bellowing orders and kicking any man in the backside who ducked for cover.

On Gibraltar, Quayle received news that the first landings had taken place; he relayed the news to Admiral Sir Andrew Cunningham. In the morning the American contingent remained in their rooms for breakfast, and so it was left to the British to have breakfast with Giraud and his aide. They listened to the BBC news while the French aide translated for Giraud.

There had been some resistance from the French but, continued the announcer, General Giraud, one of France's greatest heroes from the First World War, was at that moment on French North African soil, issuing the call to his countrymen to follow him to victory with the Allies.

The general heard the translation, and fell silent.

Quayle recalled that 'Mason-Mac had to placate Giraud and, after two hours and plenty of sherry, Giraud was eager to be on his way to North Africa.'

Two days later General Patton flew in without notifying the ground he was on his way. A number of the Rock's guns opened fire and Patton's pilot quickly radioed through his identification.

Quayle recalled:

Patton walked into Government House with his pearl-handled revolvers strapped to him, so I politely reminded him that he didn't need to be armed. I thought he would probably shoot me, but he simply removed his revolvers and laid them on a chair.

Eisenhower asked him how morale was in North Africa.

'Very high,' replied Patton, and then he explained that there had been only one disciplinary case which had to be dealt with. A lieutenant had left his foxhole against orders. He hadn't deserted; he'd gone to rescue his sergeant who was lying wounded, but he had his orders to stay put and Patton said, 'He had no damn business leaving his foxhole.'

Patton said he'd had the lieutenant shipped back to the States but he wouldn't be court-martialled. He said, 'I reckon you can crucify a man, but there's no need to rivet the nails.'

No wonder they called him Blood and Guts Patton.

The *Aurora* arrived at Gibraltar's harbour where Kenneth More stood on deck among the officers, watching very proudly as the flag of Admiral Sir Andrew Cunningham was raised. The pipes sounded and the admiral came on board to be transported to Algiers.

Following the success of Operation 'Torch', Lieutenant General Montgomery's 8th Army had orders from Churchill to 'destroy the German–Italian Army commanded by Field Marshal Rommel'.

Spike Milligan, with 19 Battery, 56th Regiment, Royal Artillery, was sent to help. He had not asked to be sent to war. He had been quite happy playing trumpet at St Cyprian's Hall on dance nights, but in the spring of 1940 he was conscripted and spent the next two and a half years at Bexhill-on-Sea.

When his regiment was ordered to board a troopship bound for North Africa, all the men were told they were not to bring any musical instruments. They took them just the same.

News of this blatant disobedience reached the ears of a major during the voyage. 'Despite orders to the contrary,' the major told Milligan, 'you musician chaps have brought your instruments. Is that right?'

Milligan confessed. Then the major surprised him by asking if he and the other musicians would play at the officers' dance in the officer's mess. When the dance was over the major went around with the hat and made a collection for the band.

As the convoy entered the Bay of Biscay, a German U-boat attacked, sinking two of the outlying destroyers. It was a balmy night when the troops finally disembarked.

On 14 January 1943, Churchill and Roosevelt met in

Casablanca. In the east, Rommel was on the run from
Montgomery's 8th Army. They were confident that a new
push from the west in the spring would drive the Axis forces
from North Africa, and then would come the invasion of
Sicily and Italy. By late January, the 8th Army was close to the
Tunisian border, having pushed Rommel's Afrika Korps and
the Italian forces into Tunisia.

Milligan could never recall his exact location when he had
his first taste of war, but he was trying to get a telephone line
up between two trees on a hill, in full view of an enemy observation post. He was suddenly fired upon by a .88 gun. The
shell landed behind him, and 'like a bloody fool' he decided to
go and inspect the damage. Another shell landed behind him,
and this time he took off, running down the hill.

He was trying to find cover when a squadron of Stuka
bombers flew over. The world around him began exploding
and he dived for a hole only to find it already full. The inhabitants were Irish troops, 'big, enormous warriors wearing Kaili
beards'. An Irish sergeant grabbed him and hauled him down,
saying 'Don't worry lad, you'll be as safe as houses here with
me.'

He later said that he took the war personally because if it
had not been for Hitler he would have been back at St
Cyprian's.

The Allies pushed forward and the Afrika Korps withdrew.
At Jabul Mahdi, Milligan and his platoon captured some
Germans. They surrendered and came across a hill in their
neatly pressed uniforms, carrying a white flag. Milligan's sergeant took the flag and blew his nose into it.

The prisoners were put into some three-tonne trucks and
the small convoy began the drive along a precarious narrow
mountain road. The lead truck broke down, and when the
British troops failed to get it going, the German officer asked
Milligan's CO if he was having trouble.

'Yes,' said the CO. 'The bugger won't start.'

'Would you like me to have it mended for you?'

Milligan felt they were being reduced to idiots as the CO
accepted the German officer's help. In no time at all one of

the German soldiers had the engine running. The prisoners were put back on the trucks and the platoon drove on. Milligan felt, 'We were the losers, they the ones in charge.'

On 16 April, Milligan celebrated his twenty-fifth birthday on the same day the Afrika Korps were routed at Tripoli.

Into the North African campaign came Private Audie Murphy who had been stuck at Fort Meade since 1941. His outfit was sent as a replacement for an infantry company, but instead of getting into battle he found a further course of training. Finally, his outfit was told to prepare to move on to Tunis but before they pulled out, news came that Tunis had fallen to Montgomery's 8th Army on 7 May 1943. The Americans had simultaneously taken Bizerta. On 12 May the Axis forces in North Africa surrendered. Eisenhower moved his headquarters to Algiers to prepare for the invasion of Italy.

With him went Douglas Fairbanks Jr who had arrived to make contact with British 'A' Force of Combined Operations which had been responsible for various deception tactics during Operation 'Torch'. He had been in the States organizing units of the US Amphibious Force to be able to practise the deception tactics he had developed at Combined Operations.

His work was top secret and vital to the success of the war. Among other things, he helped in 'the man who never was' ploy in which a corpse, with the false identity of a Royal Marines officer, was purposely washed ashore in Spain in May 1943, with a briefcase full of false papers which claimed that an attack on Sicily was just a cover for the real target of Sardinia.

Rex Harrison's divorce from Collette had come through in the late summer of 1942, and on 25 January 1943, he married Lilli at Caxton Hall Registry Office in London. Now they could not be separated and she was no longer considered an enemy alien.

After I married Lilli, I was trained as a Flying Control Liaison Officer at 10-Group Operational Command which was at Rudlow Manor (near Bath) where my cousin Bat Tongue and her husband Buster lived, so I felt very much at home there. I was there for a number of months and it was a rather demanding course which I passed, and was then transferred to 11-Group Headquarters at Uxbridge. So we were settled into a normal married life at last.

You know, I don't think I was ever happier than when I was in the RAF. I felt useful at last, which is, after all, what I think everyone who joined up wanted to feel. I worked in the operation room which was underground for obvious reasons. It was a large, round room with a huge table with a map of the countryside showing all the land from the Wash in Norfolk to Southampton, and the coasts of Belgium and France.

At around dawn our bombers would return from their missions and then we'd really be busy. I sat behind glass overlooking the map table, and I had five telephones which I used to guide in aircraft which had reported an SOS. That was my job, to help guide returning bombers to the nearest air strip or send out sea-rescue units to where a plane would have gone down.

Sometimes we'd have up to twenty planes all in trouble, and I would contact each of them to guide them down. I took great pride in my job and it was very satisfying, if exhausting, knowing I'd helped to save valuable lives. Of course, things didn't always turn out for the best and we sometimes lost air crew. But if you managed to get all the SOS planes down safely, you felt bloody good.

Lilli, meanwhile was making films, which I envied, I must admit. But when I stopped to think about it, I was doing something that was probably more important.

His job took him to other aerodromes where the emergency services would be tested with mock operations. While at RAF Manston in the south-east of England, he took part in a real emergency when a damaged aircraft reported it was approaching. He helped to guide it in over the radio and assisted in getting the crew out.

Lilli's film work was temporarily terminated when she became pregnant. One afternoon in the spring of 1943, the couple were entertaining director Harold French and actress Deborah Kerr at their house when the air-raid siren went off. They didn't flinch and continued chatting. Harrison went over to the window and saw a German plane breaking through the clouds and dropping a bomb. He realized the bomb was heading their way.

He called 'Get down' and they dropped to the floor. The bomb landed in the garden and virtually sank into the rain-sodden ground before exploding, cushioning the enormous blast which threw all four against the far wall. The room was thick with smoke.

An air-raid warden broke down the door and helped them to their feet. Harrison received a cut to his forehead. Lilli suffered only a cut wrist. Deborah Kerr and Harold French were covered in debris. They were all lucky not to have been killed. Lilli was particularly relieved that the unborn baby was unhurt.

Meanwhile Lieutenant Richard Todd had escaped from the backwater of Berwick-on-Tweed when an old friend of his, Major R B Freeman-Thomas of the 42nd Armoured Division, had him transferred to the headquarters of the division as a liaison officer.

He took the opportunity to join the newly forming 6th Airborne Division. There followed extensive training in parachuting and then in signals. He was getting to be known as a 'Course King' because of his success in passing so many courses.

The film world was shocked in June of 1943 when a plane carrying actor Leslie Howard was shot down. He had been persuaded by Anthony Eden in April to undertake a propaganda tour of Spain and Portugal. At the end of the tour he boarded a plane at Lisbon on 1 June, and *en route* to London the plane came under a calculated and deliberate attack by two German fighters. Howard's plane, which was unarmed, was brought down, and when the Germans were asked to give a reason for their action, they gave several excuses, none of which the British government accepted as plausible.

In England, Trevor Howard's training to be a Red Beret came to an end on 2 October 1943, when he was found to be unfit and invalided out of the force. Having wasted three years, he was angry, but what made him even more furious after the war was when a film studio publicist released a story that Howard had won the Military Cross.

He said:

It was just a load of crap for the sake of building up my image as some kind of hero. Obviously it was good copy for the papers, but there was never a grain of truth in it. I was bloody furious about it, and even now [in 1979] I still read about what a bloody noble hero I was supposed to be.

The truth is I never saw any action. Would have loved to, not because I wanted to be a hero. I just wanted to do my bit like anyone else.

14

The Hope of Poland

'The visual and mental vistas that were opened up to me by those terrible German movies almost made being in Cracow worth it.'

Roman Polanski

In Cracow, Poland, in early 1942, Roman Polanski had to brave the daily prospect that he might be discovered as a Jew, although the fact that he sold newspapers virtually on the Gestapo's doorstep may have been the best cover for him.

A small underground resistance to the German occupation had become organized. It did not go so far as to create sabotage and chaos for the Germans, but it did try to encourage the populace to oppose the Nazi regime. Partisans followed people who went to see the German produced movies – the only films being shown in Cracow's cinemas – and harassed them by painting slogans on their houses, calling them traitors and collaborators, and breaking their windows.

Roman didn't care about the content of the films he went to see. He later said:

Going to see films in Cracow during the war was the most sublime sensual experience. Except for watching films, there was absolutely nothing else to provide any sort of pleasure to an eight- or nine-year-old boy. The visual and mental vistas that were opened up to me by those terrible German movies almost made being in Cracow worth it. Had there been no Germans, had there been no war or occupation, I probably would have ended up a merchant. And hated every minute of my life.'

He gave all his earnings to the Koslewskis and, with no money of his own, he continued to sneak into cinemas. One evening he was caught by the cinema manager who promptly turned him over to the police. The Cracow police usually made Jewish-looking males strip to discover if they had been circumcized. Those who were were handed over to the SS unless they could prove they were not Jewish and had been circumcized for medical reasons.

Roman was fortunate in that he did not have the obvious dark looks of most Eastern European Jews, so on this occasion he was not made to strip and was allowed to go home. The Koslewskis told him that if he got into any more trouble he would be thrown out to fend for himself. The whole family were in danger of being put to death for harbouring a Jew.

Roman did stop sneaking into cinemas and, instead, began to pay for his entrance. But to do this he had to withhold some of his earnings from the Koslewskis. One of his cousins found out and informed on him, and he was again threatened with expulsion. To make sure he paid over all the money he earned, a family member stayed with him all day, every day, at his street corner, counting how much he took in newspaper sales and confiscating his earnings at the end of the day.

Desperate to find money to enable him to go to the cinema, he joined a gang of older boys who broke into garment ware-houses and sold their goods on the black market. To combat black marketeers, the Cracow police had undercover agents who arrested Roman and his gang. At the police station two of the boys who were Jewish were made to strip and taken away. Barely in their teens, the two boys were beaten into revealing the identities of any other Jews they knew of in hiding. Roman felt sure they would give them his name, but they didn't, and he was released while the two boys were handed over to the SS.

Fearing he might still be betrayed under the expert interro-gation of the SS, Roman hid in the cellar of an abandoned building for several days before daring to return home. All he had for light in his hiding place was a candle. One night, as he watched how the hot wax dripped on to his finger and cooled, he had the idea of using melted candle wax to fashion a foreskin. It made for an effective disguise and only a close inspection of his penis would reveal that his foreskin was merely a wax imitation. Whether he actually invented the fake foreskin or had already heard about it is arguable, although many insist he was the originator. What does seem certain, though, is that Jewish men in hiding heard about the trick and adopted it.

During the winter of 1942, Roman was on his way home after a visit to the cinema when he was stopped by a gang of young men from the underground movement. They beat him up and warned him not to see any more German films. From then on, he made sure that whenever he left a cinema, he remained undetected.

On Christmas Eve 1942, he tried selling a black-market sweater to a man who said he needed something special as a Christmas present. The customer turned out to be an undercover policeman and Roman was again arrested and taken to the police station where he was thrown into a cell with several other boys. He suddenly realized that he was not wearing his fake foreskin and he was terrified that he might at last be ordered to strip. He told them that his surname was Koslewski and the police sent for his 'father'. Mr Koslewski had to pay a small fine and then Roman was released without having to strip.

Again Roman was told by the Koslewskis that he would be turned out, and again they let him stay on. But their patience would not last much longer.

When the Germans occupied Poland in 1939, Hans Frank, who had been head of the Nazi party's legal division, became governor general of the western half of Poland, leaving the eastern side under Russia's jurisdiction. He set up his headquarters in Wawel Castle near Cracow and was responsible for the extermination of Poland's Jews. He also sent the entire teaching staff of Cracow University to internment or death, making Poland into what he described as 'an intellectual desert'.

Then, in June 1941, the Germans suddenly launched Operation 'Barbarossa' against the Soviet Union. Now the western half of Poland fell to the Nazis, and Hans Frank was made governor general of all of Poland. But he never held sole power because overall the country was in the grip of the SS, and by 1942, virtually all his power was gone, although he remained in office as little more than a figurehead.

Former Polish prime minister and army general, Wladyslaw Sikorski, was in Paris during the invasion of Poland, taking command of Polish soldiers who fled to France. When France fell, Sikorski went to England where many Poles – Jewish, Catholic, Protestant, agnostic – also arrived to enlist in the British forces. The RAF formed special Polish divisions. Their incredible courage and determination earned them the admiration and respect of the British airmen.

The Polish pilots had one single goal: to drive the Nazis from their country. When Michael Bentine, the British-born comedy actor who became famous as one of *The Goons* on British radio, television and cinema, met up with them, he learned that their credo for winning the war was, 'You fight it twenty-four hours a day'. The Poles, Bentine wrote, ate, drank and slept it, devoting their whole attention to it.

Bentine had been turned down by the RAF at the outbreak of war because of his father's Peruvian nationality, but in 1942 they finally accepted him. Because his eyes were poor, he was rejected as a pilot but given the chance to volunteer for MI9, a relatively new section of the British Secret Service, its purpose being to foster escape and evasion attempts. He was sent on a course which included many men of different nationalities who had escaped from the Germans' *blitzkrieg* across Europe.

He found the Poles were particularly religious and believed in guidance through prayer. He came to feel a particular fondness for Poles who 'fought valiantly and died in hundreds of thousands, and they deserved better,' he said.

He joined two Polish squadrons in May 1943, at

Hemswell, Lincolnshire. They flew Lancasters, Halifaxes and Stirlings, and took over the long-range night offensive of Bomber Command. He noticed that the intellectuals among them discussed how they believed the Nazi hierarchy were using rituals for their mass mind manipulation of the German population. Bentine said that this concept was later confirmed to him by other men in the intelligence service, as well as members of the various resistance movements and even from Germans. 'They are mad dogs,' the Poles told Bentine. 'You have to bloody shoot them.' What the Poles taught Bentine, and what was later confirmed by the evidence of his own eyes, was that 'the Nazis were criminally insane'.

Anthony Quayle had prepared for battle and a siege of Gibraltar, but neither had come. Now, however, the Rock's defenders began to strengthen the fortress in the event that Hitler attempted to close the Straits, with or without Spain's help.

Mason-MacFarlane's health was poor; he had suffered spinal damage in a car crash in 1933 and paralysis was affecting his movements. Yet each day he made long tours of the tunnels to keep morale high, although sometimes he stumbled and fell, cutting his knees. An Australian neurologist, Sir Hugh Cairns, told Quayle that the general needed to be operated on or face total paralysis, and he urged Quayle to persuade the general to retire. Quayle told Cairns that he couldn't envisage Mason-MacFarlane ever doing that.

Quayle took on many of the general's duties, including going into Spain to continue Mason-MacFarlane's attempts to seal good relations with the Spanish Army. The general told Quayle that they were to expect the arrival of General Wladyslaw Sikorski, President of the Polish government in exile and a warm personal friend of Mason-MacFarlane.

Sikorski had formed close ties with Churchill, and when Germany turned on the USSR, Sikorski persuaded Stalin to reinstate Poland's pre-war borders and free thousands of Poles who had been seized in 1939.

However, in the spring of 1943, the bodies of Polish

officers – their hands bound, shot in the back of the head – were found in seven mass graves in the Katyn Forest near the Russian city of Smolensk. In all, 4,500 bodies were found. The USSR denied responsibility, even though the local peasantry reported that during the early months of 1940, before that area had fallen into German hands, they had seen hundreds of Polish prisoners being taken into the forest; the witnesses said they had heard gun shots.

In 1942 German slave labourers uncovered a dead, uniformed Polish officer buried in the forest, leading to the discovery of the mass murder. An investigation concluded they had been shot in the spring of 1940. Another 11,000 Polish prisoners were never found.

In July 1943, General Sikorski arrived in Gibraltar with his daughter and several of his staff. They intended to spend the night and leave for London the following day.

It so happened that Mr Maisky, the Russian ambassador, stopped briefly during Sikorski's stay, causing an embarrassing situation as Sikorski and Stalin had just broken diplomatic relations following the discovery of the massacre at Katyn.

Mason-MacFarlane, whose sympathies were with the Poles, assigned Quayle to take care of Maisky on his arrival and stay with him until he departed later that day. He was to prevent Maisky from meeting Sikorski.

Maisky's plane arrived on 4 July. Quayle took the Russian on a tour of the Rock. The ambassador asked him what he thought the future of Spain held.

Quayle replied, 'I think there is only one solution for this unhappy country – the restoration of the monarchy.'

Maisky paused and then said, 'I do not think this is the time for restoring the Spanish monarchy.'

They drove back to Government House in silence, collected the ambassador's suitcase and then drove to the runway and Maisky flew off. Later that evening, the Polish guests boarded their plane. Quayle and Mason-MacFarlane watched from the tarmac as the plane took off. All seemed well but to their horror the plane dived into the sea.

They drove to the end of the runway and turned the car

headlights on, but they could see nothing but the dark sea. Searchlights were switched on until they found, half a mile out to sea, a wing of the plane. Rubber boats were launched. A young Polish pilot looked on, sobbing and beating his head with his fists. 'This is the end of Poland,' he cried.

The bodies of Sikorski, one of his companions, and a British brigadier were recovered. The pilot was found alive, but both his legs were broken.

The next morning Mason-MacFarlane gave Quayle the task of arranging for coffins. This he did, not without a little trouble as the dead of Gibraltar were usually weighted down and buried at sea. Sikorski's body was put aboard the *Orkan* while a band played the Polish national anthem. A seventeen-gun salute sounded and the ship sailed off to England for the funeral in London.

To the Poles, General Sikorski had been their greatest hope for the future. But to nine-year-old Roman Polanski living in Nazi-occupied Poland, there seemed no hope in the summer of 1943.

He had finally been thrown out by the Koslewskis who sent him to relatives, the Borocowskas, in central Poland, almost a hundred miles from Cracow. The Borocowskas were simple tenant farmers who barely eked out a living from a few acres of land, and who were strictly orthodox Catholics. The Koslewskis told them that Roman was the son of a Polish soldier, killed during the Nazi invasion, and that his name was Raimund Borocowska, one of the Cracow Borocowskas. Roman was told that under no circumstances was he to let the Borocowska know that he was a Jew.

With no room in the dilapidated farmhouse, Roman slept in the straw loft of the barn. He had to work for his keep, rising at dawn to begin his farm chores, and finally finishing exhausted at dusk. He had to attend church weekly, Bible study three times a week and prayer sessions three times each day.

He actually preferred the deprivation and danger of Cracow than this gruelling, religious life. Instead of Germans

– for there were relatively few in the countryside – there were priests and nuns whose antipathy towards Jews made them just as dangerous in his eyes. They regarded Roman as a bad influence on the local youth, warning them to avoid him as he seemed to be resistant to their religious instruction.

But the boys and girls were initially fascinated by this new arrival from the city, and they questioned him. A couple of times he nearly revealed his true identity through slips of the tongue, but the ignorant peasant children failed to understand anyway.

He chose to make few friends, and few wanted to be involved with him in any case, scared of the consequences after the local church warnings about him. But one girl, Eva, was quite captivated by him. For a thirteen-year-old she was buxom, and very much a rebel in her teachers' eyes. When Roman, then turned ten, boasted to her about his fake foreskin, she demanded to see it.

He took her into a neighbouring farmer's barn and showed her his trick with a candle. Before he knew what was happening, she was seducing him in the barn loft. In their fumbled passion, Roman accidentally knocked over the lighted candle which dropped on to the hay below. Within minutes the barn was in flames.

Roman and Eva ran naked from the inferno. Field workers who came rushing towards the barn saw them, and soon Eva's father, a pillar of the Catholic community, was demanding to know what she had been up to.

She told him about the candle. 'What were you doing with a lighted candle in a hay barn?' he demanded.

She just blurted, 'Papa, he is a Jew.'

Eva's father marched round to the Borocowska farm and hammered on the farmhouse door. 'You are harbouring a Jew,' he ranted.

Roman heard the commotion from where he slept in the barn's loft, and through a rack in the wall he watched as Eva cried to Borocowska, 'He is a Jew. The boy from Cracow is a Jew.'

'You are crazy.'

Eva's father said, 'I will prove it. Where is he?'

Borocowska pointed to the barn and Eva's father came in and found Roman cringing in terror. The man dragged the screaming boy down on to the ground and ripped off his pants. 'There you see, it is the sign of the Jew.'

Borocowska demanded to know the truth and Roman was forced to admit his true origins. Eva's father said that he would turn Roman over to the Germans but Borocowska was afraid of being punished for harbouring a Jew. He needed the boy, anyway, to work on the farm since his own sons had been taken by the war.

To placate Eva's father, Borocowska gave him a litter of new-born piglets. But Roman was warned never to go near Eva again.

Roman was now told that if he expected to remain with them, he had to undergo Catholic instruction and baptism. A few days later, Roman officially became a Catholic. He knew he was a Jew, and he felt his roots and traditions as a matter of course. But he had never felt in any way submissive to Jewish religious teaching and he would not submit to Catholic indoctrination.

His biggest misery was missing his mother. He felt lost without her. As for the war, it had become a way of life that would never end. For Roman Polanksi, aged ten, there seemed no future.

15
The Yanks Are Coming

'I know there was this saying about being oversexed, over-paid and over here, but I always found the English so kind.'

James Stewart

In the early months of 1942 the US 8th Army Air Force under General Carl Spaatz began arriving in Britain. The AAF force grew by the summer and was based in hastily constructed airfields, mainly in East Anglia.

Unlike the British Air Force, which bombed at night, the American Flying Fortresses made daylight precision raids in close-flying formations. Each plane flew at slightly different levels for maximum gun cover against the German fighter planes without fear of shooting the closest Flying Fortresses. In January 1943 it was decided by the Allied Command that the chief aim of bombings would be 'the progressive destruction and dislocation of the German military, industrial and economic system and the undermining of the morale of the German people to a point where their capacity for armed resistance is fatally weakened'.

Major William Wyler arrived at AAF headquarters in High Wycombe towards the end of 1942. With him he brought famed cameramen William Clothier, Harrold Tannenbaum and William Skall. His immediate commander was Lieutenant Colonel Beirne Lay. There was little film equipment to speak of, just an Eyemo camera, but Wyler didn't wait around and immediately went off to the 91st Bomb Command at Bassingbourne to get his first look at the Boeing B-17 and talk to air and ground crews. He watched as the first American bombers took off on 17 August 1942 for the first all-American mission. General Ira C Eaker, in command of the 8th Air Force, led the assault on the marshalling yards at Rouen in northern France.

Wyler's much-needed film equipment was supposed to be on its way by ship. Meanwhile he and his crew received training in how to use a machine gun and recognize aircraft. Eventually half of the film equipment arrived; the rest was sunk by the Germans.

Wyler and his unit took off on their first mission, not over Germany as Wyler had hoped, but over St-Nazaire and Lorient on the south coast of Brittany; their targets were the naval yards. Despite the heavy anti-aircraft flak and the attacks by German fighter planes, all of Wyler's men returned to base to celebrate New Year's Eve and see in 1943.

Determined to film a bombing raid on Germany, Wyler urged Colonel Stanley Wray, commander of the 91st, to inform him in secret of any forthcoming raid. The plan was that someone would phone Wyler, and if Wyler was asked, 'How's the weather in London?' he knew it meant that Germany was the next target.

That call came through and Wyler and his unit jumped into a jeep and drove over to Bassingbourne by night to be ready for take-off at dawn. The first raids on Germany began in January 1943. Wyler and his unit were on board for the attacks over Kiel, Hamburg, Schweinfurt and the Messerschmidt plants in Regensburg.

Wyler recalled that the flak 'was terrific – so thick that at 26,000 feet the blue sky looked like a punctured sieve'.

Lieutenant Clark Gable arrived in England with his 'Little Hollywood Group' in April 1943 to join the 351st whose entire complement of B-17s was ready by early May. Gable's presence in England was kept a secret but German intelligence discovered he had joined the 8th Army Air Force. 'Lord Haw Haw', the traitor who broadcast in English from Germany, welcomed him to England.

The 351st still needed to undergo training before being committed to operations, preventing Gable from getting down to work as he needed his group to get experience of combat conditions. General Ira C Eaker, Commander of the 8th AAF, offered his assistance and arranged for Lieutenant Gable to visit other operational air bases.

At Molesworth in Huntingdon, on 4 May, he climbed aboard a bomber with the 303rd Bomb Group and took off in a B-17F 'Eight Ball Mk II' on his first combat mission, purely as an observer. Their target was Antwerp in Belgium.

Combat in a B-17, as Gable quickly discovered, was nerve-wracking and physically exhausting. In a compartment beneath the flight deck was the escape hatch through which the five-man crew had to squeeze if the plane was hit. If the plane went into a spin, no one could get out. Gable wondered what was the chance of escape with additional men on board taking film. He learned that the crews were becoming increasingly aware that the chances of any of them surviving a completed tour of twenty-five missions were hardly more than one in three.

When German fighters attacked, Gable wanted to fire back, so he took over the radio-room gun. Anti-aircraft fire hit his bomber with a 20mm cannon shell, but no one was injured.

He was relieved to return to Molesworth in one piece and elated at the danger and excitement of combat flying. John Huston told me, 'It was said that he seemed enthusiastic to see the German war machine being decimated on his first and subsequent missions, as though in revenge for the loss of Carole.'

A month later the AAF made public the fact that Clark Gable, now a captain, was serving with the 8th in England. He reluctantly accepted orders to meet the press. To confuse enemy intelligence, he was photographed standing by a B-17 of the veteran 91st Bomb Group from a different station. It is said that Hitler, previously a fan of Gable's, put a price on his head, offering any German pilot who brought his plane down immediate promotion and a cash reward.

During May, just a few days before the 351st at Polebrook

became operational, Gable and Andy McIntyre heard a tremendous explosion. They rushed out to discover that two Fortresses had collided in the air. They captured on film the grisly results of the flaming wrecks which fell on the airfield. Both crews were killed, one of the pilots being a squadron commander.

Then, on 14 May, the 351st took off on its first mission during which it lost another squadron commander.

According to Marjorie Bennett, a nurse during the war, Gable turned up on Malta at some point during May 1943. She told author Eric Taylor that she was stationed on Malta where there was a shortage of food and water. Lunch for the nurses usually consisted of hard cheese, dates, army biscuits and a cup of tea.

American airmen on Malta invited the nurses to their base for a dance. The shutters had to be closed and the room, crowded with around forty Americans and twenty nurses, was very hot.

A handsome lieutenant asked Sister Bennett to dance. She recalled that he was a good dancer but he sweated a good deal. At the end of their dance she found that his perspiration had made her wet down the front. She was so cross that when the lieutenant asked her for another dance she turned him down.

Someone told her that she had just danced with, and then rejected, none other than Clark Gable.

At the 91st, William Wyler had come up with an idea to film the twenty-fifth mission of the 'Memphis Belle' which was named after the girlfriend of the aircraft's captain, Robert K Morgan.

The 'Memphis Belle' took off on its final mission on 19 May 1943, to Kiel. Vincent Evans, bombardier of the 'Memphis Belle', later recalled how William Wyler walked the open catwalk of the bomb bay five miles above Germany. The temperature was 45 below zero and he had to breathe out of a walk-around oxygen bottle while trying to point his camera at flak bursts and German fighters.

Over the intercom Wyler, who was frustrated at missing shots of the flak, asked Captain Morgan if he could possibly get closer to the flak. The captain told him what he could do!

At some point Wyler passed out. He later wrote that he thought he was actually dead. He regained consciousness to find he was lying between the pilots and the plane's nose. He made his way back to the pilots' compartment only to find that while he was unconscious they had already hit their target. A couple of days later, Wyler flew in 'Our Gang' and was glad to note that the radio operator passed out.

One of the planes which Harrold Tannenbaum flew in was shot down over France. Wyler had to write to Tannenbaum's family regretfully informing him of his death.

General Eaker had become concerned that if Wyler were to be shot down and captured, he would, as a Jew and as the director of *Mrs Miniver*, receive particularly harsh treatment at the hands of the Germans. He told Colonel Lay to ground Wyler, but Wyler immediately got on a B-17 bound for a raid on Hamburg. When he returned Lay reprimanded him, threatening him with court martial. Wyler said, 'If anybody wants to court martial me for doing my job, I'm willing to leave that to the judgement of the readers when they see the headlines.'

Lay kept from Eaker the fact that Wyler went on one last mission. Then, on 25 May 1943, King George and Queen Elizabeth came to Bassingbourne to meet the crew of the 'Memphis Belle'. Wyler talked with the queen for several minutes, while the king and gathered generals waited. The queen told him that she loved *Mrs Miniver*, and, he said, she proved most charming.

Shortly after, Wyler returned to the United States to put together his film, *The Memphis Belle*.

On 10 July Captain Gable was involved in a mission over Villacoublay where the squadron came under heavy attack. As the months passed, the original contingent of crews were rapidly depleted through losses. Gable had come to know many of the men personally. He was a gregarious man who enjoyed the companionship of his comrades, and they found him immensely likeable. Because he was so much older than most of them, they had come to call him 'Pappy'. He was noticeably moved by the deaths of so many of his young friends.

On 12 August he flew in the lead plane piloted by Major Theodore Milton. There was little enough space in the aircraft so Gable, with his camera, had to stand throughout the six-hour flight. Over Gelsenkirchen the weather was so bad that they had to seek a last-resort target with little success.

During the summer he went to visit David Niven who was living with his wife Primmie and their baby son in a thatched cottage near Slough. Niven was out when Gable arrived unannounced, so he sat down and played with little David Junior and drank David Senior's whisky. Niven remembered coming home 'to find Clark Gable in his American Air Force uniform sitting in *my* deck chair, playing with *my* son, drinking *my* last bottle of whisky being served to him by *my* wife!'

It was a happy reunion and Niven noticed how Gable had 'in his deep misery at the loss of Carole found it possible to rejoice over the great happiness that had come my way, which was very generous of him, and just like him'.

Niven said that Gable found it rough 'being Clark Gable. He wanted to be just an "ordinary guy" in the Air Force, because there were those who sucked up to him because he was Clark Gable, and those who wanted to bring him down because he was Clark Gable.'

Gable admitted to Niven that during the bombing raids he was always 'scared stiff', and that what frightened him most was the thought of being captured by the Germans and what Hitler might do to him. 'That sonofabitch'll put me in a cage and charge ten marks a look all over Germany,' Gable said.

He became a frequent visitor at the Nivens. It seemed that he was gradually getting over Carole Lombard's death, but he was sometimes overwhelmed by Niven's own family happiness and one evening he disappeared into the garden. Primmie found him sitting on an upturned wheelbarrow, his head in his hands, crying.

This was not a side to Clark Gable that any of the men of the 351st ever saw. Perhaps it was the actor in him that held him together during the five combat missions he flew. More likely it was his desire to get back at the Germans for causing Lombard's death.

His next mission was in a B-17 called 'Ain't I Gruesome?' which was hit fifteen times over the Ruhr. Standing on the flight deck, he came within two feet of being hit in the head by a heavy piece of shrapnel that struck the upper turret.

He flew his last combat mission on 23 September in 'The Duchess'. The target was Nantes in France. He was filming from the waist gun positions and took over one of the guns when a German fighter attacked the plane. He didn't hit the German, but it was this sort of determination and aptitude that earned Gable the admiration of the crews he flew with. He returned the admiration in full, later telling interviewers that the people they should talk to for a good story were those men.

In October 1943, he was ordered back to Washington where he was interviewed by General H H Arnold who informed him he was to be awarded an Air Medal for his operational services. In May 1944, he was promoted to major and the following month was honourably discharged, but he continued to work on putting together five training films from all the footage he and his crew had taken.

While most of the Hollywood film stars and directors who joined the American Air Force were given the job of making films, James Stewart actually piloted a Liberator. As a major, based in Tibenham in Norfolk, he led twenty day-time bombing missions.

He had already risen high in his profession before volunteering for the air force. For him, there was no other choice but to be a pilot.

He told me:

I've just loved flying ever since I first flew as a passenger – it had to be in 1920. It was after the first war when aviation was just getting started. America had a training aeroplane that was built for the war called the Curtis Jenny, and a lot of pilots bought them and did what they called barn storming, and they'd appear at country fairs and they'd land in a meadow outside of the town, and their price was a dollar a minute to take you for a ride. And they were all dressed up like they are when they show them in the movies with silk scarves and goggles; I remember it very well.

I paid my dollar and I just thought I had to learn to fly these things myself, so I learned to fly in 1935. I got a private licence and then a commercial licence and then I flew in the war. It's a tremendously interesting thing to me – the whole thing of flying and the development. So when we went to war, I knew I had to enlist and there was no question of my not being a pilot.

I joined up in 1942, and after I did my basic training I was sent to England in 1943 and was there in 1944. I was a major of the 445th Group at Tibenham in Norfolk.

In those times when you lost some crews, the local people were always there with encouragement, always there to almost replace the family of so many of the men that were lost. And this was such an impressive thing to all the rest of us who kept on going because it was a tremendous help in so many ways, having to do with the feeling of and the dedication to the job we had to do.

The local people really did treat us well. I know there was this saying about being oversexed, overpaid and over here, but I always found the English so kind. They some-times brought us real eggs; you know, we only had powdered egg which was sort of like eating rice. And the *taste*! After nearly fifty years I still can taste it. And there was this wonderful thing that every once in a while, after maybe a bad mission, the next morning they would send us real eggs, real wonderful tasting eggs.

The American airmen were occasionally overwhelmed by what they saw as being peculiarly English. Sergeant Walter

Matthau, a radioman-gunner, recalled, 'Once I won about 20,000 dollars at cards, and I took everyone in the barracks to the Palace Hotel in Norwich. And I saw the tablecloths and the silverware, and I started crying because it was so beautiful. And the maître d' kept giving us napkins and spoons and every time he would give us something he would say, "Thank you. I said to him, "Why do you keep saying thank you when you give us something? We should be saying thank you to you."

'And he said, "It's tradition, sir; tradition."'

The son of Jewish–Russian immigrants and a struggling actor of twenty-one when America went to war, Matthau found his own way of coping with the constant threat of being killed in action. 'What was it – sixty per cent killed? I had a great buddy and I took all his possessions home when I went back to New York, and it was very hard. I think that unconsciously there is some kind of a wall that is erected by the survival instinct and that wall prevents you from falling apart and fainting and dying. What you really say is, "Thank God it wasn't me".'

There can be no knowing how many potential movie stars, not only in America's air force, army or navy, but also the military forces of other countries were lost in the Second World War. Had Walter Matthau been killed, he would have ended his days as just one of the war's casualties, never to be even considered a world-famous actor.

One lucky survivor was Jack Palance who piloted a bomber that was shot down. He was severely burned before bailing out, and the subsequent plastic surgery to repair his face gave him the gaunt, taut features that helped to make him one of the screen's favourite heavies.

On 7 January 1944, Major James Stewart made headlines when he led forty-eight Liberators of 445th Group in a daylight raid on Ludwigshafen. At first there was nothing particularly unusual about the mission; there was an attack by enemy fighters, but his group's defences fought them off without any loss.

On the way back he saw that 389th Group, the lead group

of the raid, had taken a wrong bearing home across German fighter airfields in France. Radio contact had been lost, so Stewart decided to go after the wayward group. German fighters were attacking the 389th as Stewart's 445th arrived to give covering fire. Eight of the strayed Liberators were lost, but it was generally agreed that the losses would have been even greater if Major Stewart had not gone to their rescue. His own group returned intact.

Rarely willing to speak about the war, James Stewart said, 'I think that whole military experience that I had was something I think about almost every day and one of the greatest experiences of my life – greater than being in movies.'

He had entered the air force as a private. After the war he remained in the Air Force Reserve as a brigadier general, making him the highest ranking entertainer in the United States military.

16
Push into Italy

*'I looked up into the sky and directly above me was a bomb
coming right down on top of me.'*

Kenneth More

In the small Italian village of Pozzuoli, the little eight-year-old
girl who would later be known as glamorous film star Sophia
Loren, along with her family, felt the direct effects of the
Germans' desperation to keep the Allies at bay. The young, fit
men of Italy were conscripted into the army and some were
taken to labour camps in Germany.

Two of Sophia's uncles, Guido and Mario, had to leave
their jobs at the munitions factory in Pozzuoli and go into hiding. As well as the devastating loss of income for Sophia's
family, there was the constant fear that the two men would be
found and sent to the labour camps.

Sophia became ever more withdrawn and found her only
comfort was to hide herself away from the war in the thick fol-
iage of a fig tree in her front yard. She somehow felt secure up
there, and she sat in the tree for hours.

The Allied bombing raids on Pozzuoli became so intolerable that the Germans began pulling out. Rumours spread
that the American ships were going to shell the harbour; the
mayor signed a proclamation to evacuate the town within
forty-eight hours.

Sophia and what was left of her family gathered a few
clothes and blankets, and caught the train to Naples where

154

Sophia's grandmother had her only known relative, a cousin by the name of Mattia. As Sophia, her mother, sister and grandparents waited for the train at the station in Pozzuoli, the two uncles came out of hiding to join them.

Half-way to Naples the train stopped and was swarmed by Germans searching through the compartments for men to transport to the labour camps. Two nuns hid the uncles under their habits and the Germans missed them. But those men who could not find a place to hide were rounded up.

In Naples Sophia's family found that the city was subject to bombing raids even more intense than anything they had experienced in Pozzuoli. The Mattias accepted their refugee relatives reluctantly. The two uncles were put into a store-room which was hidden by a large cupboard full of china. Sophia, her mother and sister had a single room with a balcony. Sophia's only contact with the outside world was from that balcony during her time in Naples because her mother feared that if they all went out, the Mattias might not let them back in. So Sophia and her sister Maria had to remain indoors.

Each night when the air-raid sirens sounded, Sophia's mother, her nerves shattered by the war, began screaming, scaring little Sophia even more than she already was.

Maria came down with measles and then typhoid. There was little to eat, and what there was the Mattias kept for themselves, going so far as to hide all their food. Sophia's family had to live on rice and potatoes, sometimes only mouldy, maggot-infested bread, which Sophia's mother and grandmother had to beg or steal. Sophia fortunately didn't catch any of Maria's diseases, but she was thinner than ever.

There were the body lice; fat, white creatures that had to be picked off individually. Sophia found a perverse pleasure in squeezing them between her fingers until they popped. They were a species of lice that had never been seen before, and a rumour spread that they had been purposely dropped by the Allies. There seemed no end to them without proper sanitation. Sophia's skin and scalp bled from constant scratching.

The Mattias didn't even allow Sophia's family to have what

little clean water there was, so Maria's fevered thirst had to be quenched with dirty rain water which her mother collected in a pot on the balcony. When the rain water ran out, she went into the street and drained water from the radiator of a German truck. The driver discovered what she was doing but, finding amusement in this desperate act, he let her go.

As Italians looked forward to liberation from the Nazis, the German soldiers began public executions. Sophia, from her balcony, watched as people were rounded up and beaten, and taken away to be tortured or sent to concentration camps.

She later wrote, 'My young eyes saw one appalling, gruesome spectacle after another.'

In another Italian town, Fontana Liri, someone Sophia would become close friends with as a film star became a victim of round-ups. Marcello Mastroianni was the twenty-year-old son of poor peasants. He worked as a draughtsman during most of the war, but was taken by the Germans to be sent to a labour camp. He managed, however, to escape to Venice where he hid in an attic until the war was over. Thousands of other Italians, both Jew and Gentile, were sent off to Germany, many of them never to return.

Kenneth More, on board the *Aurora*, had been given the job of organizing the ship's concert parties. His ship was now based in Bone Harbour in Algiers. Their task had been to disrupt supply lines to Rommel's Afrika Korps between Sicily and Tripoli, leading 'Q Force' with two other cruisers, the *Sirius* and the *Argonaut*, and two destroyers, the *Quiberon* and the *Quentin*.

'One night our force sank two enemy destroyers and four troop ships,' More recalled. 'After that we were constantly dive-bombed. Every night the harbour was ablaze with burning ships and oil tankers. Ours was the only ship that never got hit, which was incredible.'

The *Aurora*'s next task was to pipe both Admiral Cunningham and General Eisenhower on board, and sail for the Sicilian Channel. The invasion of Italy, beginning with landings on Sicily, was scheduled for 9 July 1943. But first the airstrips and underground hangers on Pantelleria, one of the outlying Italian islands, were to be pummelled by a tremendous bombardment.

Kenneth More recalled, 'At half past ten in the morning we opened fire on the island. Soon you couldn't even see it for the smoke. There were a hundred Flying Fortresses bombing it and the blasts were so tremendous that our ship trembled from the force even though we were three miles out to sea.'

The *Aurora* was then sent to Tripoli to receive on board King George VI and take him to Malta. 'He talked to each of us,' More remembered, 'and then went to his quarters. He was suffering at the time from gyppy tummy, and he was treated by his personal doctor and remained for the most part in his quarters.'

They arrived at Malta on 20 June 1943. The people of the island had, the year before, been awarded the George Cross, the highest award for bravery that any civilian can earn. The Maltese had withstood twenty-two months of bombing and they had subsisted on near starvation rations. Now the king had returned personally to thank the island's defenders for their courage and endurance during the long siege.

The *Aurora* returned to Tripoli with the king who, before leaving ship, made Captain Agnew a Commander of the Victorian Order in recognition of his special transportation responsibilities.

As the *Aurora* returned to normal duty, Agnew realized that, under battle conditions, the men below decks who had no idea what was going on became demoralized. So he gave Kenneth More a new job. 'Because I was an actor, he decided I could do the job of giving the ship a running commentary of any action.' He was relieved of his duty with the anti-aircraft guns and stationed on the lower bridge with a microphone connected to the ship's Tannoy system.

His first commentary job came when twelve Stukas came at the *Aurora*, approaching on the port quarter:

These Stuka pilots were experienced men from the Battle

of Britain and I thought at the time we had little chance
of surviving this. I told the whole story through the
Tannoy as we fired on them with our six-inch guns and
somehow managed to miss every target. At one point I
looked up into the sky and directly above me was a bomb
coming right down on top of me. I hit the deck because
there was nowhere else to go. There was a Paramount
News cameraman in front of me who didn't know we
were about to have a bomb fall on us, and I yelled for
him to get down. He threw himself beside me and I told
him to move over a bit because we were on a narrow part
of the bridge and there was no room to breathe.

The bomb actually hit where I would have been standing had I still been on the anti-aircraft gun. A piece of the
bomb actually came through to the bridge and the
cameraman had his head cut; he wouldn't have been hit
if I hadn't told him to move over, but that's how it is in
battle and war – you can never know if the next shell has
your name on it.

The *Aurora* was not damaged enough to prevent it from
sailing to Sicily to give cover, on 9 July 1943, for the amphibious landings on Sicily. Some 1,200 British airborne troops
were sent over Sicily in gliders, their objective being to take
bridges, airfields and high ground. Out of 144 gliders, 70
landed in the sea and 200 men were drowned. Simultaneously
2,781 American paratroops were scattered across the island to
little effect.

Then came the amphibious forces which proved much
more successful. The Americans, landing at Licata, met no
resistance from the Italian defenders who gave up without a
fight. But at Gela, tanks kept the Americans at bay until the
following day when American artillery battalions landed and
pushed the German tanks back.

In the US flagship *Monrovia* with Admiral Hewitt was
Lieutenant Douglas Fairbanks who went ashore with the third
wave of infantry to find themselves on an totally unused
stretch of beach. Fairbanks walked off in the direction of a

beachmaster who was waving madly. But it was too late to get off the beach by the time Fairbanks realized that the beach-master was trying to let him know that he had been walking through a minefield.

Patton called for 2,000 extra men from North Africa. They landed at Gela on the night of 11 July, among them Audie Murphy. As the Allies pushed across Sicily, Murphy proved a ruthless GI. He was sent out with a scout patrol and came across two surprised Italian officers who attempted a quick getaway on horseback.

Murphy dropped to one knee and shot them both.

His lieutenant was furious and asked why he had shot the Italian officers.

'What should I have done?' Murphy retorted. 'Stood here with egg on my face waving them goodbye?'

At the Furiano River, on the road to Messina at the southern tip of Sicily, Murphy came under artillery fire for the first time. He just kept his head down and said later that he quickly acquired a healthy respect for the Germans as fighters.

On 25 July a new Italian government was set up and Mussolini was arrested, while in Sicily General George Patton and General Montgomery were competing in a race to reach Messina. Patton got there first, on 17 August, two hours ahead of Montgomery. Audie Murphy, now a corporal, was suffering from bouts of malaria. When he collapsed on the roadside at Messina, a major stopped his jeep and asked him if he was sick.

'No, sir,' Murphy replied, 'I'm just spilling my guts for the hell of it.'

On 3 September the Italians capitulated to the Allies in Sicily and six days later the Allies landed on the Italian mainland at Salerno. Following the first assault there, Corporal Murphy landed and was in action north-east of the town in an attack on a machine-gun emplacement by a blown bridge. During the battle his friend, Steiner, was killed.

Lieutenant Fairbanks took part in a number of hit and run

'beachjumping' operations, such as at Civitavecchia which was about fifty miles behind enemy lines.

He drew up plans to take the island of Ventotene where it was thought the Italians would surrender without a fight. But when Fairbanks landed with the force's commander, a captain and three other officers, they discovered the island was held by 400 Germans. The small group set up loudspeakers and remained throughout the night, simulating a full-scale attack with flares, smokescreens and sound effects to keep the Germans busy while the captain returned for reinforcements.

On 12 September, Fairbanks's force took Capri without a shot being fired. He made Capri the base for a number of harassing raids during which he captured an Italian admiral and was consequently awarded the Silver Star.

Now a lieutenant-commander, Fairbanks landed on Corsica and, setting up a new base and with French troops under General de Lattre de Tassigny, he helped to take Elba, for which he received the Croix de Guerre.

In Naples the public executions increased as the Allies advanced towards the city. Sophia, now aged nine, watched as young boys, hardly older than she, attacked German tanks with petrol bombs by stuffing crude explosives into gun turrets. These boys came out of the slums, were incredibly organized and were armed with bombs made from bottles filled with gasoline and with rags serving as fuses.

Sophia saw two German soldiers escaping from their burning tank, their clothes on fire, running after the boy who had blown their tank up, firing at him with pistols even though their hair was in flames. They disappeared down an alley and Sophia never knew what became of the boy although she heard continuing gun shots.

These boys attacked tanks, trucks, anything that would create destruction and chaos as the Allies continued their advance. They dropped rocks and paving stones from rooftops. Some boys had managed to get hold of hand grenades. Some were blown up by the explosions they caused, some were shot; but they kept up this guerrilla warfare for four days.

Then the Germans began to withdraw from Naples, blowing up the sewers and the water system. By the end of the fifth day, they had all gone, taking with them most of the food and fresh water.

A line of people began to form at a food shop next to the house where Sophia lived in the hope of getting anything that the Germans had overlooked. German snipers in the hills above killed and wounded many of the old men, women and children who queued. But the desperation of the people was such that they continued to line up along the street.

Two days later, on 5 October 1944, Allied tanks rumbled into Naples. The people, including Sophia, poured into the streets to welcome them. GIs handed out presents of biscuits and sweets. Sophia was given a piece of chocolate; she'd never had any before. She managed to catch a can of instant coffee which she gave to her grandmother who was mystified what to do with it at first. Then she discovered that all she had to do was add hot water.

The food the Allies brought began to turn up on the black market. Sophia's family were unable to afford any of it. The joy of liberation was short-lived. The Allies requisitioned the building where Sophia's family were staying, and even the Mattias were turned out. The railways had been destroyed and so Sophia's family began the long walk back to Pozzuoli, sharing the road with hundreds of other refugees. Uncle Mario carried the sick Maria on his back, the others carried their few belongings. Sophia began to feel elated once more at the thought of going home.

There were reunions with old friends as they drew near to Pozzuoli and they heard news of people who had survived and of others who had been killed. Years later, Sophia Loren would relive those experiences as an adult in the film *Two Women*.

They found Pozzuoli virtually destroyed. But their house, though badly damaged, still stood. Repair work began and the US Army provided food as well as setting up an aid station where a single treatment with DDT killed the lice which Sophia had carried home with her. That for her was the end of the war. Life with all the familiar poverty that she had known before the war was henceforth normality.

17

The Battle for San Pietro

'There was a boot with part of a leg in it. There was a burning torso. Parts of what had only an hour before been living beings were scattered about.'

John Huston

For the Allied forces in Italy, the war was far from over. Beyond Naples ran the Volturno River which was held by the troops of Albert Kesselring, Commander-in-Chief of all Axis forces in the Mediterranean.

In October, the Volturno became swollen by rain as Major General John Lucas, the new commander of the US VI Corps, prepared to cross.

On 10 October 1943, Corporal Audie Murphy and a squad were sent downstream to act as a decoy. They came across a German position and cleared it with a grenade. They dug themselves in and came under enemy fire from the far side of the river. They were pinned down there for three days while Lucas made his crossing. By midday of 13 October the Americans had gained the high ground and attacked the Germans who had kept Murphy's squad pinned down. The corporal and his men then followed across and joined the VI Corps in its advance towards Mignano.

The British, too fought at Volturno. Bombardier Spike Milligan was there, having just been released from hospital after treatment for sandfly fever.

In Washington, William Wyler screened *Memphis Belle* for

President Roosevelt who thoroughly approved of the film. Wyler was consequently recommended for the Distinguished Service Medal and was ordered to Italy. The night before he was due to leave, he was waiting in line for a cab outside the Statler Hotel in Washington when someone in the queue got into an argument with the bellhop before entering a cab.

The furious bellhop turned to Wyler and said, 'Goddam Jew!'

Wyler told him, 'You're saying that to the wrong feller.'

'I didn't mean you, I meant him,' replied the bellhop, pointing towards the passenger in the cab as it drove off.

'That doesn't make a goddam difference,' said Wyler, and he punched the bellhop.

The next day Wyler was summoned to an air force base for an enquiry into the incident. He was reminded of the articles of war and asked if he understood the expression, 'Conduct unbecoming an officer and a gentleman.'

Wyler replied that he had been a gentleman long before he became an officer. Asked if he had legal provocation for hitting the bellboy, he replied, 'I sure did. He said "Dirty Jew".'

He had to admit that he had not acted in self defence but added, 'This kind of thing is one of the reasons I am in uniform and subject to these articles of war.'

The following day he received a letter from General H Arnold in Washington outlining the charges and giving him an option between a court martial and an official reprimand. He was all for defending himself at a court martial, but an officer friend persuaded him to accept the reprimand since he did not have a chance of winning his case. He was anxious to get to Italy, and so he accepted the reprimand which went down on his record.

He was finally allowed to leave for Italy, but the recommendation for the DSM was cancelled.

He arrived in Naples to join Major General Ira C Eaker who was commanding all Allied air forces in the Mediterranean and was based at Caserta. With him, Wyler brought writer Lester Koenig, who had written the script of *Memphis Belle,* and film cutter John Sturges who later directed the classic war film *The Great Escape.*

According to Captain John Sturges, General Eaker didn't entirely disapprove of Wyler's conduct with regard to the bell-hop incident. 'You had the feeling that the general and the officers there, who all knew about Wyler's charge, had a sneaking regard for what he'd done.'

Wyler, Koenig and Sturges began rigging 16mm cameras on P-47s – the Thunderbolts – of the 12th Air Force's 57th Fighter Group based on Corsica.

Said John Sturges, 'The Thunderbolts flew each and every day, trying to pound the German defences, and they were perfect for getting really intense footage of battle. We had Eyemos attached under the wings, to the tails and in the cockpits with simple stop-start buttons so the pilots could operate them. Not every pilot wanted these cameras, and we didn't force them to carry them if they didn't want to. Some said cameras were bad luck.'

Captain John Huston was in London, collaborating with the British military on compiling a film about the North African landings, when he was told to proceed to Italy and document the triumphal entry of the American forces into Rome. But, as Huston was to discover when he arrived in Italy, Rome was still in the hands of the Germans.

He told me:

In London I had become great friends with writer Eric Ambler [who had written the screenplay for the army-sponsored feature film *The Way Ahead* which starred David Niven], and suggested he come with me to Italy to help me write the script as we went along. We arrived to find that our troops were a long way from Rome.

The whole Italian campaign had ground to a shuddering halt.

Our troops had got as far as Caserta, north of Naples, but bad weather and the Germans held our forces back.

I was distressed to find Naples broken and despoiled. Small boys offered their mothers and sisters to soldiers for money. There were packs of rats which you had to walk around. The little girls were filthy. The people were starving. The city was rife with typhus and cholera. It was, indeed, an unholy city.

Our headquarters were in Caserta. It was a large, once glorious palace now packed with soldiers. Myself, Eric and about thirty-five other men slept in one room. My only complaint was Eric's snoring.

There was a photographer called Bob Capa. I had met him at a New Year's party in New York before the war. I met him again in Naples. One day we were walking along a Naples street when the air-raid siren went. As always, at the first sound of a siren, the streets emptied. Bob and I pulled into a doorway to escape, not the bombs, but the shell fragments raining down from our own anti-aircraft fire.

Suddenly a hearse came charging round a corner. It was the traditional Italian Baroque hearse, pulled by six black horses. The driver was on his feet, whipping the horses. The hearse was passing the doorway where we were taking shelter when the back doors of the hearse flew open and coffins began falling out, bursting open as they hit the ground, the corpses of those who had died of typhus and cholera littering the street.

It was a grotesque sight, but it was also funny. In war, when you have seen so much death, so much deprivation, so much horror, you learn to laugh at things that would in peace time be perfectly horrific. But this was funny, and we could only laugh.

Huston, Ambler and a camera crew of six were sent to the front line. 'We were to make a film that would explain to American audiences why we were no longer advancing in Italy,' explained Huston.

Field Marshal Albert Kesselring had his men dug into the rugged ribs that outline the mountainous landscape of Italy. The few roads the Allies needed to use were open to attack from the hills. Armoured vehicles could hardly move, so virtually every inch had to be won on foot. The 143rd Infantry

Regiment of the 36th Texas Infantry Division, to whom Huston and his crew were attached, had been the first troops to enter Naples, had crossed the Volturno and were now fighting in the Liri Valley. It was December 1943.

Highway 6 was the only main route to Rome, running through the Liri Valley. To enter the valley the 143rd had to take the village of San Pietro. Before the village four German battalions were entrenched. Another battalion had the high ground north-west of San Pietro on Mount Lungo. All approaches were heavily mined. Huston learned that experienced officers said that the German position was impregnable to a frontal assault. Yet that was precisely what the 143rd were ordered to do.

Said Huston:

The night before the attack our own artillery blasted the valley and the village, but the Germans were so well dug in that only direct hits had any effect on their defences. I took the opportunity to interview some of the men who were going into battle in the morning. Some of them spoke eloquently, saying they were fighting for what the future might hold for them, their country and the world.

The following morning our troops went forward and within 200 yards were brought to a virtual halt by barbed wire. They crossed the wire only to be brought down by heavy fire and mines. The attack never got more than 600 yards forward and a lot of men died for nothing.

We attacked again, and then once more, and still we lost men as the Germans blasted us with mortars, artillery and automatic fire from the ridges and from the heights.

Patrols of volunteers made the attempt to push ahead and throw hand grenades into the strong points, but none of the men came back. Then somebody who was probably at the back of our lines and didn't know a damn about the terrain ordered sixteen tanks to advance on San Pietro along a narrow dirt road with hairpin bends and a drop to one side.

The Germans allowed the tanks within a few hundred yards of the village before destroying the two rear tanks with anti-tank guns. Three other tanks were stopped by mines and the rest were then hit by artillery and anti-tank guns. We watched as our tanks exploded and burned, and the men inside tried to run for it. Only four tanks were able to make it back.

When the battle was over myself and my crew crept forward to film the results. There was a boot with part of a leg in it. There was a burning torso. Parts of what had only an hour before been living beings were scattered about.

A lot of the men I had interviewed the previous night were dead. The bodies that could be reached and retrieved were laid in a row in the bedrolls and identified where possible and then covered. I had my cameras placed so that as the bodies of the men I had interviewed were lifted, their faces were in close-up, and later when I put the film together, I used their voices over the close-ups. Later, we considered the emotional effect these scenes would have on the families of the men and decided not to include the shots.

While lives were being wasted in the assaults on San Pietro, Huston, Eric Ambler and his crew were living in a smaller village, Prata, which nestled in the hills and went virtually untouched by the bombardments. 'We got to know Pietro who owned the wine shop and his wife and four children. We gave his wife all our rations and she cooked for us, giving us pasta and wine, and I tried to repay Pietro for his kindness, but he wouldn't take any.'

An assault on Mount Lungo on 16 December proved a costly success. Intelligence reports said that the Germans were, by then, already pulling out of San Pietro. Huston immediately headed for the village intent on getting film of the US troops entering it.

'We moved through the battle area towards the village. It had rained the night before and all the machine-gun emplacements, guns and equipment were glistening in the early morning sun, and all around were the dead. We saw more dead that day than living.'

The camera crew reached the outskirts of the village. Suddenly a machine gun opened up on them from above. They ducked behind a wall. Intelligence had obviously got it wrong. Huston and his crew tried to figure out what to do. Mortar shells began falling around them, causing enough smoke and dust to block their escape from the view of the Germans as they ran back to their own lines.

When the Germans, shortly after, withdrew from San Pietro, Huston and his crew were the first back into the village. 'We went in by jeep, squeezing past the crippled tanks. We were able to film the advance patrols of American troops entering. Down from the hillsides swarmed the old men, women and children of the village who had taken refuge in caves while the battles had raged. There wasn't a single young man among them; they had all long been taken away.'

Before long the enemy began shelling the village and sending over its bombers. The American artillery, still outside the village, thought that the Germans must still be occupying the village, so they opened up on San Pietro. 'The ground literally jumped and heaved,' Huston recalled.

He, his crew and the troops ran with the villagers back to the caves.

In the cave there was a little girl who must have been about seven who sat on my lap and stroked my clean-shaven face. I don't think she had seen a man clean-shaven before because all the old men had stubble.

I glanced over at my cameraman and he was shaking from head to toe. He told me, 'I'll be all right, captain. I do this sometimes, so don't worry about me. I'll get over it.' I think he must have been claustrophobic, and he didn't stop shaking. The bombardment on the village stopped as both sides concentrated their fire on the surrounding countryside. I told my sergeant, 'Come on, let's go outside and get some shots.'

So we went out and I had him do a panning shot, but

he shook the whole time. I told him to do it again. He was a little steadier, so I had him do it a third time and this time he got a superb full 360 degree pan of the encircling ring of fire. It was a great shot and he had stopped shaking.

We could see the Germans counter-attacking in the valley and, figuring there would probably be a flanking movement as well, we decided to get the hell out of San Pietro. We made it back to our jeeps, and my crew went in the advance jeep and Eric Ambler and I got in a jeep driven by a lieutenant.

We were squeezing past the tanks again and trying not to go over the side of the road when we saw an American command car coming towards us. It stopped about fifty yards ahead of us. We were shouting to them to keep moving, but a shell had a direct hit on it. The jeep and the men just disintegrated. Our lieutenant put his foot down and we drove on, but we couldn't see a single sign of the command jeep.

We came to a metal bridge made of two beams spanning a gully. The beams were spaced especially for trucks, and our jeep had a narrower wheelbase, so the jeep didn't quite fit and we stalled.

I said, 'Jesus, lieutenant, didn't you see what happened to that command car? Get us the hell outa here.'

The lieutenant turned to me and said, 'Do you want to drive, captain?'

Eric just sat there in his casual manner and said, 'Really, lieutenant, this is most precarious. We really should get off this bridge as quickly as possible.' He was one of the coolest men I ever met.

The jeep just kept stalling and I figured we'd had it. The Germans certainly had time to zero in on us and I expected a direct hit any moment. But finally the lieutenant got us moving again and we got off the bridge and round a bend to safety.

While the 36th were attacking San Pietro, the 15th and

30th Texas Infantry Divisions had been attacking German defences on Mount Rotondo. Between Mount Lungo and Rotondo ran the railway. Corporal Audie Murphy and his squad were sent on a reconnaissance mission and unknowingly found themselves overlooking a German tank camouflaged at the edge of a grove.

They walked towards the tank and the first they saw of it was when the barrel began to lower. The Germans suddenly pulled back the camouflage net to reveal the tank and it fired.

Murphy's squad scattered as the shell landed. They made it into a gully, dragging one of their wounded comrades. From the gully Murphy watched as a head appeared at the tank hatch and looked around. The Americans were out of sight, so the tank began to turn and move away.

The fighting around Mount Rotondo was as intense as the battle to win San Pietro. Time and again Murphy and the others moved forward, but each time they were thrown back. Then the 15th attacked from the southern side while the 30th came at the Germans from the rear. This time they were successful.

Murphy's 1st Battalion was detailed to take Hill 193, a rocky elevation at the base of Rotondo. At dusk, Murphy heard footsteps. Peering into the darkness, he realized they belonged to approaching German soldiers. He threw up his rifle and opened fire. The Germans fell back and the GIs scrambled up the slope to take shelter in an old quarry.

The following morning they saw Germans slowly climbing the rocky path. The GIs kept low with their rifles at the ready, holding their fire until the Germans were almost upon them. Then they opened up, killing three Germans and capturing four others.

The Germans finally withdrew from the mountains and John Huston returned to San Pietro with the troops. The villagers gave them a tremendous reception of welcome and gratitude.

'They had hidden all their cheeses and wines from the Germans and now they brought them out and gave them to us. I looked around at the rubble that used to be their homes

and wondered what they had to celebrate. But they were very
happy people.'

He went looking for the little girl from the cave. 'I thought
she was an orphan and I wanted to adopt her. But I was
happy to find out she still had her family and was living with
her parents.'

Christmas came and Huston and his team stayed with
Pietro and his family in Prata, filming the children singing
Italian Christmas songs, while in the background was heard
the sound of distant battle.

18

Albanian Mission

'I had the communists and the Ballists to contend with, and
you just didn't know who was betraying who.'

Anthony Quayle

During 1943 Anthony Quayle had become increasingly
unhappy because 'I just really wanted to do something positive for the war effort. Then a friend in SOE said, "Come and
join us," so I did.'

He told Mason-MacFarlane about his decision. 'You're a
fool,' the general said affectionately, 'but if you must, I'll do
what I can to help. Sorry to lose you.'

While Mason-MacFarlane was in London during the summer of 1943, he succeeded in finding Quayle a posting at
SOE headquarters in Cairo. When Quayle received this news,
he put on civilian clothing, got into one of the Government
House cars and drove through the frontier into Spain for a
few days absence without leave. Then he flew to Cairo where
he reported to the SOE office.

His orders were to go to Albania. But first he had to be
trained in explosives, ciphering, deciphering and speaking
Albanian. No one knew very much about what was happening
in Albania so two British officers were parachuted into Greece
close to the Albanian border to investigate.

They returned with the news that Albania was close to civil
war with various political groups claiming to be harassing and
killing the enemy, who were the Italians until the Italian

173

surrender. To the officers it seemed the groups were more intent on killing each other. A small number of British liaison officers were dropped in but they were few, widely scattered and out of communication. A properly organized operation could drop men, stores and ammunition by plane, but it was almost impossible to get out, even by way of Greece where the occupying Germans had blocked off sea escapes.

Quayle with two others, Brian Ensor of the Irish Fusiliers and Gordon Lazell, a gunner, were chosen to be dropped. Gordon was the first to fly out and was dropped by parachute in his allotted zone. But he slipped on a rock and the sub-machine gun he was carrying went off, causing fatal head injuries.

Quayle and Ensor meanwhile were sent to Taranto in Italy and from there made their way to Bari on the Adriatic coast where they set up an SOE base – Force 266. Quayle began learning how to drop by parachute.

Finally, in November 1943, it was decided he would go by boat across the Adriatic and make his way by foot across country to Pogradec. His assignment was to look into the possibility of seaplanes landing on Lake Ohrid, mainly for the purpose of getting people out of Albania.

Immensely relieved to be going at last, he boarded the *Sea Maid*, a fishing boat manned by a volunteer crew dressed to look like Italian fishermen. They cast off mid-afternoon so as to be half-way across the Adriatic by nightfall to make the final run-in under darkness and hopefully avoid being spotted by a German E-boat.

They arrived on schedule, a mile off the coast. They watched for the designated signal from 'Sea View', a base set in a narrow inlet in the rocky Albanian coast, but it never came. Eager to leave before morning, the fishing boat turned and went back to Italy.

Quayle had to hang around Bari again for a few more weeks. Then word came from 'Sea View' and the crossing was again undertaken. But again no signal came from the shore. They turned back. By this time the wind was strengthening, so the captain decided to head for the little Italian harbour of

Otranto. There, moored up behind a Royal Navy minelayer, they spent the next week waiting for the storm to drop.

On Christmas Day, the captain of the minelayer invited Quayle and the 'fishing crew' aboard for Christmas dinner. It lifted their spirits, and when the storm had died down, they set off for Brindisi.

They were not there long before orders came for Quayle to get to 'Sea View' as quickly as possible. Major Field, the SOE officer based there had been injured in an accident with some gelignite and needed to be evacuated. Quayle was to take over Field's job although exactly what his job was he didn't know. What he did know was that he he had to be 'a bloody nuisance' to the Germans, and to keep the 'Sea View' base open.

On 31 December he set off again in the fishing boat. The heavy sea rolled during the crossing but became calmer when they came close to the shore. This time they saw the signal – a fire. The captain steered the boat into the narrow creek, barely dodging the rocks on either side.

Ahead the beach was hidden by sheer cliffs. The fire was blazing and a few men stood on the beach. Quayle got into a small rowing boat and came ashore. Field lay on the beach, his head wrapped in bandages soaked with blood.

'You'll be back in hospital soon,' Quayle assured him.

Field told him hoarsely, 'I wish you joy of the damned place,' and was put in the rowing boat to be taken on board the fishing vessel.

Quayle explored the small caves a few hundred feet above the sea which served as HQ. There, Sandy Glen, a naval commander in MI6, was plotting the harbour defences of Valona. Dale McAdoo, an American major of the OSS, was involved in his own intelligence work.

Field's radio operator, Bombardier Crane, told Quayle that he and Field transported the transmitter and charging motor around the country on pack mules. Some of the mules occasionally got eaten by wolves.

Said Quayle:

I hadn't a clue then how I was going to accomplish what I'd been sent to do. I met with the elders of Dukati, a village through which ran a supply route for the Germans in Greece. Field had asked them to attack German traffic but they had refused to do so because of the threat of reprisals by the Germans.

So I asked if they would approve if I and my men carried out attacks, but they were equally alarmed that their village would still suffer the consequences. The situation was further complicated by the constant threat that the anti-communists known as Ballists, such as these elders, and the communist Partisans who engaged the Germans in the mountains, would succeed in destroying the country themselves by their constant struggle against each other for superiority. They wouldn't even allow me to arrange for delivering arms to the Partisans across Ballist land.

The Partisans were also difficult to deal with. An Albanian who had been of help to Field took me as far as he dared to the mountain where the Partisans hid out. They felt they had been betrayed by Field who, they claimed, had delivered arms meant for them to the Ballists, which wasn't true at all, but that's what they believed and the only way they were going to cooperate was if I made sure they got the arms they wanted, otherwise they were likely to attack Dukati to get guns.

The only way to get arms to the Partisans was to establish a new coastal base in Partisan territory, so I moved down to Vuno taking one other man with me called Gray.

It took several days to reach Vuno where his hiding place, an old monastery, lay within half a mile of a road constantly used by Germans. He left Gray there with a trusted Partisan called Pavlo and went back to 'Sea View' to signal for a delivery of arms to be sent to Vuno.

On the journey back to 'Sea View' he stopped for a night at a Ballist village called Dhermi where he was given food and a bed. In the middle of the night German trucks arrived. Someone had tipped the Germans off that an English spy was in the village and Quayle had to dive out through a back window as the Germans burst through the door. He managed to escape up a hill in the dark.

At 'Sea View' wounded Italian soldiers, one of whom was a doctor whose badly injured arm had become gangrenous, were taking refuge. The Ballist lookouts had deserted and one of the OSS officers, an Albanian communist, had been murdered. Knowing they were now at risk of being discovered, Quayle established another base, half-way between 'Sea View' and Vuno, at Grama Bay. While he was gone, the *Sea Maid* arrived at 'Sea View' and evacuated the Italians, but by then the Italian doctor had died.

News came that the monastery at Vuno had been attacked, with Gray being taken prisoner and Pavlo shot dead. Quayle sent a signal to cancel the delivery of arms to Vuno and to inform HQ at Bari that he had moved to Grama.

'I felt totally responsible,' Quayle reflected, 'and I suppose one can say that was war, but it was more than that. I had the communists and the Ballists to contend with, and you just didn't know who was betraying who.'

The move to Grama was hampered by snow, but the camp had local herdsmen to act as lookouts. 'Thanks to those herdsmen, we were warned that a small patrol of Germans were coming and we literally took to the hills. Some of the men wanted to fight it out with them, but I knew the Germans would be able to warn its unit by radio, otherwise I would have killed the three Germans myself.'

The unit moved back into camp and a few nights later, on 13 February 1944, a trawler carrying supplies for Quayle's unit arrived. The captain was Sterling Hayden, a Paramount contract player who had joined the Marines and was now working under cover as a trawler skipper. Despite Quayle's assurances that he could safely enter the bay, Hayden refused to come any closer to collect some of the Italians who were still with Quayle. Several Italians tried to swim out to the boat. Three drowned.

Two passengers from the trawler came ashore. Giuseppe Manzitti was an intelligence officer who had assisted Field and had been responsible for directing Italian soldiers to 'Sea View'. 'We called him Munzi for short,' Quayle recalled,' and he really seemed to care for his fellow man. It's corny to say, but he became like a brother to me.'

The other arrival was Captain Peter Rous who was to become Quayle's second-in-command. At the same time Dale McAdoo left as the OSS had become alarmed at the fact that the Germans were actively searching the coast for enemy spies.

Into camp a few days later came one of the Ballist leaders, insisting that no arms should be given to the communists. Quayle maintained that the British government would give arms to whomever was willing to fight the Germans. The Ballist demanded arms for his people to attack the Germans once they began withdrawing, but Quayle knew the Ballists would use them to attack the Partisans.

Deciding it was dangerous to remain at Grama any longer, Quayle sent the Italians back to 'Sea View' while he prepared to move camp. Then news came that the German garrison at Dukati was preparing to comb the forests and ravines.

Taking only the radio transmitter and headphones, Quayle's unit followed Albanian guides into the mountains to hide, aware that their guides could well betray them if given any reason. They also had to pay exorbitant prices to local herdsmen for food.

They slept in underground caves and huddled together to keep from freezing. It rained constantly, but they could light no fires or dry their clothes.

One of the trustworthy Albanians brought news that Ballists from Dukati had joined the Germans in attacking Partisans. On the last day of February 1944, Quayle watched helplessly through his field glasses as the Italians he had had to leave behind were marched along the road to Valona under guard.

The next day, Quayle's men crossed the same road and climbed a mountain at Trajas, taking shelter in a group of goat pens on a grassy plateau. They were all exhausted and Quayle was suffering from a fever. That night they awoke to discover that one of their guards had gone and so was the pack which carried their money.

They were out of radio contact with Italy but had to pretend otherwise because their guides would certainly betray them if they knew how isolated the men had become. While they waited four days for one of the trusted Albanians, Zechir, to bring the batteries and charging motor which they'd hidden at Grama, they made a pretence of sending messages on the transmitter.

Zechir returned with the batteries and charging motor, and even managed to acquire petrol from a German truck.

Quayle sent a message to Bari for medicine to be dropped by plane as one of the other men had become seriously ill. But the plane never arrived. Then a message came through that a delivery would arrive at 'Sea View' on 14 March for the men of Dukati. After that the batteries ran down.

The good news was that the elders of Dukati sent mules to carry the heavy equipment back to 'Sea View'. On 14 March no supplies arrived. Two days later Quayle received a message that a boat had anchored off the coast the previous night but no contact with 'Sea View' had been made. 'I was convinced the transmitter operator in Bali was an idiot,' Quayle said, 'and the whole thing was just impossible. Morale sank to an all-time low and we had to contend with fleas and lice.'

He arranged to meet with Partisan leaders on 20 March and on the 18th he set out across snow-covered mountains to Gumenica. *En route* he collected the sick soldier, now recovered, whom he'd had to leave on the plateau at Trajas. His meeting with the Partisans was bitter as they complained that he had promised them arms and none had come. The Partisans had been hunted by the Germans and many had been killed or wounded. One of the Partisans even drew his revolver in anger, but Quayle managed to placate him. Before leaving the next day he had reassured them their arms would arrive.

As Quayle and his man made their way towards the plateau

of Trajas, Ballists fired at them. Quayle knew they were sending a message not to deal with the Partisans. During the
journey supplies of food and ammunition had arrived at 'Sea
View'.

On 26 March Quayle received a message from Bari to
return to make a personal report. A boat finally arrived to pick
him up on 3 April, by which time he was sick and delirious. 'I
remember nothing of being put in the boat or the journey, and
didn't come to until I was on my way to hospital in the back
of a truck. I tell you, it actually hurt with joy to be safe. I was
sure for a while that I was going to die and I literally wept
with gladness.'

19

The Long Road to Rome

*'If Patton had been in charge of the operation, we would
have taken Rome earlier than we did.'*

John Huston

While Anthony Quayle was beginning his Albanian mission,
John Huston was moving up with the US Army from San
Pietro, through the Liri Valley and on to Monte Cassino, a
tremendous hump of rock towering over the town of Cassino
and crowned by a medieval monastery. The German commander knew the Allies would wear themselves out trying to
take it.

Bombardier Spike Milligan saw in the new year of 1944 at
Lauro, on the advance towards Cassino. His division dug into
the mountain, wishing each other 'Happy New Year.'

There was no time for celebrations, and little to celebrate.
The battle was ferocious, and Milligan said, 'I was terrified,
everybody was. Everybody was scared stiff, but what can you
do?'

He was hit by mortar fragments in the leg and lay there
unable to move. Nobody was able to get to him with shells
landing all around, but finally a friend managed to get to him
and help him to the nearest first aid post. A major there who
was in a state of shock accused Milligan of malingering and
had him demoted.

Milligan was suffering from battle fatigue but was sent back
up to the front line too soon. It was quickly clear that he was

physically and mentally unable to carry on, and despite his protests to be allowed to remain with his division, he was sent to Afrigola and Banio for rehabilitation, and then on to an officers' rest camp near Naples where he was made up again to bombardier. But he was not to see the front line again, and towards the end of the war he was assigned to Stars in Battledress.

The battle for Monte Cassino began on 17 January 1944. Blizzards raged through the mountains, exhausting the men of Lieutenant General Mark Clark's 5th Army. The 36th Texas Division, to which Huston was attached, attempted to cross the Rapido River, but they walked straight into an area that had not, despite information to the contrary, been cleared of German mines.

Huston recalled:

The 36th was pretty well demolished. I remember standing by the side of a road with a West Point major who had been over the Rapido and back again. Half of his right hand was blown away and wrapped in a bloody bandage. As his troops passed in straggling groups, they saluted and each time they did, the major, dead on his feet, bent in agony, straightened and returned a full salute to them all, snapping his hand against his helmet. After seeing this, I never gave a sloppy salute again.

Huston went to Caserta for a well-earned break. He was in the street when a jeep turned a corner, its tyres squealing. Huston 'hit the dirt'.

'It sounded just like a .88 shell coming in. I got up and brushed myself off. I told myself, *Christ! Don't let that happen again.* Another jeep came round the corner and I hit the dirt again.'

While at Caserta, he was invited by members of the US Rangers to a party in Naples. They were celebrating their imminent departure to establish a beachhead at Anzio. These landings had been the idea of Winston Churchill; he wanted a swift push from the beaches to the Alban Hills, south-east of

Over here, overpaid and overwhelmed by a British welcome:
Colonel James Stewart and Major Clark Gable both flew bombing
missions over Europe.

General Mike O'Daniel, Commander of the 3rd Division, shows Lieutenant Audie Murphy the Congressional Medal of Honour Murphy is shortly to receive from General Alexander Patch.

When Audie Murphy became an actor he recreated his own true-life war experiences in the film *To Hell and Back*.

Rome, to cut the main German supply routes for the western end of the Gustav Line, where the Allies were held down before Monte Cassino. It was hoped that the Germans, threatened from the rear, would withdraw and allow Monte Cassino to fall into Allied hands.

But US Major General John P Lucas, commander of the Anglo-American forces which were to make the Anzio landings, was convinced the Germans would counter-attack swiftly, so he waited until his initial force of 40,000 men had been reinforced with 60,000 more.

The landing was planned for 22 January 1944.

Huston arrived at the Rangers' party:

It was held in a former nightclub on a hill overlooking the bay of Naples. It had a rotunda with a balcony overlooking the main floor. From the ceiling, several storeys high, hung the biggest crystal chandelier I'd ever seen.

The Rangers were pretty wild and raring to go, and after a few drinks they began playing some wild game. One of them took a running jump at the chandelier and began swinging from it. Then everyone below threw plates at him, the idea apparently to see if they could hit him on the head and knock him off. When he fell, another took his place until there were several men lying unconscious on the floor.

Finally the whole chandelier came down. I am sure that some of those it landed on must have been killed, but I didn't stay to find out.

The next day the Rangers began climbing on to the transports and kids were running alongside yelling, 'So long, Anzio! goodbye, Anzio!' How the secret invasion of Anzio was kept secret from the Germans I'll never know, but the Germans were taken completely by surprise. I didn't go with them, though. I headed back for the front.

For three days prior to the landings, the troops had trained. Corporal Audie Murphy was ready to go, but as his unit prepared to pull out he went down with malaria again and was confined to hospital with a temperature of 105 degrees.

As Churchill had hoped, and as Huston said, the Germans had not expected the Anzio landings, and by late afternoon of 22 January, most of Lucas's force had landed, including the British 1st Infantry Division, two commando battalions, the 46th Royal Tank Regiment, the US 3rd Infantry Division, a tank battalion, a parachute infantry battalion and three battalions of the US Rangers. Audie Murphy fought off the malaria in less than a week and was one of the replacements who arrived at the beachhead.

The road to Rome now lay open. Huston said, 'If Patton had been in charge of the operation, we would have taken Rome earlier than we did.' In fact, Lucas decided to stay put. Churchill commented, 'I had hoped we were hurling a wild cat on to the shore, but all we got was a stranded whale.'

Lucas's decision allowed the Germans time to reinforce the routes the Allies had hoped to capture. Some 40,000 German troops were sent to Anzio to hold back the advance. The battle for Anzio raged for weeks.

Murphy met up with his division just past the Mussolini canal. A good many men had been lost, and the unit was down to only thirty-four. Murphy was instantly promoted to staff-sergeant.

That night he took two men out on a reconnaissance patrol towards the Cisterna–Sessano road where an assault was planned to expand the bridgehead that still lay within the range of German shells.

The 3rd US Rangers were to be spearheaded by three Ranger battalions. The 1st Battalion of the 15th Infantry, led by tanks, were to advance two miles to the right of the main attack to clear the right flank.

Murphy's B Company of the 1st Battalion, advancing to clear a sector of road into which the Germans were dug, walked straight into a barrage of 20mm shells. The GIs panicked; Murphy and another soldier scrambled under a fence and were held down by a sniper. Before Murphy could see where the shots were coming from, a shell landed next to him, tossing him into the air and killing the other soldier. Murphy was miraculously uninjured.

The battle continued through the day but at dusk the Americans were forced to withdraw. One hundred and fifty men of the battalion were lost, including the commander, leaving Audie Murphy in charge. He had to be promoted to lieutenant.

On 30 January 1944, the 15th Battalion succeeded in taking Isola Bella; the Anzio beachhead was being extended inch by inch.

Despite his nickname 'Baby Face', Sergeant Murphy was quick to establish his authority among his men. He ordered a team to bury some dead cattle, but one of the men, Jakoby, refused. There was a brief argument as Murphy tried to persuade the soldier. Finally, the lieutenant punched Jakoby in the mouth; thereafter he never argued again. When Murphy was questioned about the incident by superior officers who reminded him about regulation regarding the striking of men, Murphy replied, 'We left the regulations in the rear. They were too goddammed heavy to carry.'

South of the rock of Monte Cassino, the freezing rain and driving snow bogged down American tanks, and by 11 February 4,145 British and 10,230 Americans lay dead. At Anzio the Allies were trapped on the beaches.

Said Huston:

At Monte Cassino there was one frontal assault after another, even though we all knew this method of attack was useless. Finally orders were given to bomb the monastery [on 15 February 1944]. Wave after wave of bombers dropped tons of blockbusters and the artillery pounded the hell out of the rock. We succeeded in destroying the monastery along with its library which was one of the greatest in the world. And it was all for nothing.

Still the Allies were unable to advance on Cassino. At Anzio the attempts to extend the bridgehead were not going well, and Lieutenant General Mark Clark relieved Major General Lucas on 22 February.

Around this time Huston heard that Humphrey Bogart and his wife Mayo Methot were in Naples, meeting the troops.

> I went back to Naples to see them and we had a grand, boozy reunion. The first thing Bogie said to me was, 'You sonofabitch! Leaving me tied to a chair.' He had already managed to get himself into trouble; he loved to drink and play the roughneck. He threw a party in his hotel room for a large group of enlisted men, and it sort of got out of hand. A general across the hall objected to the noise and complained. Bogie told him, 'Go fuck yourself!' Bogie was shortly thereafter shipped out of Italy.

Huston was ordered back to the United States and *en route* he stopped at London where he met up with director William Wyler. With Wyler was a young female companion. 'She had lived through the worst days of the blitz,' said Huston, 'but she was happy and laughing. Her name was Deborah Kerr.'

In Washington Huston began to put together his film, *The Battle of San Pietro*. During the first screening of the film for high-ranking officers, a general got up and stormed out three-quarters of the way through. The other officers followed. 'I shook my head and thought, "What a bunch of assholes! There goes *San Pietro*",' Huston told me.

Furious complaints that the film was 'anti-war' led to it being classified SECRET and filed away.

General George C Marshall heard about it and demanded a viewing. After seeing it, he said, 'This picture should be seen by every American soldier in training. It will not discourage but rather will prepare them for the initial shock of combat.' Suddenly everyone was praising the film. Huston was awarded the Legion of Merit and promoted to Major Huston.

He tried to adjust to normal civilian life in New York, but began to suffer psychologically:

I thought I was a seasoned veteran, a real soldier. I had seen the dead in great numbers, I was alive instead of dead. But I couldn't sleep. I'd wake up in the middle of the night in the St Regis Hotel, and eventually I'd have to get up and have a drink or go out for a walk. I'd find myself walking through Central Park with a .45 pistol in my waistband, hoping that some bastard would try and jump me so I could shoot him.

Suddenly I realized that, emotionally, I was still in Italy. I couldn't sleep because I couldn't hear the guns. I was suffering a mild form of anxiety neurosis. I had to put my life back together again.

William Wyler returned to his unit in Italy to decide how best to get footage from the ground of the Thunderbolts in combat and of the damage they inflicted.

Said John Sturges:

The only way we could figure it was to get in a jeep and drive to the front. So that's what we did, Wyler and I. We found ourselves driving up terraced hillsides and through olive groves; all very picturesque, except the war had pitted them all with craters.

We reached a British unit and asked a colonel there to take us up to the closest point to their front line. We crawled forward and got a pounding from artillery shells; we had to throw ourselves into muddy ditches for cover. The shells kept getting closer and we knew they were getting our range. I was sure we'd be killed then, but the shelling just stopped. Wyler kidded that the German firing at us must have stopped to light a cigarette!

To get even more exciting aerial shots, Wyler managed to acquire a B-25 and a pilot, Captain Barnett Bartlett, who had done two tours of duty and was assigned to low-risk flying. He welcomed any chance to get some action and with Wyler and his cameramen on board they set out to film the Allied fleet that was gathering in Naples harbour in preparation for an invasion of the south of France.

Wyler wanted to get a shot of Mount Vesuvius so Bartlett circled the volcano and, on Wyler's word, flew over the crater, coming in so low the plane barely skimmed the crater by little more than eight feet. The plane suddenly dropped, sucked down by the difference in air current. Bartlett pulled hard on the stick and they only just made it over the far rim of the crater.

Although the fleet had blimps overhead to prevent air attacks, Wyler asked Bartlett to get in closer. He did, flying between the cables, skimming over the water and tipping the plane to avoid getting his wings clipped off by the cables. Wyler called it 'the goddamndest ride I ever had'.

Late in 1943, French actor Jean Gabin finished filming *The Impostor* in Hollywood. It was the tale of an escaped murderer who dies heroically while fighting for the Free French. It was a subject close to his heart for he had resisted all advances from the French régime under Marshal Henri Pétain and hoped to join the Free French under Charles de Gaulle.

RKO wanted him to star with Luise Rainer in *The Temptress*, but he insisted he would only make the film if Marlene Dietrich was his leading lady. The studio head cancelled the film, paid Gabin his salary in full and swore that the French actor would never work in Hollywood again.

Gabin met with Sacha de Manzierly, the Free French representative in New York, and enlisted. Marlene Dietrich went with him to a secret port near New York and there they swore eternal friendship 'like two small children', as she decribed it. She kissed him goodbye and he boarded a destroyer bound for Morocco.

The ship never reached its destination. It was sunk and Dietrich was heartbroken, believing Gabin had died. But she later learned that he had survived.

In 1944, she enlisted in the US Army, and on the night of 4 April she was put on an ageing C-45 transport plane with young troops who had not yet seen combat. Her instructions were sealed. They took off and hit a violent hailstorm. Survival instructions were given in case they had to make an emergency landing in the sea. Once airborne, she was permitted to open her orders; her destination was Casablanca. With her in the plane was a young comic called Danny Thomas, a tenor who snored in his sleep, an accordionist, and Lynn Mayberry, a singer from Texas.

They touched down first in Greenland, then the Azores, finally landing in Casablanca on a blacked-out runway. The troops got out and then soldiers from the base came on board and questioned Dietrich and her troupe – 'Who are you? What unit do you belong to?' They hadn't expected the entertainers and didn't seem to know what to do with them.

'Let's just stay calm and wait here,' Dietrich told her troupe. A colonel showed up and announced that he had not been told of their arrival but would find them quarters.

They gave their first performance on 11 April in the Algiers Opera House, and then visited the bases in North Africa before being moved on to Oran. They were not being kept only in safe areas; often they came under fire during their shows. They quickly learned that three things counted out there; eating, sleeping and taking cover. Dietrich's shins were bruised from the times GIs threw her on to the ground during raids. She learned, also, that sometimes the gunfire they came under was from their own ranks.

'Thank God there was always a GI nearby to give me a shove,' she wrote.

She also visited the front-line hospitals, where among the injured GIs she would find German soldiers. The wounded GIs would ask her to go and speak to them, and when she did the Germans looked at her in amazement and asked, 'Are you the real Marlene Dietrich?'

Her memories of those hospitals were of rows and rows of beds and hanging jars of blood.

In May she and her troupe were flown to Naples where they performed for the 15th and 20th Army Air Forces. They usually flew in and out of the service camps on the same day. They were never far behind the front line.

She heard how the battles around Cassino continued until 13 May 1944 when Polish resistance troops, crossing mountains and attacking the Germans from the rear, took Monte Cassino.

Anthony Quayle recuperated in Naples, having arrived back from Albania suffering from malaria which put him in hospital for a few weeks. General Mason-MacFarlane was now in Naples, in charge of Allied Military Government, but in poor health. He would have welcomed Quayle's assistance, but in May Quayle was summoned to Bari and from there was taken by the *Sea Maid* back across the Adriatic to Albania.

He had wondered what had happened to the friends he left behind, and now he found them on the beach at 'Sea View' in poor condition. The American radio operator, Kukich, was half out of his head, threatening to shoot anyone who tried to steal his boots. Munzi, the Italian agent, was also there, 'looking like Ben Gunn from *Treasure Island*', and caring for a group of Italian soldiers.

It turned out that the Germans had blocked off all escape routes and searched the whole area, driving the agents into various holes, always having to keep on the move.

All were put on board the boat and taken back to Italy. Quayle returned to Naples and was asked by Mason-MacFarlane to remain and help him. Rome was soon to fall, and then the Italian people would want their own government. Mason-MacFarlane's job was to help them in the process.

The Americans finally broke out of Anzio on 23 May. They moved towards Cisterna and Campoleone, but once again Lieutenant Audie Murphy came down with malaria. He returned to his unit two days later to help take Cisterna. During that battle, a friend of his, Private A H Johnson, was killed at his side. Marlene Dietrich's troupe arrived in Anzio where she sang on the beach littered with shells.

On the night that the 5th Army smashed the German's final defences of Rome, Anthony Quayle was sent with two of Mason-MacFarlane's political advisors into Rome, knocking on the doors of the politicians who had been forced into inactivity by Fascism. Then he returned to Naples to report to Mason-MacFarlane.

The next morning, 4 June 1944, Allied forces entered Rome with General Mark Clark at their head. Marlene Dietrich and her troupe were put into a jeep to follow the troops into the Eternal City. She was in the convoy of jeeps and tanks, and later wrote, 'It was like an Easter Parade. The boys threw cigarettes and chocolate.'

She had been suffering with a sore throat which by this time had turned to pneumonia. She was ordered into hospital at the seaport of Bari and treated with penicillin.

Wyler, Koenig and Sturges were also there. 'We had thought there would be an almighty battle for Rome,' said Sturges, 'but the Germans had decided to spare the city. We arrived virtually with the first armour and infantry divisions and we had a great time celebrating under Mussolini's balcony at Piazza Venezia.'

Burt Lancaster was also in Rome, having fought with the 5th Army in North Africa, Sicily and now mainland Italy. 'To be honest,' he told me, 'I was never in any real danger because I had a pretty wonderful time seeing Europe as a page-turner for one of our men who was a pianist. We would go up to the front line, sure, and put on a show during a break in the firing. It was the best way to see a war.'

Lancaster had a few times been promoted to sergeant, but he kept getting busted down again for insubordination. When a lieutenant with acting aspirations told Lancaster how to be an actor, Lancaster, who was about to be promoted, told him, 'Get the hell out of my hair!' The lieutenant saw to it that his promotion and the increased pay that went with it were cancelled.

In Rome a buddy of Lancaster's wanted to see Pope Pius XII but there was such a large crowd waiting outside the papal audience chamber that he knew he'd never get the chance. So Lancaster used an old circus trick, propelling his friend over the heads of the crowd and landing at the front.

On 8 June, Anthony Quayle flew back into Rome with two

leading Italian politicians, Benedetto Croce and Ivanoe Bonomi, for a meeting with other Italian politicians to decide finally who would lead the new government. Winston Churchill had made it clear to Mason-MacFarlane that he wanted Marshal Badoglio, who had signed the armistice, to be prime minister. But the majority of the Italian politicians agreed that their government would come under the leadership of Ivanoe Bonomi. Mason-Mac was recalled to London to face the anger of Churchill.

Quayle was summoned back to Bari to join Mason-MacFarlane's number two, Ellery Stone. In the HQ mess, he saw Sterling Hayden who had refused to bring his trawler into Grama Bay during the Albanian mission. Quayle had no desire to speak to him, and left. During the ensuing weeks, he recommended Munzi for an Italian decoration, and took two weeks' leave in England.

For Audie Murphy and his unit, the liberation of Rome meant a period of leave, but then they were to begin training for Operation 'Anvil' – the invasion of the south of France.

While Marlene Dietrich was going up close to the front to cheer the GIs, the British soldiers were not being forgotten. Faith Brook, Kenneth Connor and Geoffrey Keen were sent by SIB to Italy to perform *Someone at the Door* for the exhausted British soldiers.

Although they were entertainers, they were never to forget that they were soldiers. They had to be on parade by seven each morning, with hair two inches above the collar and, for Faith Brook, not a sign of nail varnish.

The tour of Italy was supposedly being routed by ENSA, but they discovered on arriving in Naples that there was a complete breakdown of communication between ENSA and the army. It turned out that there were about sixty ENSA companies in Naples not doing anything, so Basil Dean made a personal visit to find out what was going on.

Actor Nigel Patrick, a colonel in the army based in Naples, had the unenviable job of trying to organize ENSA and SIB units. He sent them out with no particular plan, just to get them out of the way before Basil Dean arrived. Brook, Connor, Keen and their small company were sent to Rome where they found there was no venue and no one expecting them. They moved on to Florence and almost immediately turned around to return to Naples. Colonel Patrick put them on a lorry in a convoy bound for Bari, a trip which took them right across to the Adriatic coast.

They got to a place called Puglia which was under thick snow. The actors' truck had no snow chains on its tyres so it got stuck. Faith Brook recalled, 'We sat in the back of the lorry for thirteen hours with no food and freezing to death' until they were transferred to another truck and driven back to Naples.

Colonel Patrick met them at his headquarters. 'Oh, you're back, are you?' he said. Faith Brook remarked that he 'stood there very nonchalantly as though he were playing in a Noël Coward comedy'.

She was frozen, hungry and exhausted from the wasted trip. 'I blew my top, telling him in no uncertain manner how we felt about our dreadful trip.' She also told him what she thought of his 'stupid organization'. He responded by putting her on a charge for insubordination.

'In the end I apologized and he forgave me,' she said, 'but I did say I'd been provoked because of sheer exhaustion.'

When the weather brightened, they went back to Bari and were stuck there for what seemed like endless weeks, so they used the time to tour the Adriatic coast. 'The area had housed thousands of British prisoners of war from the North African campaign until the Italian surrender,' recalled Faith Brook. 'The places were empty of people and the only sign of war I saw was the remains of the bombardment of Monte Cassino, and that was awful.'

Noël Coward also met the troops in Italy, although his tour seemed much better organized. He visited a hospital in Tripoli where he did his routine as a Desert Rat, only he was, in the words of producer Peter Daubney, who was one of the patients, a 'Cartier Desert Rat'. At first the men were insulted by his appearance, but in the end 'they stood and cheered and cheered'.

Peter Daubney wanted to meet Coward and found his makeshift dressing room. Seeing how heavily bandaged Daubney was, Coward asked, 'What's the matter with you?'

Daubney explained that he had lost his arm at Salerno. He noted that Coward 'was much more compassionate than I was', and that seeing all the wounded in the hospital Coward 'was so deeply moved'.

Coward insisted on taking Daubney back to his ward. He was, said Daubney, 'an enhancer of the spirit and not a diminisher in any way'. That encounter 'helped me enormously to get well'.

20

Normandy

'I saw a German soldier lying by the roadside. It was just the torso; the legs had been blown off.'

Richard Todd

Rex Harrison returned home from 11-Group on 19 February 1944, and found that Lilli had gone into labour. An ambulance rushed her to the London Clinic while he followed in his car.

That night London experienced one of its worst air-raids as Harrison paced up and down in the waiting-room, praying that the clinic would not be hit. To the tune of the bombs, Lilli gave birth to a boy; they called him Rex Carey Alfred.

The very next morning, unwilling to expose his family to another night of heavy bombing, Harrison collected Lilli and the baby and took them back to Denham.

'The RAF put me in a film called *Journey Together* with Edward G Robinson and Richard Attenborough which the RAF Film Unit produced,' said Harrison. 'Then they cut my scenes.'

Shortly after, Harrison's duty with 11-Group ended. 'The Air Ministry decided that with sufficient men queuing up to take my job, I would now serve the war better in front of a camera.'

He was honourably discharged from the Royal Air Force in the spring of 1944.

★

In Eastern Europe, there had been some of the most ferocious fighting of the war at Stalingrad. The Germans had first broken over the plains of southern Russia in August 1942. Stukas and Junkers dive-bombed Stalingrad, devastating the city. On 23 August, Hitler ordered the city's capture. But General Friedrich von Paulus, in command of German forces, found the advance slow going, with his panzers hemmed in by ravines. It took until the end of August for him to break through the Russian defences and begin the attack that was supposed to finish Stalingrad on 13 September 1942. But the battle, with its street by street fighting, lasted until early 1944. It ended with Paulus's surrender to the Russians on 31 January 1944.

Over a million people had died. For Germany, it was the first great disaster of the war.

By spring the Red Army was pushing back the boundaries of the Nazi empire. The effects were felt in Poland where the Germans attempted to shore up the eastern front against the Red Army. Throughout Poland the resistance organization had been growing, and the SS, in its efforts to break the underground, intensified its oppression of the ordinary citizens.

The only oppression which adversely affected Roman Polanski, now ten, was from the Catholic, farming life-style of the Borocowska family. He stubbornly remained resistant to their religious teachings and, unable to bear it any longer, decided to run away in the spring of 1944.

He walked south-west, which he believed was the way to Cracow. After about eight miles he came upon an intersection where he found the road from the central Polish city of Lodz to Cracow. He tried to hitch a lift but no truck would stop.

A German car pulled up at the intersection and two soldiers emerged to set up a roadblock, stopping trucks and checking papers. Roman saw his chance to move along the line of waiting trucks, begging for a lift. He was spotted by one of the soldiers who called him over. 'Where are you going?'

'Cracow,' Roman mumbled.

The soldier asked the driver he was checking if he would take the boy. The driver agreed.

'He will take you part of the way,' said the soldier. Roman was relieved. Then the soldier added, 'But first show me your identity card.'

Roman did not have such a card. He shrugged and tried to stifle his growing panic. *'Papers!'* insisted the soldier.

Roman began to back away. 'Halt!' ordered the German, removing his pistol. Roman dived under one of the trucks, scrambled to the other side, and took off into the woods. The two soldiers ran after him as Roman ran blindly on through the wood. He could hear the soldiers behind him, ordering him to stop. They began firing but he kept running, expecting at any moment to feel a bullet in his back.

The soldiers finally gave up the chase but Roman kept on running until he was too exhausted to run any more. Rain began to fall and he found a large uprooted tree to shelter behind for the night. He was cold, soaked and terrified.

The following morning he decided that he would be safer just to go home. He arrived back at the Borocowska farm with a fever and told the family that he had gone for a walk in the forest and had become lost.

All Borocowska said was, 'You have missed two days' work. You will pay', and then began beating Roman to the floor. From then on Roman pretended to accept the family's religious doctrines to avoid further beatings.

By early 1944, Bombardier Frankie Howerd had become restless at Penclawwd. Four times he auditioned for Stars in Battledress – four times he was turned down. He told me:

> I went to the CO and asked *please* could I do something positive for the war effort. I thought that the only way I might get my name in the newspapers was as one of yesterday's casualties. So he sent me down to Plymouth where I found myself training to be a Commando. Me! Up and down rope ladders and leaping over assault courses. Actually I was very fit and some genius decided I

ought to be promoted to sergeant and they gave me a few
lessons in how to drive a truck. They put me behind the
wheel of the world's largest lorry, jam-packed with soldiers who had their life in my hands, and I managed to
drive straight into a hedge. So they changed their minds
and never let me behind a wheel again.

During the early spring of 1944, David Niven was ordered
to report to General Sir Frederick Morgan in Sunningdale.
Niven arrived at the carefully camouflaged HQ in the
middle of a wood where Morgan, as Chief of Staff to the
Supreme Allied Commander, had been working on pre-
liminary plans for Operation 'Overlord' – the invasion of
Occupied France.

Niven told me:

The first and most important decision Morgan and his
staff had to make was exactly where to land on the
French coast. Information was supplied to him that had
come from the French Resistance about the German
defences, and he had hundreds of photographs taken by
the RAF. He ruled out landing in Norway, the
Netherlands and the Bay of Biscay, and he had to choose
between France and Belgium. The Germans knew that
the most obvious landing on the French coast would be
at Calais, crossing from Dover, so Morgan knew he had
to plan further down the coast, and at some time (in June
1943) had arrived at the conclusion that Normandy
would be the point of invasion.

The date had originally been set for some day in June,
1944, and it was shortly before then that I was summoned to Sir Frederick's secret headquarters.

He told me that because I had spent a great deal of
time in America and I liked Americans, he was taking me
out of Phantom and promoting me to lieutenant colonel
and assigned me to an American general called Barker
with whom he'd worked on the initial invasion plans. I
found General Morgan's Nissen where he told me he had

been given the task by Eisenhower of making sure there were no weak links between the various Allied forces.

'From now on,' General Barker told Lieutenant Colonel Niven, 'you take orders only from me, and when the invasion comes you will be working only for me. We will be liaising between the British and American forces. You're going to be in the thick of it.'

Through his work with General Barker and General Morgan he came into personal contact with General Sir Bernard Montgomery who was to command the Allied landing force in Normandy.

'I did know Monty slightly,' Niven told me. 'In his HQ he had a huge blackboard on which he'd written, "Are you a hundred per cent fit? Are you a hundred per cent efficient? Do you have a hundred per cent binge?" No one ever dared ask him what he meant by binge!'

John Ford was sent from the Far East to London, there to prepare for very special filming of the D-Day landings. In fact, much of the preparation had been performed by his aide, Mark Armistead, who had spent the past two years in London, installing a secret laboratory at Denham Studios for developing classified film stock.

Armistead had also helped to develop an aerial reconnaissance technique known as 'low-level-oblique' so that any area of land could be photographed from fixed cameras flying at a height of 200 feet, resulting in precise images from which the sizes of bridges and buildings could be accurately calculated. Even the depths of rocks in the sea could be estimated. Because the War Office had no detailed maps of the Normandy beaches, low-level-oblique reconnaissance was able to provide the necessary data.

To capture unique film of the landings, Armistead had 500 clockwork Eyemo cameras mounted on to the front of landing craft so that they would be triggered automatically by the ramps being dropped on the beaches, removing the need for cameramen.

Ford himself wanted to cross the Channel before D-Day to complement the photographic maps supplied by Armistead. US Navy Commander John D Bulkeley, whose exploits became the subject of Ford's war film *They Were Expendable*, agreed to take Ford back and forth across to the Bayeux area in a PT boat. They crossed the Channel using only a single engine to drop off an agent or sometimes collect information, and then return to England. Ford asked director George Stevens, who was preparing to take his own film unit into Europe, if he wanted anything from France. Stevens asked for two bottles of booze, and he got them.

According to Andrew Sinclair, Ford assigned two cameramen, Brick Marquand and Junius Stout, to go in the day *before* the landings with a few Rangers to choose their camera positions and to dig in.

The 'Course King', Lieutenant Richard Todd, now assistant adjutant of the 7th Parachute Battlation, led his men in training on a stretch of land at Topsham in Devon in preparation for the Normandy landings. They practised parachuting over two parallel rivers and capturing the bridges there. The exact targets were kept secret from the men, but Lieutenant Todd, as assistant adjutant, was informed that their targets were the River Orne and Caen Canal bridges. He set to work on schedules and planned for himself to go in aircraft 33.

In a flat in Victoria, London, Lieutenant Dirk Bogarde studied maps and photographs of the Cherbourg peninsula and Normandy coast. Aged twenty-four, he was in army intelligence; his job involved pouring over low-level-oblique photographs, looking for hidden clues that revealed the secret installation of defence guns.

Bogarde had originally begun army life in the Royal Corps of Signals in 1941, been sent to Officer Cadets' Battle School in early 1942, and emerged as a full lieutenant in July 1943. While the army tried to decide what he was best suited at, they made him a liaison officer for the infantry. Then he became unofficial ADC to a brigadier before attending a War Intelligence Course in October 1943, from which he emerged as a brigade intelligence officer and air photographic interpreter. From the flat in Victoria, he was moved to Odiham RAF Station and seconded to 39 Wing of the Royal Canadian Air Force.

The invasion had originally been set for 5 June 1944. Richard Todd's parachute unit was sent to Fairford aerodrome, near Bristol, ready to go. At Odiham, Lieutenant Bogarde received news that a German Panzer Division had moved into the Bayeux area. He scoured new photographs, coming in by the hour, to try to locate the division. This, and the awful June weather, convinced Eisenhower and Montgomery to postpone the invasion.

The following day, the Allied Command decided to launch Operation 'Overlord' – D-Day had come: 6 June 1944.

A last-minute decision put Lieutenant Todd into aircraft 1 instead of number 33, and he was chosen as the first man of the battalion to jump. They took off as night was falling. As they crossed the coast of England, they could see the largest armada ever assembled.

The previous day Sergeant Howerd was granted a twenty-four-hour pass to visit his mother in London. 'You didn't have to be a genius to know something was in the wind,' he said, and the next morning he was on a train to Tilbury and immediately put on a merchant ship which was ferrying troops across the Channel. 'Because I had been in the Royal Artillery they put me in charge of a Bren-gun on the conning tower, and we set off across the Channel.'

Niven recalled that on the night before the invasion he and Primmie 'clung together miserably'. He told her he would not leave until after they had had breakfast together. It was a kind lie. She finally fell asleep just before dawn, and he quickly and quietly dressed, took one last look at her and their baby son who lay in the cot beside the bed, and left.

Earlier that morning, gliders carrying light infantry under the command of Major John Howard landed close to the Caen Canal. Their object was to capture Benouville Bridge, later to be known as Pegasus Bridge.

Six hundred and ten British parachutists were ready to

begin their drop. In aircraft 1, Lieutenant Richard Todd stood ready at the exit. For some reason the pilot had to take avoiding action and as the plane tilted, Todd very nearly fell out before the signal was given.

Ready at last, he jumped, loaded with a kit that included an inflatable boat in case an assault crossing of the rivers had to be made. He landed in a cornfield about half a mile from the planned position which was south of Amfreville on the east bank of the River Orme. There was German fire coming from the town of Ranville.

As the rest of his battalion landed, he took his bearings from the direction of the aircraft, found his commanding officer and arrived at the rendezvous in a quarry within ten minutes of landing.

Above, wave after wave of aircraft transporting the rest of the battalion came under heavy fire from the German defences around Caen. Many planes were hit, and Todd knew it was very likely that aircraft 33 had been brought down.

The depleted force of parachute troops started towards the bridges from where they could hear the sound of small-arms fire.

He recalled, 'We made our way towards the bridge and I hadn't gone very far when I saw a German soldier lying by the roadside. It was just the torso; the legs had been blown off. Normally that would have been enough to turn my stomach but, I don't why, it didn't then. I just had the feeling of mild curiosity and thought *poor chap*, and then I went on.'

Further along he saw someone lying behind a little hillock and thought it might be a sniper. He crept down to the river which was on his right and crawled carefully along the river bank out of sight. At the hillock he discovered that his sniper was a dead British parachutist. 'I went to look at him and saw that he was a young teenager I remembered well by sight. He had just a little hole in the middle of his forehead. No blood, just a little hole.'

They came across the first bridge over the Orme which the airborne troops, who had been transported in the gliders, were holding. On the second bridge a German tank was ablaze.

Lieutenant Todd personally presented himself to Major John Howard.

Recalled Richard Todd:

> We had to get to the other side of the bridge and get dug in because the German counter-attack was beginning to gather force and there was a lot of activity going on.
>
> Our orders were that in the event of the bridge being captured by us intact, we were to establish a bridgehead on the far side of the waterway from the 6th Airborne area and hold until relieved, and that meant hold no matter what happened because the bridge was absolutely crucial because our little battalion bridgehead was on the main line of attack of 21st Panzer Divison coming up from Caen and they were quite formidable.

On HMS *Belfast* was Hollywood director George Stevens. He had been invited to head an Army Signal Corps film unit and was put in charge of the combat photography in Europe. D-Day was his first assignment. He had brought with him from Hollywood 16mm colour film stock to record his own personal record as well as supervising official black-and-white 35mm film coverage. As a lieutenant colonel, Stevens commanded an élite team of about thirty cameramen and directors from the film industry. Among them were novelist Irwin Shaw and screenwriter Ivan Moffat.

By 5.30 am the German coastal defences were within range of the Allied fleet's guns. The bombardment began. Stevens turned his own personal camera on the 6-inch guns on the X and Y turrets of *Belfast* as she opened up on the German defences.

The Normandy beaches had been split into five sections. The first landings were by the Americans, at 'Utah', close to the town of Ste-Mère-Eglise. Just after 7.00 further American forces landed at 'Omaha' near Port-en-Bessin. That was where John Ford's two cameramen were dug in.

At 7.25 the British and Canadians landed at 'Gold', at Arromanches. Twenty-five thousand men fought their way up

the beach towards Le Hammel where they were held back.
But by nightfall they had broken through and had taken
Arromanches and had reached the outskirts of Bayeux.

'Juno', to the east of 'Gold', was taken by Canadian forces
while 'Sword' at Ouistreham was taken by French 4
Commando and various British commando and Infantry
divisions.

Dirk Bogarde arrived by being parachuted from a Dakota
into a cornfield at St Sulpice. His flight lieutenant,
Christopher Greaves, an air photographic interpreter with 39
Wing of the Canadian Royal Air Force, told Bogarde to dig
himself a hole in a nearby hedgerow and ordered someone
else to make some tea.

A few hours after the first landings on 'Juno', George
Stevens and his crew came ashore, landing at the village of
Bernières at the centre of 'Juno'. There he came across a
British Sherman flail minesweeping tank of the 22nd
Dragoons of the 79th Armoured Division. It had been dis-
abled by a landmine but the crew were unhurt. Stevens had
the cheerful crew pose on the tank holding a German sign
warning of mines.

Because the Special Coverage Unit was attached to the
Allied Supreme Headquarters, they could move about the
battlefield as they wished, allowing Stevens in particular to
shoot what proved to be some of the most evocative film footage of the war, in colour, and never intended to be seen by the
public.

He found the village had been blown apart in the bombardment. But the French occupants were delighted to see the
Allies, and he captured scenes of French Resistance fighters
triumphantly waving French flags.

On 'Omaha' John Ford's cameraman, Brick Marquand,
heard his name being hailed over the beachmaster's bullhorn.
'There's a crazy guy out there on a PT boat who wants to
know how you are and to tell you to get your ass back to
England with the stuff.'

The crazy guy was John Ford. Marquand packed up his
camera and film stock and made his way back to Portsmouth.

He received a Silver Star but much of his film was never seen because Roosevelt had a restraining order on material shot by the Field Photographic Branch. The official film of the landings was in the hands of the George Stevens unit.

On board an American destroyer was actor Robert Montgomery, a lieutenant commander. He had been commissioned as a lieutenant in the US Naval Reserve where he began his friendship with John Ford which led to their collaboration on *They Were Expendable*, filmed towards the end of the war when Montgomery had to replace Ford as director for a while because Ford was ill and exhausted from his war exploits.

Lieutenant Colonel Niven and General Barker boarded the *Empire Battleaxe* at Southampton. Already casualties were being ferried back to England. 'Hundreds of wounded GIs were being helped off a tank-landing craft,' he recalled, 'their eyes wide with shock, boys who had grown old in just a couple of hours.'

A GI watching from the deck of *Battleaxe* said gloomily, 'That's a helluvan encouraging send-off for us.'

When the *Battleaxe* arrived off the Normandy coast, Niven was ordered into a landing craft and put ashore. 'The beach was marked with white tape to shows the paths around the minefields. The dead rolled in the surf and littered the beaches. I try not to remember it now. What I do remember is lying in a trench that first night, hearing the nightingales over the gunfire.'

At the bridges held by the Airborne and Parachute Battalions, the 21st Panzer Division came, as expected, down the road from Caen. The British officers in charge of the machine guns and mortars had been killed, so Lieutenant Todd took over their duties even though all their machine guns, mortars and radios had been destroyed. He was dug in between the little church of Le Port and the canal. A company commanded by Major Nigel Terry, who had lost a leg in the battle, was under fire from Germans who had managed to get between Taylor's company and the others at Le Port.

Said Todd, 'This very lightly armed para battalion had only hand-held weapons with which to face Panzers. But we held due to the enormous bravery of all the men involved and jolly good leadership from their officers.

'Out of the 610 that we dropped of the 6th Para we had, by mid-morning, 240 left. I lost two of my closest friends. Then we lost a lot more in the battle; we lost about sixty killed or wounded that morning around the bridge.'

While waiting for Lord Lovat to relieve them, Lieutenant Todd made a reconnaissance towards Ouistreham to check on a unit further down the canal towards the coast. He saw a boat drifting up the canal. Suddenly, the Germans hiding in the boat opened fire on the thinly stretched-out British, but a return of fire quickly saw off the surprise German attack.

Two and a half minutes later Todd heard the unmistakable drone of the bagpipes of Lord Lovat's approaching commandos. The bridges had been held, and that evening the heavy equipment arrived to push back the Panzers.

Todd recalled that 'each battalion had its own medical section, and our medical section was all staffed by Quakers – non-combatants who wouldn't carry arms. But they were extremely brave and did terrific work under fire. We admired them especially because of the fact that they never carried a weapon. They had guts.'

Now relieved, and with the Panzers retreating, Todd's unit moved forward to the eastern side of the River Orne to extend the bridgehead. On 11 June, he was ordered to report to Divisional HQ at Ranville which then moved to the quarry where the 7th Parachute had rendezvoused, and there Lieutenant Todd remained, waiting for the Normandy breakout.

During the first day, the invasion force held the beaches. Four days after landing, Dirk Bogarde discovered a severed leg on 'Gold'. It was hardly more than a foot and shin strapped into a boot. Some American soldier had lost it at 'Omaha' and the strong current had carried it down the coast and washed it up at Arromanches.

He watched as a flock of gulls swooped down on to the sea and began pecking at the severed leg. Then he clambered up the beach through the twisted barbed wire.

The US 101st Airborne Division had landed near Carentan at the beginning of the invasion where many had drowned in flooded areas around the Douves River. The landing forces at Utah Beach pushed up towards Carentan where there was a small bridge; the one vital link between the US forces and the British further east. Lieutenant Colonel David Niven, in maintaining personal contact between the Americans and the British, used this bridge which came under constant shellfire.

I had to make the crossing quite frequently, and I was trapped by the shelling on one crossing. There were fox holes either side of the bridge which I had to dive into and cower as the rain just poured down, filling my fox hole until I thought if I wasn't blown to bits I'd probably drown. The rain stopped and I dared a peek out over the top. A few yards away in another fox hole I saw a head and to my delight and surprise it was an old friend of mine, John McClaine, who had been a reporter in New York and was a lieutenant in the navy attached to the OSS.

He pinned an Iron Cross on my chest which he'd acquired when a delivery of the medals had been parachuted to the German soldiers in Cherbourg but had fallen into McClaine's hands instead. Then he gave me a ride in his command car to a small inn in a backwater that was untouched by the war. We became the first Allied combatants the three ladies who ran the inn had ever seen. They gave us a bloody good meal washed down with bottles of Bordeaux. Then we headed back for Carentan and the war.

George Stevens set up his own base at Carentan, living, like all the other US troops, in tents. He kept his men in order, even down to maintaining regulation haircuts. His team called themselves the 'Hollywood Irregulars', even though it consisted of men of different nationalities. To others they were the 'Stevens Unit'.

Ivan Moffat of the Stevens Unit noted:

> The overwhelming impression was one of extraordinary logistical power – the thousands of ships and hundreds of thousands of tons of material being landed twenty-four hours a day. If there was victory, which of course we assumed there would be, this is what victory would be made of; it was truly the sinews of war, and one almost felt that such things as regimental traditions, individual gallantry, élite brigades, all that was hardly to be reckoned with against the scales of this amazing accumulation of stuff – equipment, transport, artillery.

Sergeant Frankie Howerd manning a Bren gun on a troop-ferrying merchantman had caught flu. The actual day he arrived off the French coast was probably on or around 18 June. He said:

> When we arrived the sea was so rough that the DUKW landing craft couldn't even come alongside of us to take off the troops, so for the next eleven days I lay on the floor of the conning tower with terrible seasickness while the rusty old bucket pitched and rolled in the dreadful conditions. We ran out of food except for biscuits but I was so sick it wasn't a problem for me although I was terribly thin when we did finally get off.

A Channel storm had begun on 18 June and lasted for five days. Ships sought shelter from the crashing seas in the partially completed 'Mulberry' harbours. These were pre-fabricated harbours which were towed across the Channel and slotted together. Two were erected, one for the Americans off 'Omaha' and the other for the British at 'Juno'. Frankie Howerd told me that by the time the British Mulberry harbour was erected it was so crowded with ships seeking shelter from the heavy seas that there was no room for his merchantman. During the five-day storm, the American Mulberry was destroyed and the British harbour badly damaged.

Wherever the front line was, the Stars in Battledress were not far behind. Comedienne Janet Brown, in the ATS, found herself performing on two tables in a field, surrounded by troops who sat on the grass. She did three shows a day, starting off at ten in the morning. She remembered that there were 'a tremendous lot of wasps' which she tried to fend off while washing out of a biscuit tin.

Sergeant Charlie Chester landed at Luc-sur-Mer on D-Day plus six. The houses were empty so he and his SIB unit took over some and waited for further orders. A sergeant turned up and told them, 'Some of these houses may have been mined and booby-trapped by the Germans before they left.'

The SIB unit wasted no time packing and getting out. Charlie Chester recalled, 'We found out later the sergeant was right.'

21

Normandy Breakout

'The sight of destruction is the thing I'll never forget – villages absolutely smeared to the ground, large towns like Caen just piles of rubble.'

Richard Todd

The Allies had hoped for a swift advance through to Paris. Makeshift airstrips had to be constructed as close to the front as possible. Dirk Bogarde and Chris Greaves interpreted every sortie flown. They had a truck complete with two desks and a few lamps which served as their office in which they usually spent endless hours working.

At St Sulpice, the cornfield was flattened and turned into an airstrip. The farmer who owned the field turned up, shouting in French and waving his fist, furious at the destruction of his land. They were, Bogarde wrote in a letter home, supposed to be the Liberating Allies, but here was this old farmer and his wife who didn't see them as Liberating Allies but as a pestilence destroying his hard-grown crops.

Only when the weather was too bad for flying did Bogarde and Greaves get a break from work, and often on those occasions they took a jeep and drove off into the broken countryside. Greaves was a professional artist and Bogarde had had some training at the Chelsea Polytechnic, so they spent their free hours painting. Any paintings they produced, which covered virtually the whole of the Normandy landings, belonged to the Air Ministry and it was only after the war that their works were returned to them.

Their job required them to drive through Europe in the wake of their Forward Recce Squadron taking photographs. One day Bogarde and his driver found themselves being fired on by mortars as they drove down an open road. They pulled into a farm, took shelter behind a barn and saw a middle-aged woman running towards them. She led Bogarde into the barn where there were two younger women, one of them pregnant and writhing in agony.

Bogarde knelt by the pregnant woman's head and held her shoulders down while the other two women delivered the baby. Bogarde later wrote that the screams of the pregnant woman virtually drowned out the sound of the falling mortars. After the delivery, Bogarde went to the barn door to breathe some fresh air. The mortars had stopped, and all he heard was the baby's cry.

The older woman tugged his arm and led him to what remained of the house where, inside, she gave him a small glass sphere set on a white china base.

Bogarde went back to his driver.

'What was all that about?' the driver asked.

'I've just had a baby.'

Then they drove back to the airstrip.

The expected rapid advance through France did not happen. The historic town of Caen should have been taken on D-Day. But there was a Panzer division in the way. Unless General Montgomery took Caen, the British and Canadian beachhead would remain jammed with men, armoury and equipment. This, said David Niven, sparked off the first differences of opinion between the Allied commanders.

Dirk Bogarde and Christopher Greaves decided to take a look at Caen for themselves and drove along a high road that looked down on the town. Their jeep provided the Germans below with a perfect target, and they opened fire with mortars. Greaves put his foot down, weaving and swerving to avoid the shells.

Desperate to get off the road, Greaves turned into a cornfield to their right, skidded to a halt, and they spread themselves on the ground behind a hawthorn hedge. It was twenty minutes before the Germans gave up trying to kill them.

Bogarde and Greaves were about to get back in the jeep when suddenly a group of Canadian soldiers with cocked rifles appeared from behind a high-hedged bank.

'Where the hell did you come from?' one of them asked.

'An error in map reading,' Greaves told him calmly.

Two days later, on 7 July, General Montgomery ordered a massive air attack on Caen, despite the fact that the town housed 55,000 civilians.

Dirk Bogarde and Christopher Greaves stood in an orchard close to their airstrips, watching as giant bombers roared above them, heading for Caen. The bombardment was so ferocious that the ground shook, and Bogarde hung on to a tree to keep himself upright. He could see the skyline of Caen lit up with fires and explosions and clouds of smoke billowing up into the night sky.

The air assault reduced much of the town to rubble which offered the Germans greater cover. The next day Montgomery ordered a frontal assault. British troops made slow progress but Caen fell to the Allies on 10 July.

With the invasion almost complete, the work on clearing up the dead on the beaches and throughout the countryside began. From a meadow Dirk Bogarde watched in numbed silence as bulldozers piled up the dead and mechanical diggers ripped up the ground to form mass graves. He had become accustomed to seeing dead men and he stood watching with little emotion as cheerful drivers with masks to deaden the stench manoeuvred the bulldozers and diggers, severing limbs from corpses and trying to get the job done as quickly as possible.

He felt sadness for the families and friends who had loved these men. He recalled, 'Everyone there had once belonged to someone.'

Richard Todd was also struck by the desolation:

There are sights I'll never forget. Certain sights, certain sounds. The sight of destruction is the thing I'll never forget – villages absolutely smeared to the ground, large towns like Caen just piles of rubble, and the other thing you can never forget is the stench of death that hung over Caen where literally thousands of people were buried alive under the rubble long before they were retrieved and dug out. That was the stench of death.

Shortly after the fall of Caen, David Niven came across 'B' Squadron of the secret 'Phantom' force, hidden in a wood near the Orne River. Among them he discovered actor Hugh Williams who had co-starred with him in *Wuthering Heights*. Williams informed Niven that his former second-in-command of 'A' Squadron, Hugh Kindersley, had been badly wounded by mortar fire. Niven recalled, 'Hugh and I agreed that if we had known about the German Nebelwerfer, which was a six-barrelled mortar, neither of us would have joined the army.'

Caen had not been the only stumbling block for the Allies. On 25 July, in one of the biggest raids of the Normandy campaign, 2,500 Allied bombers flew over the camp of the Stevens Unit to destroy the German positions west of St-Lô. George Stevens captured the sight of the countless waves of aircraft on film.

'The sky was full of bombers,' recalled cameraman Dick Kent, 'coming over everywhere you looked and dropping rows of bombs just ahead of where we were.'

Twelve air-raids poured bombs on to the German garrison in St-Lô. Afterwards, Stevens drove forward to see for himself the devastation. St-Lô had once been a picturesque market town. The garrison had been destroyed, but Stevens found that the whole town had also been flattened.

On 28 July, Coutances was liberated by the US First Army. French civilians saw George Stevens and his crew in uniform and presented them with flowers in gratitude for their liberation, despite the fact that their town was in virtual ruins.

Stevens set up his own personal camera and was filming in the shattered town when, just down the road from where he stood, a jeep hit a landmine left by the *Wehrmacht* who were leaving mines and booby traps in the path of their advancing enemy.

The explosion shook Stevens and sent GIs scattering. As the smoke cleared, Stevens moved in close to the shattered jeep and watched as medics tended to the driver who lay seriously injured, blown completely out of the jeep in the blast.

As the German resistance began to crumble towards the end of July, Stevens filmed German soldiers surrendering, many of them smiling for the camera, happy their war was over. Makeshift PoW camps had to be hastily erected out of barbed wire to maintain the thousands of prisoners whose fighting spirit had collapsed.

As the Allies pushed forward, around 300,000 Germans and their vehicles crammed the roads and lanes in their desperate attempt to reach the River Seine and escape across on the ferries. The Allied forces had the retreating army surrounded between Falaise and Argentan – the 'Falaise pocket' – making them easy targets for Allied aircraft.

The town of Falaise fell on 17 August and on 21 August the 'pocket' was closed. Fifty thousand German soldiers were captured.

Dirk Bogarde admitted that, like hundreds of his comrades, he believed at first that the Allies had won a magnificent victory and was sure there couldn't be enough fight left in the enemy to beat off the Russians mustering on Germany's borders. He expected the war to end before autumn.

But the Germans were not about to surrender and they would fight all the way back to the Fatherland. What Bogarde eventually came to realize was that while the Allied generals argued among themselves, they had 'left the back door open' for the Germans to escape in their thousands, complete with their armoury.

In fact, some 30,000 Germans managed to escape across the Seine, 'including sixteen German generals,' noted David Niven.

In the south of France, another invasion took place. Operation 'Anvil' was originally planned to coincide with D-Day, but this led to further disagreement between the Allied leaders. The Americans liked the idea, arguing it would

Marlene Dietrich of the US Army literally risked life and limb entertaining the GIs on the European front lines.

After an initial rejection by the army because of a heart flutter, Mickey Rooney was finally accepted in 1944 and sent to Europe where he entertained an estimated two million GIs.

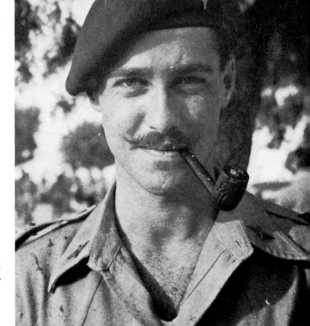

Lieutenant Richard Todd pictured on duty in the Middle East just after the war.

trap the Germans between converging attacks through France. But the British, especially Churchill, preferred to advance through Italy towards Germany. The Americans won the argument and Churchill insisted the operation be given the new code name 'Dragoon' because he had been 'dragooned' into it.

Shortage of landing ships resulted in a postponement of 'Dragoon' until after D-Day. The Americans took three infantry divisions from Italy in June 1944, including Lieutenant Audie Murphy's division, as well as forming an Anglo-American 1st Provisional Airborne Division from units in the Mediterranean. The Free French under General Jean de Lattre de Tassigny were assigned to exploit the initial landings.

Air attacks on the German coastal defences began on 6 August while an invasion fleet assembled at Naples where Audie Murphy boarded one of the 880 ships.

The fleet arrived off the southern French coast on 15 August where the American infantry divisions stormed ashore on beaches between Cannes and St Tropez. There was little resistance and the beaches were soon secured.

Commander Fairbanks, involved in an elaborate deception operation, was aided by his personal knowledge of the area. Leading seventeen other vessels in the gunboat *Aphis*, he landed French troops ashore between Nice and Cannes to cut the coast supply road from Italy.

The Fairbanks unit sped west to join with the rest of his force for diversionary attacks around Toulon and Marseilles. Three aircraft, with the aid of cunningly scripted radio traffic, persuaded the Germans that they were three whole squadrons. Radars were jammed by dropping so-called 'windows', and dummy parachutists loaded with rockets that exploded on impact – invented by Fairbanks – had the enemy fighting off the 'invasion'.

In his gunboat, Fairbanks came under attack by an Italian destroyer and an armed yacht. The *Aphis* was badly damaged and virtually immobilized but as German shells pounded the sea on every side of him, Fairbanks set up a smokescreen and manoeuvred unseen into a tactically superior position. He opened fire on the enemy vessels and scored direct hits, sinking both ships.

For this action Fairbanks was awarded the Legion of Merit with Valour Clasp. His commendation stated that 'the success of the operation as judged by subsequent intelligence reports was to a considerable degree due to the conception and thorough development of the special plans produced and to a considerable extent executed with considerable heroism by Lieutenant-Commander Fairbanks'.

He also received the British Distinguished Service Cross and the French Légion d'honneur.

This was his last action in the war, and in August 1944 he was recalled to Washington for staff duties with the Strategic Plans Division of the Navy Department.

Audie Murphy, in the main part of the invasion, landed on Yellow Beach at Ramatuelle, then moved inland. Two friends with him were hit and killed. Alone, he turned a corner and came face to face with two Germans. They hesitated, and Murphy shot them both with his carbine.

He found himself in a one-man battle against Germans with automatic weapons dug in on a hill. Knowing his carbine was inadequate, he rushed to a nearby farmhouse and borrowed a machine gun from a squad of GIs. He ran to a ditch and set up the gun but found he was too low down, firing way over the heads of the enemy positions. He moved out into the open, despite lack of cover, fired several bursts and then advanced with the machine gun in his hands. He took out a number of the enemy and withdrew back to the ditch.

He was joined by Private Brandon who had been with him since Sicily. The Germans shouted that they wished to surrender. Before Murphy could warn Brandon, the private stood up and was shot. Murphy held him as he died. Thirsting for revenge, he stood up and rushed forward throwing hand grenades and wiping out a German MG42 machine-gun post.

He picked up the machine gun and started up the hill, charging the German position which had killed his friend.

Firing from the hip, he killed the entire gun crew. Further resistance on the hill was destroyed by other advancing GIs.

Murphy and two of his men set out across country to join other units of their division which were driving further inland. In the wood, Murphy and the two GIs came across a German observation post manned by eight soldiers which they promptly captured.

French forces headed west for the ports of Toulon and Marseilles, and spurred on by the thought of liberating their homeland, they secured both ports on 28 August, by which time the Germans were retreating northwards up the Rhône Valley. Murphy, now with the rest of his division, approached Montélimar. Lieutenant General Alexander M Patch, hoping to trap the Germans, ordered the infantry divisions to bypass Montélimar and attack from the rear.

During the fight for Montélimar, Murphy found himself pinned down by two 88mm guns and heavy small-arms fire. He managed to acquire a bazooka and fired three shells into the German ammunition dump. The resulting explosion allowed the American infantry to advance swiftly with tanks, and the Germans surrendered.

During a house-to-house search for hidden snipers, Murphy entered a room and came upon what he described as 'a terrible looking creature with a tommy gun. His face was black, his eyes red and glaring.' Murphy opened fire without a second thought. Glass shattered before him. He had shot his own reflection in a mirror.

A GI who came up behind him said, 'That's the first time I ever saw a Texan beat himself to the draw.'

Moving up towards the border with Switzerland, Murphy was among the troops who took Besançon. As he stood talking to two friends, a mortar landed at their feet. All three were blown into the air. When Murphy regained consciousness, he found he was sitting next to a crater with a broken carbine in his hands. The other two men were dead. Three others standing nearby were wounded. He had injured only his foot and had to be hospitalized for a few days.

22

From India to the Pacific

'Then he shot me in the ass, although I didn't know exactly
where I was hit, only that I was hit.'

Lee Marvin

The Japanese in Burma had had little to fear from the Allies
since 1942. The war in Europe had been placed first in priority, the Pacific second and the China–Burma–India campaign
last. America wanted to drive the Japanese from China and
use the country as a base against Japan, but Britain had no
interest beyond recapturing Burma and Malaya.

The newly formed 14th Army under General William
Joseph Slim, which became known as the 'Forgotten Army',
pushed south through the jungles and malaria swamps of
Arakan's Mayu Peninsula on the coast of Burma near the border in January 1943. Jack Hawkins and the Cross Keys
followed the 14th who were eventually pushed back in May to
where they started.

The Indian heat, disease and bad food made it a debilitat-
ing base for the British troops. Because of logistic and
administrative difficulties planned operations for the push
back into Burma were cancelled in the dry season of 1943.
However, the combined efforts of the RAF and US 10th Air
Force in 1943 began seriously to threaten Japan's air superiority over Burma and, as the months passed, the Japanese began
to realize that its forces in Burma could no longer remain on
the defensive.

The theatre of war on the India–Burma front affected Captain Jack Hawkins only in terms of where his next show would be. With the Cross Keys in Bombay in mid-1943, he met Eric Dunstan, the distinguished broadcaster and journalist, who was in India with a small branch of ENSA. With virtually no staff of his own, he asked Hawkins to join him.

Dunstan needed permission from General John Grover who asked exactly what Hawkins's role would be. Dunstan replied that Hawkins would be his second-in-command. Grover promptly promoted Hawkins to major and handed him over to ENSA.

Not long after, the Second Division was sent to the front line in preparation for the push into Burma. Many men that Hawkins had known were lost in the campaign. He was grateful to providence that he too didn't end his days 'as a corpse in some tangled corner of the Burmese jungle'.

As with the real theatre of war, Hawkins discovered that ENSA, too, considered India as the least priority. Many entertainers who were sent to India as a mere way of winding up final months of contracts arrived exhausted, often with vital equipment and musical instruments missing. As far as Hawkins was concerned, it 'was a complete shambles'.

He received a cable from Cairo that he was to expect a company of actors who would arrive in Bombay on New Year's Day, 1944. They were picked up at the docks by Major Donald Neville-Willing, one of Captain Hawkins's staff, and taken to Green's Hotel where Hawkins came to meet them.

The first of the company he met was Doreen Lawrence, 'a tall fair-haired girl with a lovely figure who in the midst of this shambles appeared completely composed, impressing me immediately'. He was less impressed with the rest of the company who had been performing *Private Lives* in West Africa and Cairo. One actor was deaf in one ear, the stage manager had a wooden leg and the leading man was shell-shocked.

Unable to get the leading man to remember his lines, Hawkins replaced him with a young officer, Philip Ashley, whom he had seen in an amateur production of the same play in Poona.

During the two weeks' rehearsal, Hawkins became quite enamoured of his leading lady. After the successful opening in Bombay, Prince Aly Khan threw a party for the actors in his house. There were gallons of French champagne and a private orchestra which played on the terrace overlooking the sea. It created a romantic backdrop for Hawkins's romantic advances upon Doreen.

Aly Khan befriended Hawkins and Doreen, and arranged a picnic for the company at Juhu Beach. A sumptuous buffet was spread out inside a huge marquee. Gramophone records provided the music and ice-cold Martinis were served. It was the archetypal scene of British imperialism in colonial India.

During the party the shell-shocked actor, who had been reduced to playing a lesser role, got drunk and persuaded a high-born Indian lady to get into a truck with him. Her screams brought the rest of the company running to the truck where she accused the officer of attempting to rape her. He was arrested and sent back to England in disgrace.

The troops in India were in dire need of some morale. For every soldier wounded in India in 1943, 120 fell ill. Hawkins's ENSA group had no transport of its own and he had to beg lifts in military transports to take *Private Lives* on tour. But there was little enough transport available in the campaign to hold back the Japanese who were keeping the front lines hard-pressed.

The army complained of the lack of much-needed entertainment and the ENSA head office in Drury Lane, London, demanded an explanation from Hawkins as to why he was not providing 'blanket coverage' of India. Angry and frustrated, he drew up a map with India superimposed over Europe to show that the distance between Bombay and Calcutta was the same as from London to Moscow. It put an end to the demands for 'blanket coverage'.

The rising tide of illness struck the company; Philip Ashley went down with dysentery. The rest of the company couldn't get out of Bombay and it was decided that they would have to go back to England. Hawkins and Doreen had fallen in love and were desperate not to be parted. They were sitting in a bar in Bombay harbour trying to think of a way out of the situation when in walked a friend of Doreen's, actor Dominic Roche. He was doing clerical work in a transit camp and with little else to do he was able to arrange to join Hawkins's ENSA group. The following week another young actor arrived in a convoy and Hawkins quickly acquired him.

While the rest of the original company left for England, Doreen and another actress remained behind to appear with Hawkins's two new actors in a farce called *Love in a Mist*, the story of two young couples, one on honeymoon and the other on a dirty weekend. 'This was perfect entertainment for the sex-starved troops,' said Hawkins.

On the day the play was to open, the new young actor went down with a fever and Hawkins had to take his place. It was arranged so that the rest of the cast would prompt him whenever he gave the signal – a stammer – that he was about to dry up. His stammering 'gave the dirtiest meanings to even the most innocent lines', and the audience roared with hysterical laughter. After that the play was in demand, and with the young officer back in his role, the company toured the whole of central and eastern India, then Ceylon. Then they followed the 14th as it pushed across the Burmese border into Imphal which had been secured from the Japanese in July 1944 by Slim's 14th, and where Slim received his knighthood. In November the Japanese were chased back over the Chindwin River and Doreen and the rest of the small company were the first entertainers in the battle area.

Hawkins, meanwhile, expanded ENSA and moved his headquarters to Calcutta to be closer to the action. He had managed to acquire a garrison theatre and his efforts to improve the quality of entertainment were rewarded when John Gielgud arrived to perform *Hamlet*, followed by Edith Evans in *The Late Christopher Bean*.

Hawkins went to Imphal and found his small company thoroughly exhausted and in need of some leave, so he sent them to Assam to recover. Any suggestion that these entertainers did little to further the war effort by simply putting on shows is laid to rest by a a signal Hawkins received from

General Sir William Slim. It read, 'I must protest in the strongest possible terms at your withdrawal of the play company *Love in a Mist*. I insist on its immediate return.'

Hawkins went to Slim's headquarters and argued that the company needed to rest. Slim finally relented, and the company were allowed to recoup their energies before rejoining the 14th in its drive through to Mandalay.

John Ford, exiled from the Pacific because of his audacious flouting of rules and his bare-faced nerve in criticizing the US Navy over its lack of preparedness at Pearl Harbor, was sent to North Africa where he covered the first two months of the invasion.

He was recalled to New York where, on 19 September 1943, he was put, literally, on a slow boat to Calcutta. It was, in fact, a voyage calculated to keep him out of the way of furious admirals and generals. Donovan, commander of the OSS, told him he had to keep his head down, and the fifty-five-day voyage towards the Far East would do just that. *En route*, they stopped off at Cuba, Australia and Ceylon.

Ford took his camera crews up to Nazira in Assam, and then to the Burma front where he and his men came under Colonel Carl Eifler, commander of the OSS in the Far East. General Donovan also arrived to go with Eifler behind the Japanese lines with the US guerrilla fighters. Following them were John Ford's cameramen (although Ford himself probably remained at base camp as at age forty-eight and with only one good eye he was in no shape to engage in guerrilla warfare in the Burmese jungles). Donovan had been ordered to capture on film the effect of the OSS to prove to Congress that their funding and support was justified by the jungle warfare in Burma.

Ford was then sent to China, to Chungking in the mountainous west where the Chinese leader, Chiang Kai-Shek, had been driven after the Japanese overran most of the country in 1942. Ford was to take film of the US troops under the command of General Joseph W Stilwell fighting alongside the Chinese. The film would be used to influence the military and

Congress to send more reinforcements and supplies to China. What Ford's film didn't capture was why Stilwell was known as 'Vinegar Joe'. He was tetchy and quick-tempered and managed to argue with almost everybody.

Under orders from Washington, Stilwell had to act as Chiang's chief of staff, but he was angered by the corruption and incompetence widespread in Chiang's regime. He demanded that those responsible be purged and that Chiang stop fighting the communists and join with their leader, Mao Tse-tung.

Of more concern to Ford was that the first camera crew dropped by supply planes were all killed, and he had to replace them. The fact that Ford and his crews were shooting film rather than live ammunition did not make them immune from fatalities. Ford was then moved to the Pacific; even while the Japanese were being pushed back through Burma, they were also hard-pressed in the Pacific.

Following the US Navy's victory at Midway, the Allies had begun the difficult task of recapturing the Pacific islands seized by the Japanese during the first six months of 1942. Guadalcanal was won back from the Japanese in February 1943, and in May 1943, the US 7th Infantry stormed ashore on Attu Island in the Aleutians. Naval bombardment and bombing attacks failed to destroy the Japanese defences but the Americans fought on for twenty days and by the end of the month almost all of the Japanese had been killed or committed suicide. Kiska was abandoned by the Japanese and fell into American hands in August 1943.

Serving on board B-25 bombers in the Aleutians was Charlton Heston, a staff sergeant radio operator. He said very little about his war experiences except, 'I succeeded in not getting shot.' Nevertheless, the battle to win back the Aleutians in 1943 cost around a thousand American lives.

In June 1943, the Allies launched Operation 'Cartwheel' with the intention of cutting Tokyo off from its South-east Asian empire. General McArthur moved west through northern New Guinea while Admiral Halsey 'hopped' his way up the Solomon Islands.

On board the sub-tender *Proteus*, Tony Curtis had seen little action, so when he heard an officer ask the crew,' Which of you gobs want to be officers?' he immediately raised his hand. 'I rather fancied the idea of wearing a gold braid and having everyone salute me,' he said.

He reported for an interview and underwent an IQ test. A mathematical problem was set before him: seven plus four. He knew the answer, but it took him longer to come up with it than the officer was prepared to give him, and the paper was snatched away. 'How can a bright kid like you be so dumb?' asked the officer.

Curtis went back to being a third-class signalman and, determined to find a more dangerous duty, as well as one that paid better, he volunteered for submarine service. He was transferred to the submarine *Dragonette* where endless weeks of monotony at sea set in. The only film they had on board was *Gunga Din* which starred one of Curtis's idols, Cary Grant. Curtis said, 'We used to run that picture over and over until we all knew the words. We ran it with sound, without sound, and we did all the different voices. I was Cary Grant, and someone else was Douglas Fairbanks Jr, and we were all those actors.' Watching that film over and over remained his prime memory of his service on board a submarine.

Since the First World War, the Marshall Islands in the mid-Pacific had been Japanese territory. Admiral Chester Nimitz, in charge of central Pacific operations, proposed taking Kwajalein atoll which was the main enemy stronghold on the Marshalls, bypassing virtually all the other islands in the chain.

In December 1943, the US fleet bombarded the islands, and the Japanese, expecting the Americans to attack each island in turn, distributed its forces through the islands. But Nimitz intended to surprise the Japanese only on Kwajalein.

While the bombardment was in progress, in a dock at Algiers Island, just off New Orleans, a new patrol craft, number 1139, was all set to go to sea. Its crew of seventy-two were virtually all green, including Kirk Douglas as its communications officer. Only two of five officers had been to sea before. The skipper had only been once.

A small naval band played and a chaplain blessed the ship. Douglas, only just married, was officer of the deck, and his new wife, Diana, stood and watched, waiting to wave goodbye with the other wives and girlfriends. Douglas recalled:

It was the most embarrassing launch of any ship ever. We were tied alongside other boats in the dock, and when we went to pull out, our crew was so green we bounced first against the dock, then backed into a ship behind us and virtually sank it. Then we bumped against a ship in front of us and ripped a life raft from it. It was like that movie, *The Wackiest Ship in the Army* with Jack Lemmon. My wife was laughing but everybody else was embarrassed, and after that we sailed off down the Mississippi.

Douglas soon became seasick and was extremely relieved when they reached Miami where they stayed for two weeks while the ship was equipped with radar. In late January 1944, they set sail for the Panama Canal and the South Pacific.

On 1 February 1944, Nimitz launched his attack on Kwajalein. Lee Marvin was 'in that particular shindig'. He told me his story:

I was in a divisional reconnaissance company and we had to go in the night before the dawn assault and try to reconnoitre a route. We were put down by an assault personnel destroyer in rubber boats; there were around twelve guys in each boat and I guess a hundred and ten of us in all, and you can bet we lost half at sea.

So we land and then wander around and not see a fucking thing because you didn't want to see a fucking thing. All you wanted to do was get the hell off that island. If you were fired on you were supposed to throw your poncho over your head, whip out a flashlight and draw an X on the map to show where the fire was coming from. I don't think anybody ever threw a poncho over their head, and nobody fired back either because you knew that if you fired back, then the Japs would know your position and then you'd be dead, right?

So we all got lost and then we'd wait for the sun to come up – *if* you were still alive – and then you saw the whole United States Navy out there and if they thought you were the Japs they'd start shelling you. You end up getting fired on by the Americans *and* the Japs and you know if you stay on the island you won't stand a chance, so you swim out to a reef and pray and hope that God is listening. Forget all that bravery crap. You're shit scared and you never forget every shit-scared moment of it all.

After four days of ferocious fighting, the Japanese on Kwajalein capitulated. The battle to take the Marshall Islands ended in success for the Americans on 22 February with the capture and occupation of Eniwetok and Engebi atolls.

Meanwhile, PC 1139's crew enjoyed a twenty-four-hour layover in Panama before leaving on a rendezvous for a series of war games with a submarine off the Galapagos Islands. They practised tracking and attacking, and Kirk Douglas thoroughly enjoyed himself. 'It was fun,' he said, 'like play acting.'

Ready at last for war, the patrol craft escorted a cargo ship to Hawaii. All day long, the sound of the sonar searching for Japanese submarines echoed as a *ping, ping, ping* on the bridge. Before long the sonar began bouncing off a shape in the water, and the crew knew they had found a submarine. Their 'mousetraps', small bombs on a rack forward on the ship, were released. They exploded only on contact, and when they heard an explosion, they knew that they had hit the submarine.

Kirk Douglas, as gunnery officer, took up position astern while the skipper slowly turned back towards the area of the explosion.

'Release depth charge marker,' ordered the skipper. This was a green slick to mark the water where depth charges were to be dropped. Douglas relayed the message. Moments later an explosion lifted the ship, sending the crew flying, and throwing Douglas against the bulkhead.

At first they thought they had been hit by a torpedo, but it turned out that instead of a marker being released, someone had accidentally fired off a depth charge which appeared to have exploded prematurely.

The captain sent off a signal reporting a possible hit; they didn't know for sure what had happened to the submarine. Then the crew set about trying to repair the damage. Douglas, in agony and with bruises all over his stomach, tried to carry on. Another of the crew came down with appendicitis, and after Douglas radioed for instructions, they set sail for Manzanilla in Mexico. There the sick sailor was hospitalized while Douglas took the opportunity to have a feast.

When they set sail up the coast to San Diego, he felt ill and was still in severe pain. On arrival in San Diego, he stood as officer of the deck, but before long he was too ill to continue and was taken to the Naval Hospital. He had internal injuries and dysentery.

Because of the seriousness of the amoebic dysentery which showed no indication of clearing up in the near future, Kirk Douglas was discharged from the navy in June 1944. That was the end of the war for him, while that month the Americans turned their attention to capturing the Mariana Islands.

On 11 June the Americans bombed the airfields of Saipan, Tinian and Guam in the Marianas. US battleships followed on the 15th, depositing 20,000 American troops on Saipan's shores. Among them was Marine Lee Marvin who once more slipped into a rubber boat, wondering if this time he'd get his 'meal ticket'.

We landed on Yellow Beach, south of a place called Challantanoa, on the morning of the first day. We crawled forward on our bellies and made it to the beach scrub. Beyond were open fields and in the fields were planted thousands of sticks with saki bottles on them. I assumed they were used as insulators for wires that had been knocked out. I was wrong. The Japs were using them as artillery markers. They knew exactly how to checkmate us in that field. They couldn't miss as we crawled into these fields, and the artillery pounding hell out of us.

We finally got to a large trench some 1,800 yards from the shore. We just dived in as the Jap artillery threw every damn thing they had at us.

So there we were in this trench with the world exploding around us and thanking God we'd found these trenches to give us cover. Then I saw that the parapets of a trench ahead of us had slits in them and I realized they belonged to the Japs, and I was just saying 'Hey, you guys, I think this is a Jap trench', when they opened up on us.

We cleared outa there – the whole trench was emptied and it had to be 3,000 yards long.

Then it was night. There were about thirty yards between them and us. We fought through the night and we lost quite a few men. The sun came up and we were ordered to take Aslito airfield, so that's the direction we went in, going through those cane fields with the artillery blowing us up. We lost some more of our guys and they pulled us out. End of third day.

Fourth day dawns. We went into what they later called Death Valley and you could tell it was. We were going up this mountain called Tapotchau. Well, I thought, if I lived long enough I might get to the top of it. It didn't look that hard. Of course they had Japs up there, so nobody could get up far enough. They sent one company in and lost a lot of men. The survivors were called back, and they sent us in. It was night then.

I was the point man of the company so I went up there with a guy called Mike Harrison. We went one way, the second and third platoons went another way, and God knows which way the fourth went.

We were climbing and suddenly Mike got it through

the chest. I thought he'd got it in the lung because the blood was pink. I didn't know what the hell to do so I just stuck my finger in the hole in his chest to try to stop the blood coming out. I didn't know what I was doing. You just do things because you're desperate and I was desperate for Mike not to die. I was fucking mad then. I lifted my Browning automatic and just started firing at whatever was coming my way, using just one hand because the other had a finger stuck in Mike's lung. We had machine-gun fire coming at us at point-blank range. Anyway, Mike was dead and I just kept on firing. We were all firing like crazy for about fifteen minutes but I don't know if we actually hit any of 'em.

Then the Captain shouted for us to fall in. We'd had about 250 men. Now there were only six of us. I couldn't get to the rest of them, and I don't know if anyone else could because we were in this ambush and we were being decimated.

Suddenly there was this Jap almost on top of me. I couldn't see him in the dark. I was just flat on the ground. The first shot he got off at me hit the rubber heel of my left shoe. It made my leg kinda fling out and I just didn't know then if I'd been hit there. I was on my belly, and I turned my head to look up and there was a bang. He'd missed my face but he hit the ground so close that all the stuff that got thrown up by the bullet hit my eyes. I cried, 'Oh Jesus!' Then he shot me in the ass, although I didn't know then exactly where I was hit, only that I *was* hit.

'Jesus Christ, I'm hit.'

'Shut up, we're all hit.'

I yelled, 'But *I'm* hit, don't you *understand?*'

Then it got really confusing, if it hadn't been bad enough. The ammunition dumps were being blown up, we were counter-attacking, they were counter-attacking.

Two guys came and got me; Pettigrew and Shyte – what a name, Shyte! You don't know what kind of state you're in, you know. You don't know if you can move,

you don't know where you've been shot. You're just
stunned from the neck down. You could be shot through
the heart for all you know, except then you'd be dead,
but I was still alive. You go through the motions: can you
wiggle your toes? Yeah, I can wiggle my toes. Then you
try and move your feet, and I'm doing all this when Shyte
screams, 'Hey, Captain Marvel's hit in the ass' – that's
what they called me, Captain Marvel. So they got
Captain Marvel outa there and down that goddamned
mountain.

The next day they found twenty-seven gun emplacements surrounding our position. It's a wonder any of us
lived. The bullets were still flying. The MO dumped
some salt on my ass and a bandage, and he said, 'Lift
your ass so I can tie the bandage.' And I said, 'With all
that shit flying around, I'm not lifting my ass a sixteenth
of an inch higher than I need to.' There was no getting
carried outa there on a stretcher. You wouldn't have
lasted five seconds. So I had to crawl out, passing all
these guys I'd known lying dead.

I had a couple of medics with me and we got to a
clearing which was about twenty feet across, and you
knew if you stepped out there you'd get gunned down. I
was never going to crawl across anyway because I
couldn't use my legs, and the only way to get across that
clearing was to go like hell. So I told the medics, 'If you
can get me up on my legs and give me a shove, I might
make it.'

So they managed to get me on my feet and they gave
me an almighty push and I sort of half ran the first fifteen
yards and fell the last five, sliding into a scrub. I crawled
behind the biggest tree I could find and found a guy sitting there who I knew. His name was Rose. He just sat
there like there was nothing else happening and he said,
'Where're you hit?'

I said, 'In the ass.'

He said, 'Would you like some water?'

I said, 'Jesus, yes.'

He leaned over to get his canteen, gave it to me, I took a gulp, gave it back to him, he went to put it back and just then he got hit. He just went 'Oh!' and fell on top of me. I tried to get him off, but couldn't. He was dead but he just kept looking at me. By now I'm panicking.

They were bringing other guys out who'd been wounded. There was a guy called Calello. He got hit in the back of the skull. It was just a glancing blow but it made him blind. He was screaming and someone was hollering for stretcher bearers. Finally a couple of bearers got to him and while they were putting him on the stretcher, one of them was killed by a shot. Then the other got it in the back. Calello got it in the hip, and then he got hit again and again even while a couple of other guys were trying to get him on a stretcher. He was screaming kind of hysterically; he didn't know if he was alive or dead.

One guy came running by me and stepped right on my ass. I found out later I had this big hole just gaping open. They finally got me on a stretcher and I was thinking that machine-gun fire is about stretcher height, so I said, 'Do you have to put me on that?' But they carried me out, four of 'em, running real fast.

One of them said. 'Please, please', because it was too fast for him. He suddenly went down and I was all over the ground. They gathered me up again and off we went until they'd got me over a small ridge, just six feet high, and we had some cover at last. And when we get there, there's this whole battalion sitting back and smoking like nothing's happening.

One of the bearers said, 'Captain Marvel's been hit in the ass', so they took me back to battalion aid where the doc stood with a couple of Jap pistols in his belt and no shirt on.

He said, 'Do you need any blood?'

I said, 'How the fuck would I know? You're the doc.'

'Okay, put him over there.'

There were two kinds of men over there. There were

dead men over there, and there were the salvables over
here who were sitting round smoking cigarettes but you
just knew they were going to die.

They put me right behind a stack of mortar shells. We
had dumps of this stuff all over the place and every now
and then you heard one get hit and going up. I was just
waiting for a Jap mortar to hit my stack of shells.

One of our sergeants was in there. He was still walking
and they'd given him morphine, and when you're given
morphine, they mark you with an 'M', so he was walking
around with an 'M' on his head.

He said to me, 'You want some water?' He had it in a
plasma can.

I said, 'Love some, sergeant.' I took a mouthful and
suddenly WOOOOOM! About 150 yards away one of
the Japanese dumps we'd captured had been hit. I looked
up and I saw Marines flying through the air – slowly, you
know – it was like slow motion.

Then someone was shouting 'Counter-attack!
Counter-attack!'

I had no gun and I was really shit scared. They got
everybody out of there and back on to the beach. I was
one of the last four to go. They put two of us in a jeep
with the two medics, one with a pistol, and we took off.
We were really flying, except it turned out we were heading the wrong way. We were heading right into Jap
territory, and there they were right ahead of us.

One of the guys just screamed and the driver stopped.
The guy who screamed jumped out and the driver said,
'Get back in or I'll shoot you.' The guy got back in and
we turned about and we flew back the way we came, and
made it to the beach. It was about five in the afternoon
by then.

I was put in a tent, and a tent on the beach is the
worst place to be because that's where they're unloading
all the supplies and the Jap artillery is hammering the
beach. I'm asking, 'Can I get off this fucking island?'

A guy who's writing the tags says, 'Not tonight.'

But then he sees a landing craft going by and he hollers, 'Anyone going out?' Then they ran me out to the craft and put me on board.

I'm pumped up with morphine, the bleeding has pretty well stopped, and I'm face down on a stretcher and I'm really beginning to lose reality now. I can remember passing ships while we're looking for the nearest hospital ship. We pulled up alongside the *Solace* and the next thing I know I can see shiny black shoes in front of my face and I'm being lifted up and I'm put in a place with yellow walls and bright lights. The doctor or somebody is saying, 'Where are you hit?'

'In my ass.'

They got me to the urinary or some ward and put me down on a real bed. With a real mattress. And I'm saying, 'But it's got sheets on it . . . the blood from my ass . . .'

'That's okay.' And there I was on a real bed.

A guy comes along and says, 'You want an ice cream?' I've got a nine-inch hole in my ass, I'm spaced out on morphine and from somewhere I swear I could hear *Moonlight Serenade* on a piano. But I can still hear firing, and I don't know where the hell I am now.

I said, 'Can you turn the lights out?'

This guy said, 'It's okay. You're okay now.'

Now I begin to recognize some of the guys around me. They even dimmed the lights but you could still hear the gunfire and explosions on the beaches.

It all began to hit me. I started to cry. I felt like a coward. I felt like a deserter. I was ashamed. I wept because I'd run away. It really bugged me. I felt as if I'd as good as thrown down my rifle and run away. I'd fucked off. Left them to it. Of course, that wasn't the way it was at all, but all that morphine and *Moonlight Serenade* just made me feel that's the way it was, and I just cried and cried. Finally I fell asleep.

He was taken to a hospital on Guadalcanal and began

treatment for a severed sciatic nerve. Then they gave him the Purple Heart. Later he would always say, 'It's nothing to shout about. I was in this hospital ward and some guy came round and said, "What's your name?" "Marvin." He threw it across the bed and that was it. Everyone who didn't turn and run was given one.'

It turned out he had been a millimetre away from being permanently paralysed and he spent the next thirteen months in different hospitals before being discharged.

The battle to win the Marianas went on without him. Off the shore, the submarine *Dragonette*, with Tony Curtis on board, helped to keep the Japanese Navy at bay.

The battle for Saipan was won by the Americans on 9 July. Then they moved on to invade Guam on 21 July and it was in American hands by 10 August. There the *Dragonette* reloaded its torpedoes. One of the loading chains broke and Tony Curtis got in the way. His back was badly injured and he couldn't move or feel his legs.

He was taken to a base hospital where he lay paralysed, convinced he would never walk again despite the encouragement of the doctors and nurses who consoled him. Seven weeks later he walked out of hospital.

Unfit for further submarine duty, he was returned to the *Proteus* and resumed his duties as third-class signalman.

There was another yet-to-be discovered Hollywood star out in the Pacific. Paul Newman was a radio man in naval torpedo planes 'which never actually fired torpedoes,' he said. He had been selected for the Naval Air Corps Officer Training scheme initially but had been dropped from the course at Yale University after four months because he was found to be colour blind. He was reassigned as air corps radioman third class and served at Hawaii, Guam and Saipan.

There was a further Pacific campaign, to take the Palau Islands. It was a costly victory that took from 15 September to 21 October, with nearly 2,000 men lost.

Then came General Douglas MacArthur's historic landing on the Philippines. He had been forced to flee in 1942 with the famous promise, 'I shall return.' He did, on 20 October 1944.

23
Up to the Siegfried Line

'The last thing the Allies needed was a dispute between the Allied leaders. Montgomery and Patton just couldn't agree on how to bring the war to its conclusion.'

David Niven

Bodies, vehicles and dead horses lay scattered along the road from Falaise which the fleeing Germans had used as one of their major escape routes. Dirk Bogarde, travelling the road in his jeep, got out when he saw French peasants rifling through the pockets of dead German soldiers and French civilians, looking for jewellery, wallets, watches, anything of value. A small boy was holding a tin can and a woman was using a hammer and chisel to remove the gold teeth from the body. Bogarde approached the boy who showed him that his tin was full of blooded gold teeth.

A German staff car riddled with bullets lay in a ditch. In the back seat was the body of a beautiful young French woman in a silk dress and a silver fox fur. An SS officer lay lifeless across her lap, his face blown away. Bogarde was used to the sight of dead soldiers. But the sight of the attractive woman shocked him into silence.

The woman with the hammer and chisel saw him looking at the car and said, 'Sale Boche! Collaboratrice!'

He got into his jeep and motioned for the driver to carry on. The bulldozers were arriving to clear the dead from the road. He turned to see an old man wearing the silver fox fur and dancing in the road.

*

The liberation of France sped up and George Stevens and his crew raced towards Paris, crossing the Seine via the army's pontoon bridge. On 23 August Eisenhower agreed to give the Free French the honour of liberating Paris. Units of the French 2nd Armoured Division moved into the outskirts of the city. Stevens saw a unique opportunity to record the crowning moment of the liberation of Paris, and in a field he approached a Free French general to ask permission to join them on their entry into the city.

The Free French troops entered the capital on 25 August 1944. Stevens and his crew were the only non-French to be a part of it. Stevens had barely set up his cameras outside Montparnasse Station, which would act as the headquarters of Major General Jacques Philippe Leclerc of the Free French, when Leclerc arrived in his armoured car. With him was Major General Dietrich von Choltitz, the commander of the German garrison; he had agreed to surrender Paris rather than see it destroyed, despite Hitler's orders to burn the capital to the ground.

Stevens filmed as von Choltitz climbed out of the armoured car and was led inside the Free French HQ. A large crowd began to gather, making the German commander anxious for his life.

Following the formal surrender inside the French HQ, Leclerc came out with von Choltitz and called over George Stevens. He wanted Stevens to film the former German garrison commander, and he personally explained on camera that it was von Choltitz's prompt capitulation which had saved the city.

Stevens filmed other German officers being rounded up and taken off under armed escort. At 4.30 that afternoon General de Gaulle arrived to tremendous adulation from the French. Then came the US troops. The celebration in the streets was as exhilarating for French and Americans alike. 'It was intoxicating,' said Ivan Moffat.

George Stevens and his cameramen were made as welcome as any fighting soldier. Cameraman Jack Muth said, 'Unless you lived through it and had been there, you couldn't imagine how the Allies were greeted. The French populace went crazy and the girls were absolutely wild and were climbing on cars and kissing you and carrying on and giving you a drink. There were girls and more girls and more girls. They were all over the place. You had to beat them off.'

But not all the Germans had surrendered. Snipers fired down from the rooftops. Stevens took film of US troops, French soldiers and Resistance fighters taking out a sniper.

Four days later came the enormous victory parade. George Stevens set his cameramen up all over the place. For a short while it seemed that the war was almost over. Meanwhile British, Canadian and Polish troops advanced on the Channel ports towards Belgium.

Said David Niven:

The last thing the Allies needed was a dispute between the Allied leaders. Montgomery and Patton just couldn't agree on how to bring the war to its conclusion, and distorted versions of their differences filtered down to the fighting troops. Montgomery wanted to strike at the Ruhr, insisting that that would destroy the enemy's fighting capability. This upset Patton because Montgomery needed reinforcements from the US 1st Army which would have halted Patton's advance on Metz. So General Barker had his work cut out trying to defuse the rumours while General Eisenhower tried to sort out his prima donnas. The problem was not only one of strategy but also egos.

Barker told me to get to Paris with important documents which I had to deliver to an American colonel in the bar of the Hôtel Crillon. I was given a jeep and a driver – an American corporal. We got to Neuilly and got lost, but I had some friends in Neuilly and, finding their apartment, I told the corporal to wait with the jeep. He was busy anyway as the citizens of Neuilly descended on the corporal with kisses and bottles of wine.

I went inside and my old friends fed and watered me and let me bathe, and when I came back out the corporal had disappeared with the jeep, apparently borne off on the crest of hysterical grateful citizenry.

Fortunately I had the documents on my person so, borrowing a woman's bicycle and fixing two Union Jacks to it, I cycled along the Champs Elysées as the people waved and cheered at seeing what was probably the first British soldier they had seen in five years. I arrived at the Hôtel Crillon, went to the bar and there found the colonel and my corporal. I promptly delivered the secret documents and had a drink to celebrate my single-handed British occupation of Paris.

Actually, Niven may not have been the very first British soldier seen by the French of Paris. Dirk Bogarde and Chris Greaves also entered the city against all the rules.

It was Greaves's idea to take a look at Paris. 'But only the Free French and the Americans are permitted to enter the city,' Bogarde pointed out. 'It's forbidden to the British.'

'Damned unfair. We've got every right to be there. Better take a teetotal driver with us.'

On the morning of 26 August, Bogarde, Greaves and their driver climbed into the jeep and set off for Paris where they found a bar and drank to the liberation of the French capital. Only the teetotal driver remained sober.

'We must liberate another town as soon as one becomes available,' they decided.

William Wyler also turned up in Paris. He had returned to London after his Italian mission but, hoping to take part in the liberation of his home town of Mulhouse, he sent John Sturges and Lester Koenig back to the United States with their film of the Thunderbolts while he followed the Allies' advance.

In Paris Wyler met up with George Stevens and asked him if he could assign him a jeep, a driver and a camera so he could shoot film at the front.

Stevens obliged with the jeep and a driver, Leicester Hemingway, the younger brother of Ernest Hemingway. They set off north toward the Luxembourg–Belgian border. Hearing warplanes, they stopped and began filming. They continued on and when they stopped again Wyler left Hemingway in the jeep, and crawled towards an observation shack where there was a GI with a field telephone looking over the hillsides and valley below. Wyler told the GI that the place looked peaceful.

'Peaceful? It's crawling with Germans,' replied the GI.

The phone rang and the GI picked it up. 'Shit! We're surrounded.' Wyler said, 'What do we do?'

'Nothing. Just wait.'

They scanned the countryside looking for any sign of an attack. Half an hour passed. There was hardly a sound and Wyler grew increasingly nervous. The phone rang again. The GI answered it, then he drawled, 'It's okay. We're not surrounded any more.'

Wyler had thought this time he really might be killed.

The Stars in Battledress were never far behind the British lines. Sergeant Charlie Chester was standing guard at a house with all the props and the piano when a bullet whizzed past his ear. He wondered if it was from a German who had somehow been left behind. He dug the bullet out of the door where it had embedded, and kept it as a paperweight (as he still does today) as a memento of 'the one that wasn't meant for me'.

Janet Brown recalled how the rain poured down when she was about to go out and entertain the troops. The rain didn't put them off and they kept filing into the field, using their gas capes to keep them from getting too wet while Janet had to go out and get soaked. But she knew that it was worth it given what these boys had done.

The next day her unit came across an old factory the Germans had used. It seemed the best venue available with the rain still teeming down. She remembered how the soldiers 'piled in and planted themselves on the derelict machinery, on the rafters, on sandbags on the floor, and those who couldn't get in stuck their heads through the broken windows. They made it pretty plain how much they enjoyed the show. It was their first break since D-Day.'

A star in battledress who was never an official part of SIB

(but should have been) was Sergeant Frankie Howerd. He had suffered severe malnutrition from his eleven days on board ship outside Mulberry harbour. When he was fit he was posted to Lille in northern France.

He told me, 'This officer came round asking if anyone spoke French and I said, "Well, yes, a little bit." The officer gabbled something in French and I said, "Oui." He said something else – I've no idea what – and I said, "Non." He said, "Right, you're now an interpreter." So I tried to explain that my French really wasn't that good, and he said, "Never mind, we're a bit short, so you'll do."'

So off he went to Lille. Shortly after, on 3 September, the Allies liberated Brussels where Sergeant Howerd was posted, seconded to the military government.

'I wanted to know who we were governing, and they said, "The Germans soon, because we're winning the war." I said, "That's one blessing, anyway."'

He was sent to a village with a major who didn't speak a word of French:

> We were trying to make a record of expectant mothers so that they would get priority when the food was distributed. The major told me, 'It's all very simple. All you've got to do is tell them we want to know of any women who are pregnant.'
>
> I didn't know the word for pregnant, so I practised how to say, 'We'd like to know if any woman is going to have a baby.' I worked it as , 'Nous voulons savoir si une femme allons avoir un enfant'. If you speak French, you'll know the balls-up I made.
>
> So I went round the village, asking the question and adding a few 'Oo-la-lahs' for good measure. The first woman I said it to just stared at me in horror. By the time I had asked four or five women, they were screaming and running away. One returned with her husband, a huge man with big muscles, and following him were men and women with pitchforks and clubs. I repeated my question to the big man, and he looked like he was going to kill me. Well, he *was* going to kill me.

I'd been asking if there was any woman who *wanted* to have a baby, as I found out later.

I decided to raise my rifle at him – only I'd left it at the hotel. So I turned and ran, got back to the hotel and informed the major of my little mistake, and we got in our jeep and evacuated ourselves from the village.

Then we got lost in a fog and we drove around while I tried to ask the local peasantry where we were. It turned out we had driven behind enemy lines. We were damned lucky not to get found by the Germans and shot at dawn. We turned about and found our way back across our own lines.

On learning that Brussels was in Allied hands, Dirk Bogarde and Chris Greaves arrived and, to help the Belgians celebrate their liberation, shared their rations of bully beef in a restaurant.

In London, Anthony Quayle was on two weeks' leave after his mission in Albania and activities in helping to establish the Italian government. In the middle of Piccadilly Circus, he ran into Eisenhower's naval aide. As they chatted, the American told Quayle about a vast airborne operation that was soon to be launched. He thought Quayle would be perfect for looking after the reporters who were going to be parachuting in. Without waiting for an answer, the American wrote down a contact name at the War Office and told him to report that afternoon.

Quayle had no desire to go to the War Office. He did not want to be part of another mission. He went back to Rome and saw out the rest of the war from there.

After what happened, he was probably very thankful he didn't decide to take part in what was an airborne attack on Arnhem.

Eisenhower had decided to go with Montgomery's plan which depended on the Allies seizing a number of vital river and canal crossings, especially on the Lower Rhine, among them a bridge at the Dutch town of Arnhem.

Patton was furious. General Barker and David Niven stage-managed attempts to maintain communications between the British and American forces; Patton was determined to go ahead with his own plans and he had to be brought into line.

The operation – code named 'Market Garden' – began on 17 September 1944. By the 26th the bridges at Veghel, Grave and Nijmegen were successfully captured.

Although a number of bridges had been secured, the battle to capture the bridge at Arnhem was a disaster. On 27 September, after ten days of desperate fighting for the 'bridge too far', the Allies withdrew.

Of the almost 10,000 troops and parachutists dropped during Operation 'Market Garden', only 2,163 made it back: 1,200 had died and 6,642 were taken prisoner.

Dirk Bogarde, seconded to an infantry division, sat one night in the mud and ice during a long, bitter winter. The Germans, in retaliation for the Allied attempt on Arnhem, had stopped movement of food in Holland and by November the Dutch on the other side of the Rhine, as Bogarde knew well, were starving.

He stared across the river that night and saw a group of Dutch people huddled and crying as they watched the desperate Allied soldiers trying to get back across to their own side, hanging on to blackened timber and rubber dinghies. The Dutch houses were in flames. Mortars and machine-gun fire rattled on. Tracer bullets seared through the darkness. At HQ they were saying that the operation had been a ninety per cent success. If this was success, Bogarde wondered, what would a ninety per cent failure look like?

He was bitter at the catastrophe and later wrote that they 'had no need of the books the generals might later write to explain things. We saw it happen before our eyes, unwilling witnesses to a shattering disaster.'

In 1977, on the set of the film *A Bridge Too Far*, he told journalist Iain Johnstone:

If I had known at twenty-four, when I was here in Arnhem, what I know today about this campaign, I'd have gone home. But that's hindsight. I think wars are totally inevitable. I'm too old to be wise about it. Unfortunately, I think youth seems to need it. It releases some violence in the human. There is something inherent in it that has to be contained by war, by violence. I don't think things will ever change and I don't think any world will ever see total peace. I think peace would be unhealthy.

During October 1944, in the mess in a château, Bogarde came across the brigadier to whom he had once been ADC. The brigadier had resented Montgomery assigning Bogarde to intelligence and even blamed Bogarde for his 'desertion'. In the mess, the brigadier asked Bogarde, 'Have you enjoyed your cushy job?' He was bitter at having lost so many men since Normandy. He told Bogarde, 'You won't find anyone you know here. All gone. Bloody lucky for you when you got out.'

Bogarde didn't try to explain; the brigadier wasn't listening. David Niven told me:

The autumn of 1944 was described by historians as a 'lull'. Not to the British airborne troops who had to fight for their lives at Arnhem. The whole thing was a shambles, but it is true that if we had taken Arnhem, it would have shortened the war. Montgomery thought that instead of tackling the Siegfried Line he would skirt the northern end and aim for Berlin. As it is, the so-called 'lull' was the slow progress towards the Ardennes.

The Allies had to come up with an alternative plan. Patton was obviously delighted since Eisenhower accepted the 'broad front' strategy whereby the Allies would attack in four areas. To Montgomery's 21st Army of British and Canadians fell the task of driving the enemy from the Scheldt estuary, opening the way clear for supply convoys to enter Antwerp and establishing a solid base for attacks on the Ruhr. Bradley's 12th Army Group was to take the border town of Aachen in

Germany, allowing Patton, further south, to advance with the 3rd Army towards the Rhine. The 6th Army Group under Lieutenant General Jacob Devers would penetrate the Vosges mountains and take Strasbourg.

Patton and his 3rd Army were stationed at Nancy in France. He was delighted when Captain Marlene Dietrich and her troupe moved to Nancy as part of her tour of the front.

He told her, 'Good will is not enough. It does the men good to know that you're at the front. They'll tell themselves the situation can't be so bad if Marlene Dietrich is here.'

He told her that she would be entertaining the troops in a building that was hardly more than a shed in a forest near Pont-à-Mousson. 'Begin the moment you're there,' he told her. 'Make it brief. The place is under sustained fire. Get back before it's dark.'

With the Germans fighting the Americans for every inch of Bastogne, she confided to Patton, 'I'm not afraid of dying, but I am afraid of being taken prisoner. I have a captain's rank. They'll shave off my hair, stone me and have me dragged by horses through the streets of Berlin.'

Patton gave her a pearl-handled revolver and told her, 'Shoot rather than surrender.'

She got into the jeep with a comedian from Oklahoma who had replaced Danny Thomas, and Lynn Mayberry, and they drove off. Reaching the top of a hill, they heard the hiss of approaching shells and tore down the hill at speed. They were nearing the shed when a heavy shell landed close by, throwing earth all over the jeep. Someone yelled to her, 'Crawl out. Open your eyes. Get going. Head for the shed.'

She crawled on all fours under the camouflage net and into the shed. It was full of soldiers exhausted from battle. She climbed on to a couple of crates and began to sing a saucy song. For ten minutes she distracted the soldiers as a thunderstorm began. It was growing dark outside as she finished the song. The comedian told a few gags and the girl from Texas sang a song. Dietrich walked among the GIs, touching their hands and telling them, 'Goodbye for now. See you again.'

She and her troupe rushed out to the jeep as gunfire came at them. They made for the hilltop and there an American guard stopped them at rifle-point. 'Identify yourselves,' he demanded.

Dietrich gave him their names, their base and the number of her regiment.

'What's the password?'

'I don't know the password.'

He asked her how many presidents the United States had. She could only tell him three. 'Why don't you know the password?' he demanded.

'We left our quarters before dawn. The password hadn't been given. We've got a guy who's a comedian from Oklahoma in the jeep and a girl from Texas.'

'Which song was number one in the summer and fall of 1941?'

'Ask the comedian, maybe he knows.'

The comedian did know, and they were allowed to continue into Nancy. It was against direct orders for the troupe to return to Nancy after dark. She went to the shattered building where she slept in a sleeping bag, and drank Calvados on an empty stomach. Then she threw up in the toilet, and drank some more.

She was exhausted, afraid and tired of enduring this way of living. But she had to sustain the morale of her small troupe, because it was their job to keep up the morale of the GIs. Before she could fall asleep, an MP entered and told her to report to General Patton.

She knew she was in trouble for getting back late. Her head hurt and she wanted only to sleep, but she followed the MP until he left her to find the rest of the way herself through the blacked-out town. Twice she got lost, but finally found Patton's quarters.

He remonstrated, as she had expected, but he was not as severe as she had feared. He even took an interest in the problems she and her troupe faced, and he told her, 'You are badly needed here at the front. But you've got to be back at your quarters before dark. I'll make sure you get the password every morning.'

She was so tired she was barely able to keep her eyes open. The general they called 'Blood and Guts' Patton lifted her in his arms and carried her to his command car, ordering his driver to get her back to her quarters.

The following morning there was no one to give them the password as she and the troupe started out again. They drove through the forest and arrived at their destination where they were given coffee before beginning the first of four performances.

It was dark when they returned. Once again they couldn't tell the guard the password. She got out of the jeep and walked over to him, and as soon as he recognized her, he said, 'Oh, it's you. Okay, you can go on through.'

It turned out that Patton's sense of humour had led him to decide on 'Cheesecake' for the password. All Marlene Dietrich had to do was be recognized.

It rained throughout the autumn, turning the ground to mud, keeping British troops bogged down in Nijmegen.

David Niven was sent by Barker into the battle zones. He came across 'A' Squadron stationed in waterlogged fields near Geldrop and spent a few days with them before moving on to Nijmegen. There, among the Welsh Guards, he met Anthony Bushell who had been Laurence Olivier's production manager and was now a company commander.

They stood reminiscing among the tanks when there was 'an appalling explosion'. Niven dived under a tank but Bushell remained standing, laughing at Niven who appeared to be the only man who had bothered to take cover.

'What the hell was that?' Niven asked.

Bushell told him the Germans had a 'bloody great gun' in a railway tunnel across the river. Every hour they wheeled it out and fired. 'We're used to it.'

In the south some progress was made. Audie Murphy was among the US troops and Free French who attacked the Vosges mountains on 16 November. Two days later they broke through the strategic 'Belfort Gap' which lay between the Vosges and Jura mountains. By 20 November, the French had reached the Rhine north of Basle.

Again Murphy displayed his reckless do-or-die aptitude for capturing several enemy positions single-handed. When his commander went out with four men to recce the area and became trapped in a quarry by enemy fire, Murphy, armed only with a carbine and grenades, went to the rescue. A hidden German machine gun opened up on him. He simply turned on them, killing five and wounding three others.

In another incident, Murphy stalked a sniper who had killed several soldiers. He found the sniper who tried to shoot him on sight, but Murphy fired first, sending two bullets into the German's forehead.

Later, another sniper wounded him in the hip. Murphy dropped to the ground as his helmet fell from his head. He saw the sniper aim at him one last time, and coolly shot the sniper between the eyes.

The wounded Murphy was put on the bonnet of a jeep and driven to a medical tent. He lay there for three days by which time his wound had turned gangrenous and he had to be evacuated to a hospital where doctors fought to save him with penicillin injections. They also had to remove five pounds of infected flesh. There he remained while, to the north, French and American troops seized the 'Saverne Gap' and took Strasbourg a few days later.

Patton had failed to reach the Rhine but did take Metz on 25 November. Montgomery took control of the Scheldt estuary, allowing the first Allied convoy into Antwerp on 28 November.

By early December 1944, the Allies had made slow progress and a thin line of American troops held the Ardennes. Rain had turned to snow which covered the wooded hills and valleys of eastern Belgium.

Around the middle of December, David Niven reported to the US 1st Army headquarters at Spa in the Ardennes to liaise with Captain Bob Lowe, a one-time reporter with *Time* who was working in 1st Army intelligence.

Captain Lowe showed Niven to the map room of the intelligence section. Niven claimed he never forgot exactly what Lowe said, pointing through the window at some hills.

'The other side of those hills there is a forest and in that forest they are forming the 6th Panzer Army, and any day now the 6th Panzer Army is going to come right through this room and out the other side, cross the Meuse, then swing right and go north to Antwerp.'

Niven asked him if he'd mentioned this to anyone.

'We've been telling them for days, three times a day.'

The following morning, 16 December, Niven went on to Marche and the Germans launched their offensive in the Ardennes; the Battle of the Bulge had begun, so-called because by Christmas Day the Germans had managed to punch a fifty-mile dent, or bulge, in the Allied lines.

Said Niven:

There was an SS colonel called Otto Skorzeny who was attached to the 6th Panzer Army. He could speak with an American accent and, with his men in American uniforms, he succeeded in infiltrating American lines and causing various acts of sabotage. They were called the Grief Commandos, and rumours of these commandos in American uniform ran wild and it was assumed they were on a mission to assassinate General Eisenhower at his headquarters in Versailles. This led to the interrogation of many real GIs and anyone else purporting to be an ally.

The GIs used trick questions like, 'What's the name of the president's dog?' I had quite a few anxious moments in the Ardennes in my British uniform and jeep with 21st Army Group markings. They'd stop me and tell me to put my hands above my head, pointing their guns at me and asking my name.

I told them I was David Niven and said, 'The actor, you must have seen some of my films.'

But they said, 'Anyone can claim to be David Niven. Who won the World Series in 1940?'

I told them I had no idea but I had made a picture with Ginger Rogers. That satisfied them I was the *real* David Niven.

Marlene Dietrich and her troupe had been moved to Bastogne, a market town close to the border with Luxembourg. The Germans were threatening to break through to Bastogne so, as a precaution, Dietrich's troupe were moved just south of the town.

Her hands were frostbitten; forever after they turned blue under spotlights. Her stage was often nothing more than the back of a flat-bed truck. She washed her face, hair and underwear in melted snow from her helmet. She drank Calvados to keep her warm, often vomiting it up afterwards.

There were rumours that the front would be strengthened by the Free French forces and that the 2nd Tank Division was nearby. Dietrich had heard that Jean Gabin had joined the 2nd Tank Division of the Free French.

She secured a jeep and set out to see if she could find Gabin. That evening she discovered the French tank division in a field, and she walked around the camp in search of Gabin. Then she saw peeking out of the tank hatch, looking away from her, an unmistakable grey-haired head. She called out, 'Jean!'

He turned around, saw her and uttered, '*Merde!*' He climbed out of the tank and embraced her. Just seconds later the signal sounded for the tanks to get into formation and he climbed back into his tank. They all moved into formation and that was the last she saw of Jean Gabin until after the war had ended.

The 2nd Panzer Division came close to capturing Bastogne on 17 December. Marlene Dietrich was literally shaken from sleep by GIs who told her, 'Clear out, clear out.'

Dietrich asked, 'How did they break through the lines.'

'Just get going. Head for Reims.'

'But that's way behind us.'

'Anyone ask for your opinion? No, then get going.'

They gathered their costumes, climbed into a jeep and drove out of Bastogne.

American tanks were sent against the Panzers and were overwhelmed by the German advance. The US 101st Airborne Division under Brigadier General McAuliffe joined the defence of Bastogne on 18 December.

Eisenhower ordered General Patton to suspend operations against the Germans in the Saarland and reinforce Bastogne. Before he could get there the Germans outside Bastogne, now in tremendous strength, offered McAuliffe terms to surrender.

McAuliffe responded by sending a written message, 'To the German Commander. NUTS! The American Commander.'

Patton arrived on 26 December and Bastogne was saved. William Wyler and Leicester Hemingway arrived too, Hemingway at the wheel and Wyler with his camera making dramatic dolly shots of what was left of the town.

He conducted interviews with some of the men of the 101st Airborne Division and then headed for Bradley's headquarters in Luxembourg. There, Wyler met General Vanderberg who had been so impressed with *Memphis Belle* that he wanted Wyler to make a film about his 9th Air Force. He had film of the battle for Bastogne taken by his own men which he wanted Wyler to compile. He put Wyler on a plane with some captured German officers and sent him to London to view the footage. Wyler was unimpressed and managed to hitch a flight back to Luxembourg to tell Vanderberg that he could not make his film.

The winter conditions caused abject misery for the fighting troops. Among the hazards they faced was trenchfoot to which thousands of men succumbed. George Stevens's cameraman Dick Kent was ordered to make a film about the dangers of trenchfoot. He said, 'An army in winter is not very happy especially at the front; it's just miserable trying to keep warm, trying to meet the enemy, obeying orders, and Christmas away from home was demoralizing.'

On Christmas Day, Stevens and his men hung hand grenades on a Christmas tree and handed out gifts to the little children. He even received a present from his own children – a small case.

Among the 600,000 American troops who found themselves in the middle of the Battle of the Bulge was a young Jewish comic called Mel Brooks. He said:

I'm just an American Jewish kid. Eighteen years old. They put me in a uniform, they put us all in trucks, they drive us to the railroad station, put us on a locked train with the windows blacked out. We get off the train, we get on a boat. We get off the boat, we get into trucks. We're in the Ardennes. We get out of the trucks, we start walking. Suddenly all around us Tiger tanks! We're surrounded by the Germans. It's the Battle of the Bulge. And it ain't like the film, believe me.

'Hands up!' they tell us.

'Wait a minute,' I say, 'we only just got here from Oklahoma. We're the Americans. We're supposed to *win!*'

So we run like hell and they're shooting at us. And we're going, 'Oh God! Oh Christ!' I mean, he might help. He was Jewish too.

The British were there as well. Lieutenant Richard Todd had been sent back to England after crossing the Seine. But he returned just before Christmas 1944 to help defend the River Meuse bridges. The 6th Airborne Division had few men, and they drove through large areas of forests in jeeps with Bren guns mounted which they fired to make the Germans believe the area was heavily defended.

Appalling snowstorms hampered Patton's progress at pushing back the Panzers but his efforts were aided by Montgomery's advance towards Houffalize, Belgium, on 3 January 1945. On 15 January Patton and Montgomery converged on Houffalize, and by the end of the month the cream of Hitler's forces had been largely destroyed. By 20 January the enemy had been contained and by 10 February the enemy had completely withdrawn. The Battle of the Bulge was won.

24

Across the Rhine

'I had never seen such destruction – the smoking town of Wesel had ceased to exist.'

David Niven

The First French Army had reached Mulhouse, in the Alsace region, in November 1944, but the Germans had maintained its positions in the suburbs of Lutterbach, Pfastatt and Bourtswiller. For two months the population endured the artillery bombardments from both sides, taking shelter in a beer cellar.

In January 1945, hearing that German resistance in Mulhouse was dissipating, William Wyler, eager to see his place of birth, got in his jeep with Leicester Hemingway and drove to Strasbourg where the Brigade Alsace-Lorraine, under the command of novelist Colonel André Malraux, were holding out.

Malraux took Wyler to the edge of the Rhine to show him the German positions on the other side. Wyler enjoyed the experience of talking in Alsatian for the first time in years, but he was eager to move on to Mulhouse. There were only eighty miles to Alsace, but Wyler and Hemingway had to detour around the Vosges mountains, covering 300 miles while the First French Army engaged in the battle for Colmar, a German salient on the west bank of the Rhine. Northwards, the Allies had moved up to the Rhine but at Colmar a pocket of resistance still held out.

Lieutenant Audie Murphy left hospital and rejoined his unit which was fighting in heavy snow at Colmar. Fighting alongside the French, the US infantry crossed over the Fecht and L'Ill rivers and prepared to attack Holtzwihr and Riedwihr. The 30th US Regiment crossed the Maison Rouge bridge over the L'Ill but the bridge collapsed under the weight of tanks. With no tank support the 30th suffered heavy casualties, and Murphy's 15th Infantry was ordered into the attack on 26 January 1945. Splinters from an exploding shell wounded Murphy in the legs, but this didn't stop him.

The next day, at two in the afternoon, he watched as six German tanks appeared on the outskirts of Holtzwihr and fanned out into three groups, obviously intent on an encircling movement. Murphy told his men to get ready. German infantry, in snowcapes and barely visible against the snow, were approaching across a field. An American tank destroyer, trying to manoeuvre into a firing position, slid into a ditch and was stuck. The crew quickly evacuated it while an artillery observer tried to contact HQ by radio. Murphy, not wanting to risk the radio getting captured, ordered the observer to the rear.

He checked his map and on the field telephone called for artillery. 'I want a round of smoke at co-ordinates 30.5-60; and tell those joes to shake the lead out.'

The enemy barrage began, killing the US machine-gun squad. A second US tank destroyer was hit and the surviving crew bailed out. Three inside lay dead. Then an American smoke shell whizzed over and landed beyond the advancing Germans, launching the counter-barrage and felling many Germans. But the German infantry continued to advance, backed up with tanks while only forty out of the 128 men in Murphy's division were left; he was the only surviving officer from seven.

He ordered the men to withdraw, but maintained his own position, staying on the phone and sniping with his carbine. There were only 200 yards between him and the enemy. He fired the last of his ammunition and as he got up to withdraw, he caught sight of the machine gun still intact on the burning tank destroyer. He climbed on board, dragged down the body of a dead lieutenant, and began firing; three Germans fell dead. His tank destroyer received a hit, but he hung on.

On the phone he advised the infantry of the changing position of the enemy. Another shell hit the tank destroyer, knocking him over. But he got back up at the gun and opened fire again, even though he could no longer see through the thick smoke which kept him hidden from the enemy. The heat from the burning tank destroyer made his feet warm for the first time in three days.

Through a break in the smoke he saw a German sergeant no more than thirty yards away, leading a dozen of his men into the ditch. They never saw him as he turned the gun on them and killed them all.

Finally the corrected barrage Murphy was waiting for came and forced the Germans tanks to withdraw. Murphy gave a final position on the phone – his own. As everything blew up around him, he slid off the tank destroyer and discovered that his right leg was bleeding. Stunned by the explosions, he limped 'as if under the influence of some drug', as he later described it, back to his own lines, too weak and exhausted to care at that moment if he was shot.

Despite his shock and the injury to his leg, he refused to be hospitalized again, and insisted on leading his men in the next attack which finally drove the Germans from the area. After the battle, he permitted the medics to treat his wound.

With the pocket of resistance at Colmar, the Americans took Holtzwihr, crossed the Colmar Canal and captured Urschenheim, Kunheim, Biesheim and Neuf-Brisach. William Wyler and Leicester Hemingway reached Mulhouse. The store on Rue du Sauvage which Wyler's family had owned was still standing. He went searching for old friends and relatives, and drove to Lutterbach where he came across a French roadblock and, beyond it, a few hundred yards away, a German roadblock. In the no-man's land in between lay the frozen bodies of soldiers.

The Jewish synagogue on Rue de la Synagogue was still intact but the entire Jewish community was gone. Some had been taken to camps, others had joined the Free French forces. He could find no trace of any of his mother's family. He and Hemingway headed back to Paris.

After a period of rest, Lieutenant Murphy was transferred to liaison duties between the various units of the 3rd Division. He was virtually under orders now to stay away from the front, which vexed him, but he nevertheless armed his jeep with a .50 calibre machine gun, rifles and two German machine guns. He also carried a crate of hand grenades.

When the news reached him that his commander, Captain Hogan, had been killed crossing the Siegfried Line, he drove to his battalion's position where he found them pinned down in old German defences by heavy artillery fire. They had all but given up when he drove into their midst in his armed jeep, shouting, pleading, coaxing them out of the trenches and forward, smashing what was probably the very last pocket of resistance on the Siegfried Line.

Northward from Colmar, the Western Allies were ready to cross into Germany. On 8 February 1945, Operation 'Veritable', the invasion of Germany, began with a massive artillery bombardment on a single German division that stood between the Allies and Germany. The British, under Lieutenant General Brian Horrocks, took 1,300 prisoners by the time they reached the Rhine on 16 February.

On 18 February, Lieutenant Audie Murphy received the Legion of Merit for his action at Colmar. But his commanding officers made sure that he was sent further to the rear as they didn't want this real-life American hero getting himself killed, which he was very likely to do at this critical point of the war with the Germans on the run. There were a few more medals they wanted to pin on him yet.

The Americans' advance into Germany was delayed when the Germans opened dams on the Roer, flooding the countryside across which the Americans were to advance. On 23 February a part of General Omar Bradley's 12th Army Group were ready to step on to German soil.

The day before, Bradley summoned Marlene Dietrich to

his headquarters in the Hurtgen Forest. She found him in a mobile home; she recalled that he looked pale and tired.

'Tomorrow we're going to enter Germany,' he told her. 'The unit you're attached to is the one which will set foot on German territory. I've discussed this with the president, and he agrees that it would be best if you remained at the rear and visited hospitals. We don't want you to be seen in Germany. If anything happened to you, we couldn't assume the responsibility. The Germans would love to get their hands on you.'

Dietrich was distraught. She had longed for the time she could again set foot on her homeland, and she was anxious to search for the family she had left there in 1934. She pleaded with the general and said everything she could think of to 'tug at his heart strings'.

He finally gave in, but said that she could only enter Germany if she had two bodyguards to protect her day and night. She accepted his conditions and the next day she followed the 12th Army into Germany. There was little opposition, and Dietrich, rather than feeling threatened, found that the German citizens welcomed her even though they knew well that she was an American citizen. These were people who had had enough of war and of Hitler's regime, and they asked her to 'put in a good word with the Americans' for them.

She was billeted in a small German cottage in Stolberg, where the inhabitants asked her to help them, and was ordered to speak in village squares, telling the people to go home and close their shutters to keep the roads clear for the tanks.

In Aachen she and her bodyguards, who were glad to be out of the fighting, lived in a bombed-out house. She performed in the ruins of a cinema for troops who were about to be sent to Remagen and, it is said, made love to countless GIs. Whether true or not, she and her bodyguards contracted body lice. Every night the rats rampaged through Aachen; Dietrich hoped to be moved on, but their stay there lengthened, and they helped the Red Cross nurses to distribute doughnuts to liberated PoWs. Suffering from frostbite and influenza, she was ordered back to Paris to recover while the advance continued to the Rhine.

The Allies reached it during the first week of March. The biggest surprise to greet them was that the bridge at Remagen had not been destroyed and it was quickly secured by American troops. This was so unexpected that Montgomery was not ready to cross the Rhine as he needed a build-up of strength.

'This,' said David Niven, 'stoked up all the old friction between Montgomery's dedication to "tidy" battles and the American genius for improvisation. The super prima donnas were at it and the depths of idiocy were surely reached when Patton telephoned Bradley and said, "I want the world to know the Third Army made it before Monty starts across."'

Patton crossed where he was at Oppenheim on the night of 22 March while Montgomery waited until the next day at Wesel. Lieutenant Richard Todd led an advance party across the Rhine in assault boats to mark the dropping zones for the British paratroopers and gliders. Niven crossed in Montgomery's wake. He said, 'I had never seen such destruction – the smoking town of Wesel had ceased to exist.'

At Munster, the only thing he saw standing was a bronze statue of a horse. Hanover had also been ruined. The burgomaster there told him that at least 60,000 bodies lay under the rubble.

On the road to Osnabrück with the American 1 Unit, he saw a hastily erected PoW camp. He reckoned there must have been a hundred thousand men already inside. Following a night of heavy rain, the morning's sun was sending up a cloud of steam from the soaked and dejected soldiers. He felt that Hitler had begun all this but now that 'the chickens had come home to roost', he couldn't find it in him to gloat.

So desperate had Germany become that old men and boys were recruited to defend Berlin to the last. One boy was Hardy Kruger, the German actor. 'I was a schoolboy in Berlin during the war,' he said, 'and during the last six months of the war I had to join the army, at the age of sixteen. I got involved in the battle after the bridge at Remagen had been crossed, fighting in the south.'

These young boys in their black Hitler Youth uniforms were supposed to be killers. Some of them were as young as eleven. They were fortunate that many of the Allied soldiers who encountered them treated them like ill-behaved school-boys. Michael Bentine had such an encounter when he replaced an intelligence officer seconded to Typhoon Wing of the RAF during the invasion of Germany. After crossing the bridge at the Dortmund–Ems canal, the unit came under fire from a farmhouse. After a brief battle three Hitler Youth emerged from the building with their hands up.

When one of the boys stumbled, Bentine's quick reflexes had him lifting his gun to shoot the boy, but his sergeant stopped him from firing.

Then the sergeant took off his army belt and whacked each of the boys in turn across the backside. Bentine saw this as punishment enough. He wrote, 'We could so easily have shot them if they had tried to slug it out with us.'

It was an example of a nation's youth driven to such fanaticism that confirmed the stories he heard that Hitler had conducted some form of ritual brainwashing. The sights and sounds of the concentration camps which he later experienced persuaded him that the Nazis, as he had been told by the Poles, were indeed criminally insane.

While the Western Allies pushed forward in the weeks following D-Day, the Red Army had launched their offensive on the Eastern front, code named 'Bagration', on 22 June 1944.

In Poland that summer the German front in Russia began to collapse under a tremendous and merciless assault by the Red Army. By October, the Russians were forcing the Germans back westward through Poland. The ferocious battles decimated the civilian population as well as the soldiers. Air-raids and artillery bombardments devastated the land and towns.

In early October 1944, the Borocowska farm was commandeered by a German garrison. The family fled to other farms, but Roman Polanski was abandoned. He took shelter from the early winter cold in a nearby barn for a few days but was driven out by the rats and lice.

Snow came in early November. The Red Army was pushing forward, the Germans were withdrawing and refugees
took to the roads. Roman joined a group of refugees who were
heading towards Cracow. He was cold and feeble, and his feet
froze as he trudged through the snow; there were a hundred
miles to go.

About a week later they came to the Warta River by which
time Roman was sick with fever and suffering from malnutrition and lice bites. He collapsed and the refugees left him
behind, lying on the ground expecting to die. Seeing a barn
near the river, he summoned up enough strength to drag himself inside it and covered himself in a pile of manure; he felt
warm for the first time in days. Worms and maggots in the
manure crawled over him. He was delirious and weak, and on
the verge of death.

When he next opened his eyes he felt hands pulling him out
of the manure. Morning had come. He couldn't remember
where he was and didn't know who the men and teenaged
boys were who stood looking down at him. One of the group
picked the maggots from his hair. Then a heavy coat was
placed over his shivering body, and he slipped back into
unconsciousness.

One of the men, Casmierz Musial, picked up the boy and
carried him to a nearby village where a partisan family allowed
Roman to be put in a bed. He was fed, and each day after that
Casmierz came to check on him. He told Roman that he was
with a communist resistance group made up of men from
Cracow and that the barn was their headquarters. They
launched nightly sabotage missions to harass the German
retreat. Casmierz had been a medical student and he continued to nurse Roman back to health over the next three weeks.

By Christmas, while the Western Allies were engaged in the
Battle of the Bulge, Roman was well again. The Germans had
launched a counter-attack against the Red Army. In January
1945, the resistance group learned that the Red Army had
reached the outskirts of Cracow. The Germans were dug in,
having been sworn to defend themselves to the very last.

The resistance fighters decided to head for Cracow to take

part in the liberation of the city and took Roman with them. They gave him an ancient gun and taught him communist ideology. They reached Cracow a week later to find that the Germans had gone and it was now in the hands of the Soviet forces. The city was reduced to rubble, and thousands of people who had fled to the mountains were streaming back into their city, their faces shocked and weary.

It soon became evident that the communist forces, which brought with it a new government, was intent on suppressing the war-weary Poles and bringing the whole country into the communist union. Those with enough fight left in them and the will to oppose the communist regime formed new partisan groups.

Communist groups were allowed special privileges provided they helped destroy the anti-communist factions. Roman, having arrived with a communist group, was issued with special papers that allowed him to roam the city at will, acting as a messenger for a liaison unit of Polish communists.

He wanted nothing more than to find his family, so he made his way back to the ghetto and discovered his old house in virtual ruins. He began scrambling around, knocking rubble through a hole in the floor, not realizing that the bricks and timber were falling on to an unexploded artillery shell. There was a terrible explosion, throwing Roman against the wall. He lay unconscious until, a few hours later, he was found and taken to hospital. After treatment for concussion, he was discharged, and for weeks he suffered from severe headaches.

The Russians had discovered the sheer horrors of the concentration camps long before their Western Allies did. In July 1944, the Russians had liberated Majdanek in Poland. The Germans had already evacuated the death camp, but the Russians saw for themselves the evidence of the Nazis' Final Solution: gas chambers, crematoria, and the charred remains of countless bodies. In January 1945, the Russians came across Auschwitz.

There were camps in Hungary too, for politcal unreliables,

where German film star Curt Jurgens was sent. He had been making films in Germany during the war, but in 1944 Josef Goebbels, the Nazi propaganda chief, declared Jurgens a 'political unreliable' and sent him to Hungary. His incarceration was short, however, as in early 1945 the Russians drove the Germans from Hungary.

The labour camps were the first sign of extreme Nazi cruelty that the Western Allies encountered. On 11 April 1945, the Americans came across the world's largest underground V1 flying bombs factory at Nordhausen. Nearby was the labour camp of Niedersachsenwerfen which housed the 13,000 prisoners who worked in the factory. The Stevens Unit was there to record its liberation and watched as slave labourers, who hadn't seen sunlight in over a year, were brought up out of the factory.

Dick Kent recalled:

Ken Marthey and I walked through one of the barracks. There was a man lying in bed with another – two men to a bunk. We said we were Americans and one of the men was very happy with a weak, sick face. We interviewed some of the people and when we came back that man had rolled over and died. We saw some ambulatory prisoners who had bandages on them and were slowly walking around. There were many men there left to die.

Twenty thousand prisoners had died. Some worked until they dropped and were sent to extermination camps to be disposed of. Ivan Moffat spoke to a prisoner who had been a Belgian civil servant, asking him what he thought of the Germans.

He replied, 'Monsieur, you can take a dozen German soldiers and bring them before me lying here and shoot them before my eyes, and I would not blink an eyelid.' The prisoner died soon after.

The next day, 12 April 1945, President Roosevelt died after a stroke. Harry S Truman stepped into the breach. With the war so close to its end, there was little time to mourn.

Moving forward all the time with the advancing Americans was Marlene Dietrich. She was with General Patton, whom she described as 'a great man', when, a week after the liberation of Nordhausen, the German Army Group B was encircled in the Ruhr, and surrendered in their thousands to him. There wasn't enough barbed wire to fence them in. The Allied commanders had estimated they would take 150,000 prisoners. But by April they had taken 320,000 including twenty-five generals and an admiral.

Said Ivan Moffat:

It was extraordinary to see these men suddenly. They were in the fields, usually below the road, masses of them corralled together and quite co-operative in a way. They wanted to get on with it. It was an odd thing in a way with this enormous power having laid down its arms; it was a peculiar sensation, not of victory but just of this formidable machine now like a mass of sheep in a field, defenceless and unarmed, ready to do our bidding.

Patton wanted to question the generals, and took Marlene Dietrich as his interpreter. In German, she asked the generals about troop movements, numbers of soldiers, how many tanks they still had: everything Patton wanted to know about.

Patton, said Dietrich, was advancing swiftly – too swiftly for the Allied commanders, and not even an order from the General Staff persuaded him to stop. They finally ordered his gasoline supplies to be cut to prevent him going on. He told Dietrich, 'It seems that an American-Russian agreement has established the borders where Americans and Russians are about to meet.'

He was right. It had been agreed that Germany east of the Elbe River would come under Russian government. So would Poland. On 15 April 1945, the two armies came face to face at the town of Torgau on the River Elbe. The Americans were forbidden to make contact with the Soviets, but on 25 April, George Stevens saw that American and Russian troops were greeting each other and he quickly set up cameras to film the event.

Stevens encouraged Russians to pose for him. In sight of victory over a common enemy, GIs and British officers mingled with the Soviet soldiers. One old Russian officer went up to Ivan Moffat and said, 'Capitalist, Communist,' as a form of introduction.

When General Emil Reinhardt, who had forbidden his men to fraternize with the Russians, heard what was going on, he stormed down to investigate. But with George Stevens filming every moment, the general was forced to join in the celebrations.

For all the seeming friendship between the Western and Eastern Allies, George Stevens saw that beneath the surface the Soviets harboured profound hostility and suspicion towards the Americans. As far as General Patton was concerned, the feeling was mutual. The event marked nothing more than a publicity stunt to cheer the folks back home.

Further north, at Schwerin, the British 7 Paras, with Richard Todd, also met the Russians. The Allies were to go no further into Germany. The fall of Berlin was in the hands of the Russians.

The British soldiers, though aware of the death camps, were not prepared for what they found when they liberated Belsen, just north of Hanover. Dirk Bogarde was among the British who secured the two camps – one for men, one for women – on 15 April. He described this as a 'hideous liberation', and said that for such a long time he and the other soldiers had assumed that Germans were not unlike them. The sight of the emaciated inmates and piles of naked corpses, the knowledge that Jews in their thousands had died from typhus, starvation and mass murder 'erased forever the erroneous idea that "Jerry is really just the same as us." No way was he,' wrote Bogarde.

The concentration camps forever left their mark on those who saw the results of Hitler's Holocaust. David Niven told me:

You cannot begin to describe the revulsion. The sights and sounds that stay with you, the stench, all those things that you can never forget because they play like a film back in your mind from time to time, were more than even those of us who had seen all the other horrors of the war could stand.

There were also the labour camps. [Niven came across one near Liebenau.] The workers were from all over Europe – from Russia, Italy, France, Poland, Holland, just from all over Europe. The gates to the camp were open but there was nowhere for them to go. I have never seen such hopelessness. They just wandered about in a trance around the camp and outside it. There were prisoners from a concentration camp who shuffled among them, standing gaunt and lifeless, and barely alive. None of them knowing which way was home, just wandering aimlessly. It is a memory that comes to me like a snapshot, a scene frozen in time.

George Stevens, at Torgau, was ordered to drive 250 miles south to a small Bavarian town called Dachau where the Americans had discovered something on 19 April they wanted him to record on film. Near the town was Germany's oldest concentration camp and there Stevens and his crew were devasted by what they saw.

Rows of bodies, barely more than skeletons covered in pale blue skin, were laid out in the street outside the camp. Inside they found piles of bodies that had been due for cremation before the Americans arrived. Although Dachau was not a mass extermination camp, it was estimated that up to 30,000 people had died. They had been starved, beaten, tortured and subjected to medical experimentation. Stevens took film which was too shocking to show to public audiences in 1944.

Thirty-five thousand inmates were barely alive when the Americans found them. 'To a twenty-year-old young man with a sheltered life behind him,' said Dick Kent talking of himself, 'it was a terrible shock. How can one human being do this to another human being? Impossible to think of. How does one justify this mass murder? You just wanted to hate all Germans.'

Captured camp guards stood terrified while others tried to hide by dressing in the black and white striped clothes of the inmates. Stevens watched as prisoners identified the guards to an American major who could barely contain his anger as he listened to the guards' excuses. The sickened GIs shot 122 captured camp guards on the spot. Another forty or fifty were murdered by the inmates, beaten to death by shovels, clubs and rifle butts. Stevens captured these horrific scenes on film, much of it to remain unseen for decades.

In the month that followed, during which the camp had to be maintained by the Americans who didn't dare let the inmates go free for fear of spreading disease, around 2,500 people died, most from typhus, some from the shock of over-eating. Some died from sheer excitement at being liberated.

Germany was being smashed. In Italy Mussolini was murdered on 28 April. German commanders there agreed to surrender, on 2 May. On 30 April, Hitler committed suicide and the Red Army reached the Reichstag. By 3 May the last of the German resistance was put down by the Soviets and Hamburg fell to the British.

25
Victory in Europe

'They sent me and a captain to Stade as the military government – just me and this captain who ended up having a nervous breakdown, probably because he had no one else to rely on but me.'

Frankie Howerd

General Montgomery stepped from his caravan parked on Lüneburg Heath, south-east of Hamburg. Outside stood Admiral Hans von Friedeburg, Commander-in-Chief of the German Navy, offering the surrender of all German forces in the north of the country, including the two armies of Army Group Vistula which were retreating before the Russians. The last thing the Germans wanted was to surrender to the Red Army.

Montgomery was in no mood for negotiation: the German soldiers fighting the Russians would surrender to the Russians. All he wanted was the unconditional surrender of all German forces in north-western Germany, the Netherlands and Denmark.

Friedeburg refused, expressing his concerns for the civilian population and asking for assurances that the people would be cared for while the German forces withdrew. Montgomery told him that it was a little late for his concerns and reminded him of the concentration camps and the devastating air-raids on Britain.

Friedeburg, recognizing that Montgomery would accept no compromise, took the demands back to the new Reich president, Grand Admiral Karl Dönitz, at Flensburg. It was 3 May 1945.

The evening of the following day Friedeburg returned to Lüneburg to accept Montgomery's conditions. Outside the tent in which Montgomery and Friedeburg met, reporters from all over the world waited.

Sitting on a pile of logs nearby were Dirk Bogarde and Christopher Greaves, drinking coffee out of tin mugs. Montgomery came out and addressed the world's press, reading the surrender document and saying that unless the Germans signed it hostilities would resume. He went back in and at 6.30 pm the document was signed. Hostilities were to cease within 21st Army's Group area of operations the following morning at 8.00 am.

'Well, old dear,' sighed Chris Greaves, 'that's it. All done. All over.'

The two friends had hoped and had expected that they would find themselves in Berlin at the triumphant moment. It now came as an anti-climax, and Bogarde later wrote that he had never felt so useless in his life. They set fire to the mess tent in some sort of celebration, watched by two German women with their children around them. 'Kaput,' said one of the women. 'Alles Kaput.'

There came a period of time Bogarde described as 'a weird vacuum', in which after so many months of daily strain and anxiety, there was sudden peace.

A second formal surrender ceremony, that of German forces on all fronts, took place on 7 May at General Eisenhower's headquarters at Reims in northern France, effective at a minute past midnight on 9 May. The war in Europe was over, and Churchill and US President Harry S Truman agreed that 8 May would be celebrated as Victory in Europe Day.

Marlene Dietrich returned to Germany in the hope of finding some of her family and heard that her sister Elizabeth and brother-in-law Georg Will had been located at Bergen-Belsen. General Bradley had Dietrich flown from Munich to the small airport of Fassberg, and from there she was driven by jeep to Belsen on 9 May 1945.

There she met Assistant Camp Commander Captain

Arnold Horwell of the British Army who had set up his office in what had been the *Wehrmacht* headquarters. Georg Will was known to Captain Horwell: Dietrich's brother-in-law had been a special services officer for the German Army and had provided entertainment for the Germans who ran the concentration camp. He had helped a Czech actor called Karel Stepanek hide from the Nazis in Berlin and escape to London in 1943, and when the British liberated Belsen, Will made it known that he had an American Army connection.

Captain Horwell had Elizabeth brought to meet Dietrich. She had been in poor health but was overjoyed to see her famous sister. The fate of the Wills, who had both worked with the Nazis, was a matter for the military governor, but Captain Horwell promised Dietrich he'd do what he could to help.

Dietrich kept in touch with Horwell who succeeded in keeping the Wills from being charged with war crimes, but because of her sheer hatred for the Third Reich, she only ever referred to Georg as 'that Nazi', and later denied even having a sister. The end of the war had not lovingly reunited her, as she had hoped, with her family. She went back to America where she was awarded the Medal of Freedom for 'meeting a gruelling schedule of performances under battle conditions despite risk to her life'. She also received the Chevalier of the Legion of Honour.

William Wyler saw out the end of the war in Italy where he was shooting aditional footage of Corsica and Rome from the air as requested by John Sturges who was editing their *Thunderbolt* documentary. Filming from a B-25, Wyler suddenly lost his hearing. This was not the first time it had happened but his hearing had always returned to normal before. When the B-25 put down at Grosseto, he still couldn't hear. The base flight surgeon sent him to the navy hospital in Naples where he was officially diagnosed as being deaf.

It was a severe blow to him; he was sure his career as a film director was over. He returned to America where the hearing partially returned to his left ear. He returned home a depressed and desolate man. His wife, Talli, said she was 'stunned and shocked and couldn't imagine what had gone wrong'.

Doctors discovered that a nerve in his right ear had been damaged probably due to engine noise and the ever-whining wind while flying. That last flight had been the final straw. There was no cure.

In desperation, he checked into an air force rehabilitation centre in Santa Barbara, hoping the poor hearing in his left ear might be caused by emotional shock. He received sodium pentathol treatment and when Talli came to see him, she found him staggering around in a padded cell until he had fully recovered his senses. But his hearing never improved.

'It was tough getting adjusted, particularly with an injury,' he said, but he learned how to direct movies by using earphones plugged directly into the soundman's microphones. Because of his wartime injury, he forever after received sixty dollars every month from the government, tax free.

In Texas, Audie Murphy was given a hero's welcome in June 1945. A public holiday was proclaimed and crowds gathered to hear him give a speech. He was awarded the Congressional Medal of Honor, entitling him to leave the army. He quickly became the country's most decorated hero with the Distinguished Service Cross, the Silver Star, the Legion of Merit, four Purple Hearts, a Bronze Star, a Silver Star, the European Theatre Medal with seven Battle Stars, the Good Conduct Medal, the Distinguished Unit Badge, the Expert Infantryman Badge and the French Croix de Guerre and Fourragère. In 1948 he was also awarded the Cross of the Chevalier of the Legion of Honour in Paris.

He became a screen actor and wrote a book about his war exploits, *To Hell and Back,* which became a film in 1955 in which he played himself.

With the capitulation of the Germans in Holland, the Allies were free to enter The Hague. Sergeant Frankie Howerd found himself in the first convoy. He recalled:

I was told to get into a staff car, and it seemed logical to me to get in the one at the front. Somehow the trucks and cars behind got lost on the way and there I was arriving alone and first in The Hague in a chauffeur-driven staff car, getting mobbed by the Dutch people who must have thought I was Eisenhower or Montgomery. They didn't know it was Francis liberating them. They picked me up and carried me on their shoulders and they were all cheering like mad. I've often thought they were the most appreciative audience I've ever had.

The joy was short-lived by the Dutch. Despite their liberation, they saw little in the way of relief in the weeks that followed, as Dame Anna Neagle discovered for herself when she and a company of actors, including Rex Harrison, were sent by ENSA on a tour of Europe. They arrived in Eindhoven in Holland. Said Dame Anna:

I was shocked by what I saw had happened to the Dutch. They had been starving before the liberation, and although food had been brought in to them, they were still starving. Perhaps all the food had gone on the Black Market, but if so I didn't see it for myself, but what I did see was that these people just didn't have any food. My first realization of this was when I went out with some of the other girls in the company to go shopping. But there just wasn't anything in the shops.

Then I saw first hand the real deprivation these people were suffering when an officer who came to see the play offered to show us around. He told us that the town was a dispersal centre for people from concentration camps and that these people hadn't had any food deliveries for three weeks and they were plagued with disease. Neither Rex nor Roland [Culver] wanted to see it for themselves, which I thought was a shame. I think everybody should have seen what war had done to these people. I mean, to see the starving children with black under their eyes was something all people who make war should be made to confront. That was what war did.

I remember that Rex, who was never used to deprivation – come to that, neither were the rest of us – complained about the rations we did get. But we were in comparative luxury, staying in a hostel that I was told had been a brothel for the *Luftwaffe*.

For Sergeant Frankie Howerd there was one more duty to perform which baffled him for the rest of his life. 'They sent me and a captain to Stade [near Hamburg] as the military government, can you believe it? That's right, just me and this captain who ended up having a nervous breakdown, probably because he had no one else to rely on but me.'

Howerd typically played down his role in these matters as it became his style to send himself up. But he was in fact a far more competent sergeant than he ever admitted, although he claimed that his commanding officer, General Brian Horrocks, 'didn't think I was the greatest success in military government'. No doubt Howerd could have told him that, and realizing the hopelessness of his situation, Howerd quickly requested his CO to send in reinforcements. Before long there were an additional 200 men and officers. 'There were now more governors than governed.'

Germany was in every way a defeated nation. With the exception of the so-called 'Werewolves', a band of young Nazi zealots who stretched piano wire across roads in the hope of decapitating Allied soldiers, all the tired German warriors wanted to do was go home. They had begun the war with promises of great victory. Now the nation was brought to its knees and its heart torn out.

David Niven was driving along a road near Brunswick. Welded to the jeep's radiator were sharpened iron stanchions to break through any piano wire left by the 'Werewolves'. After passing through a village he saw two men in typical farm clothes on a one-horse wagon. 'But the man at the reins was wearing field boots,' said Niven.

I got out of the jeep, drew my revolver and told the corporal with me to cover me. I walked over to the wagon and motioned for the men to put their hands on their heads and in rather bad German told them to produce their papers.

The one who was wearing the field boots said, 'I speak English. This man has papers, I do not.' I asked him who he was and he told me his name and that he was a general. He said they were not armed. I saluted him and told them to lower their hands and said, 'Where are you coming from, sir?'

He said, 'Berlin'. He looked entirely dejected, totally despairing. I asked him where he was going, and he said, 'Home'. He said he was almost there. He looked to the village I had just come through. We just stared at each other for what seemed a long time.

Then I said, 'Go home', and then I added, rather ridiculously I suppose, 'but cover your bloody boots.'

He just closed his eyes, breathed a huge sigh that was almost a sob, covered his face with both hands, and then they drove on.

Niven said that he could not claim to have exerted much pressure on the 'squabbling field marshals and generals', but he guessed that he must have done his job well because that September General Barker pinned the American Legion of Merit on him.

Thousand of British PoWs liberated in the east by the Soviet Army were sent to Odessa on the Black Sea coast to await collection by British representatives. Film actor Michael Denison, who had been attached to the Intelligence Corps for much of the war as an interrogator, was given the job of going to Odessa to bring the PoWs back home. The ship he travelled on from Britain carried Russians who had been held prisoner by the Allies. Britain and the USA had agreed that all five and a half million Russian ex-prisoners of war should be forcibly repatriated.

Arriving at Odessa, many of the Russian ex-PoWs were immediately labelled as traitors for having allowed themselves to be captured. Stalin's regime was not sympathetic to its own unfortunate troops. 'The Russians were very dispirited about this, even though they were home,' said Denison. 'They did not know what their eventual fate might be. Perhaps it's just as well we didn't know.'

On the return journey to Britain, Denison debriefed the ex-PoWs. They were a lot happier at going home than the Russian PoWs. In the Soviet Union, around twenty per cent of the returned soldiers were sentenced to death or twenty-five years of hard labour. Only about fifteen per cent were allowed to return immediately to their homes; the rest either died in transit, or were sentenced to internal exile or forced labour to rebuild the Union's bombed towns and cities.

Soviet power spread and grew, swallowing up Poland. In Cracow, the group Roman Polanski had arrived with was integrated into the new communist government. Twelve-year-old Roman kept himself busy searching for his parents, but the days passed with no sign of them at all. He joined a small gang of young scavengers who managed to steal a large cache of German bicycles, most of which they sold.

Roman was cycling one day when he suddenly heard his name being called. It was his Uncle Raimund, now an emaciated old man. Roman ran to him and was struck by the terrible smell; it was, Polanski later recalled, as though his uncle's insides were leaking through his skin. Raimund had survived the Mauthausen concentration camp, as had Roman's father, Riszard.

Raimund took Roman to see his father; his condition was even worse, but he had not learned to soften his manner. With no thought for the boy's feelings, he bluntly told him that his mother had died in the ovens of Auschwitz, and he still held Roman responsible.

Uncle Raimund spent the next couple of weeks gathering what was left of the family and installing them all in a ruined house. The end of the war brought little cheer to Poland. The Allies had gone to war over its occupation by Germany, and now the war had ended with the Allies allowing the Russians to occupy it. The Poles had won nothing.

26

Victory Over Japan

'I'd see Japanese soldiers moving swiftly from tree to tree, coming towards me. But I'm lying paralysed; I can't move my legs.'

Lee Marvin

While the Germans were surrendering, the Japanese were gradually losing ground and swearing to die to the last man. The forgotten 14th of General Sir William Slim had won great victories at Imphal and Kohima in Burma, and now Vice Admiral Lord Louis Mountbatten, commander of the Southeast Asia Command, told Slim to prepare for the complete reconquest of Burma.

In May 1945 Jack Hawkins was in the Saturday Club in Calcutta having a drink with some companions including an officer from Mountbatten's headquarters in Ceylon. The news was excellent: Rangoon was about to fall and a massive sea invasion was in place to cut off the Japanese retreat. The Japanese commander had decided that Rangoon could not be defended and had pulled out. An RAF plane flying over the town saw painted messages on the roofs of Rangoon Gaol where PoWs had remained: JAPS GONE. BRITISH HERE.

Hawkins and his companions were joined by 'a tubby little air vice-marshal' who had just arrived from China where he had been meeting with the Chinese leader Chiang Kai-shek. He told Hawkins he was taking his flying boat into Rangoon the following day and said, 'Why don't you come along? Meet me at the Hoogly River at seven in the morning sharp.'

Hawkins never could fully explain why he accepted the invitation – 'maybe it was the drink' – but he was there in the morning to find a party of about twenty-five waiting to board the flying boat. Just about everyone, including Hawkins, had each brought along a case of Scotch which was carefully loaded first. Then the party climbed aboard, trying to get comfortable on the floor which was covered in old sacks.

The pilot, Hawkins observed, looked apprehensive when he saw that the plane was overcrowded, but he unquestioningly started the engine and they set off down the river. They gained speed and bumped along but the flying boat was too heavily laden to take off. They turned and tried again, lifting hardly more than a foot in the air and splashing back down again.

After the third attempt the pilot told the air vice-marshal that they would have to lighten the load. The air vice-marshal told him to dump some of the fuel, obviously deciding that the Scotch was more important.

'But there is nowhere between here and Rangoon to refuel,' complained the pilot. 'We'll be skirting an island that is still held by the Japs.' But the air vice-marshal was adamant, and gallons of fuel were released into the river.

This time they just made it into the air, barely missing the Hoogly River bridge and to the relief of all made it over the Irrawaddy River at Rangoon. The pilot saw signals flashing from below and said, 'They don't want us to land. They think the river is mined.'

'Just pretend we haven't seen the signals and take her down,' ordered the air vice-marshal.

Hawkins held his breath as they came down, hit the water and came to a stop. They were met by a party of military police who were furious at having their orders recklessly ignored. The air vice-marshal stepped out of the plane and promptly ordered the MPs to take him and his party to head-quarters before they could raise any objection.

Several jeeps and a couple of Japanese military trucks were acquired and they drove into Rangoon, pulling up outside a theatre that was still intact and being used as the headquarters.

Inside, the brigadier in charge demanded to know what Major Hawkins of ENSA was doing ahead of the 14th.

Hawkins replied in no uncertain terms, 'For a start I want this theatre. In addition, I want decent billets for the soldiers in my command, and a good central building as a hostel for my entertainers. Is that understood?'

The brigadier conceded without a word of argument and Hawkins was shown to a hostel which had been used as a brothel for the Japanese officers.

On 3 May, two days later, British and Indian soldiers marched into Rangoon. The 14th had all the supplies it needed, but the Japanese were determined to make a stand east of the Sittang River, near the Burmese border with Thailand. Slim began to divide his forces for an attack on Malaya and Singapore, code named 'Zipper'. Then the monsoon came and the operation was postponed.

After spending almost two years on HMS *Aurora*, Kenneth More left to train as a fighter direction officer, learning to guide pilots by radio to within visual range of their targets with the aid of radar screens with PPI tubes. He passed the course and went on leave in London to see his mother. He took her out to dinner and, having left the restaurant's number because he expected to receive news at any time as to his next posting, half-way through the meal a call came through for him.

Michael Hordern, the distinguished character actor of stage and screen, now a lieutenant-commander in the office of the Second Sea Lord, was on the phone. 'I've good news, Ken,' he said. 'You are going to the Pacific.'

More expressed his surprise at this sudden shift to the Pacific. 'You're a key man now, Ken,' Hordern told him. 'So you're going to fight the Japanese.'

While everybody else was celebrating the end of the war in Europe, Kenneth More boarded the troopship *New Amsterdam* and sailed to the Red Sea, there to transfer to the British aircraft carrier *Victorious*. The American fleet was gathering for what would be the final air bombardment of Japan and *Victorious* was to join it. More didn't see land for over seven weeks as the aircraft from his ship joined the American planes in heavy bombing raids on the Japanese mainland, beginning on 10 July 1945.

In Burma, Lieutenant Dirk Bogarde arrived for Operation 'Zipper'. The rains were still falling, planes couldn't take off, and with no sorties being flown there was no work for Bogarde. He sat around with nothing to do in the endless humid days.

He was given the low-down by one of the officers as to what he could expect once the rains stopped. 'You'll probably be sent to one of the divisions, I shouldn't wonder. The bloody Japs have got their backs to the wall but they will fight like hell.'

Then he began hearing the tales of horror taking place behind the barbed wire of the barbaric Japanese PoW camps. 'Bound four of our chaps with bailing wire into a tiny bundle, head to feet, doused them with petrol and set them alight.' He was strongly advised not to get taken prisoner and was issued with cyanide pills.

It was 3 August 1945. Three nights later he heard the news that an atom bomb had been dropped on Hiroshima.

'God Almighty! Now they've let the bloody genie out of the bottle,' he said, 'we'll never get it back in.'

The next day another atom bomb was dropped on Nagasaki.

The Japanese leaders met with Emperor Hirohito to decide whether to accept the Allies' offer of unconditional surrender. Finally, on 14 August, the Americans accepted the Japanese surrender, assuring them that the Imperial constitution would not be abolished. The Japanese leaders broadcast their surrender to the nation the following day.

Little known is the fact that Commander Douglas Fairbanks Jr aligned himself with those who saw the retention of the Japanese emperor as the only guarantee of an orderly peace. Others maintained that Hirohito should be treated as a war criminal. There were thousands of Allied PoWs who agreed.

Fairbanks himself drew up the draft of the Potsdam Proclamation authorized by Truman, Churchill and Chiang Kai-shek, agreeing to the establishment 'of a responsible government of a character representative of the Japanese. This may include a constitutional monarchy under the present dynasty.'

Kenneth More recalled the tremendous relief that swept through the *Victorious* when news came of Japan's defeat. He and the hundred Fleet Air Arm pilots on board 'drank ourselves silly in a phenomenal party'. They stripped naked, including the commander, and hung from the bulkheads, among the pipes, singing and drinking and 'enjoying every delirious moment'.

On 2 September Tony Curtis stood in line on the deck of the *Proteus* in Tokyo Bay. It was an overcast day, but the spirits of every sailor were high as they watched the formal surrender document being signed by Japanese Foreign Minister Mamoru Shigemitsu, General Umezu, General Douglas MacArthur (as Allied Supreme Commander), Admiral Chester Nimitz, Admiral Sir Bruce Fraser (for Britain) and General Sir Thomas Blamey (for Australia) on the quarterdeck of USS *Missouri*.

The Star Spangled Banner blared from the *Missouri*'s loudspeakers and a massed fly-past of around 2,000 Allied planes roared above.

Somebody had to be punished for the Second World War. If it were not to be the entire German nation, it had to be the men who took Germany into the war. Twenty-one defendants representing the German General Staff, German government and Nazi party were charged with crimes against humanity at the Nuremberg Trials which began in November 1945.

John Ford was directed to have two of his men, Robert Parrish and Budd Schulberg, find photographic evidence for the trials. They searched through what was left of Germany for film taken by the Germans which they had failed to destroy. They discovered that film of the torture and execution of the conspirators who had tried to assassinate Hitler in the failed bomb plot of July 1944 had been seized by the Russians.

They tried to negotiate with the Russian liaison officer but made no progress until they happened to mention that their commanding officer was John Ford. The Russian officer quickly changed his tune; he was a great fan of Ford's films and he consequently arranged for the immediate transfer of more than 30,000 feet of vital film which was subsequently used at the Nuremberg Trials. Of the twenty-one defendants, only three were acquitted; the rest were either executed or imprisoned. Hermann Göering killed himself on 15 October 1946, the day before the others were executed.

John Ford received the Legion of Merit from James T Forrestal, Secretary of the Navy, for 'exceptionally meritorious conduct in the performance of outstanding services to the Government of the United States as Chief of the Field Photographic Branch, Office of Strategic Services ... He worked tirelessly toward the preparation and direction of secret motion-picture and still photographic reports and ably directed the initiation and execution of a program of secret intelligence photography.'

While Americans were celebrating the end of the war, John Huston was seeing first-hand what war had done to many of its soldiers. He had been asked by the army to make a documentary called *Let There Be Light*. 'Its purpose being to show how men who suffered mental damage in the war should not be written off as lunatics,' he told me.

> I went to a lot of army hospitals for my research and decided to film at Mason General Hospital on Long Island which was the biggest of its kind on the east coast, and all the doctors and officers there were very willing to help out.
>
> There I met Colonel Benjamin Simon who guided me and who took me with him when he observed his patients, making preliminary diagnoses from their general appearance. I was very sceptical at first about this form of

diagnosis, but I found that with hardly any exception he was right. He could tell from posture and gestures and facial expressions what the patient was suffering from.

One in ten of the patients admitted was psychotic. Most of them fell into the general designation of 'anxiety neurosis'. I understood that a little as I had suffered from it in some small way. Some men arrived with tics and some were paralysed. I saw miracles in that place, followng one particular group of patients from the day they arrived to the day they left.

The hospital hoped to restore these men within six to eight weeks so that they could return to civilian life, but there was never any pretence of effecting complete and lasting cures.

I saw men who arrived unable to walk given back the use of their legs. Men who couldn't talk found that they could. You see, these disabilities were mainly hysterical symptoms. And because the mental state of these men had much to do with their inabilities, they had to be carefully monitored because a man who suddenly found he could walk was capable of going to an open window and jumping. In some cases, a patient might overcome one anxiety only to have it replaced with another form.

Shock therapy was used on schizophrenics and catatonics. It wasn't something that we could use in our film, but I decided we ought to photograph it for the record. It was a very severe form of therapy in which the patient would arch his body so violently from the shock that half a dozen people had to hold him down; not to stop him running away but because he could break his back. It was that severe. And the sounds these men made when given shock therapy was really unnerving – a primal scream.

There were men there who thought they were Christ or under instruction from God or some deity. And, funnily enough, I found my time at Mason General about the nearest thing I ever came to a religious experience, because it made me realize that the main tool in psychological health is love. Now that may sound corny and out of fashion, but that's the way of it.

I thought it really said something important, that film, but the War Department saw it and decided it couldn't possibly be shown as they wanted to maintain their myth of the 'warrior' which said that we sent out boys to the war and they came back men; it was only the weakling that fell by the wayside. Well, that may have been the principle of Patton, but this experience taught me better. And it was truly the most joyful experience for me, and I felt like I was going to church every day I went into that hospital.

In a sense, the Second World War gave many British actors who were also true war veterans steady employment for many years. John Mills, Richard Todd, Kenneth More, David Niven, Denholm Elliott, Sam Kydd and many others all found a niche in British-made war films. The war did not have a noticeably damaging effect on the careers of those who had gone into uniform already famous, and from the PoW camps came a number of men who had caught the 'acting bug' and wanted to do it for real.

Only in Hollywood was there some trepidation among the previously established film makers who had temporarily aborted highly lucrative careers.

'I think all of us who had worked in Hollywood before the war and then came back to it after the war returned different men,' said John Huston. 'It was difficult to adjust, to know that there had been those who had stayed safe at home, making movies and money while others had done whatever they could to secure peace in the world. I think we resented coming back to find the new faces at the studios who had taken our place and we wondered if there would be a place for us.'

William Wyler had found that the war had been 'an escape to reality'. His values had changed and he found that the things that really mattered were human relationships, 'not money, not position, not even family. Only relationships with people who might be dead tomorrow were important. It's too bad it takes a war to create such a condition among men.'

George   Stevens   returned   concerned   that   post-war

Hollywood would not need him. Colonel Frank Capra didn't wait to be left on the shelf. The day after VE Day he and producer Samuel Briskin formed Liberty Films which would unite producers and directors of stature into an independent company, free of the studio system.

John Sturges said that he was lucky still to be able to continue working on *Thunderbolt* when the war ended, 'even though nobody was really interested in it by then. The war stopped too soon for us.'

On 31 October William Wyler was released from the air force as a lieutenant colonel. *Thunderbolt* was completed but put on the shelf because no one was interested any more; he remarked that he had sacrificed his hearing for nothing. To reflect his mood, he made *The Best Years of Our Lives*, the story of three men who came home from the war to try to rebuild their lives. One was played by real-life war veteran Harold Russell who had lost both hands in action.

John Ford was still in the navy when he made *They Were Expendable* which finished filming early in 1945. He had demanded, and received, a sum of a quarter of a million dollars from Louis B Mayer, whose MGM studios were financing the film, for the purpose of opening the Field Photo Farm, a recuperation centre for OSS veterans and paraplegics. Ford saw Mayer's money as 'conscience money' because Ford and his Hollywood army had been combating the Nazis while Mayer and his studio had stayed home to make money.

Ford then returned to Europe to see out the end of the war and came back to America in October 1945, suffering from an injured leg and exhaustion. He found it difficult to adjust and for some weeks had to walk with the aid of crutches. He continued to subsidize the farm with an annual payment of $10,000 and was never able to forget what he and his men had experienced during the Second World War. William Corson, a leading historian of American military intelligence, told Andrew Sinclair, 'You can see it in the subsequent films. All were acting out some of the themes subsumed on the Second World War.' He was marked by it for the rest of his life.

'We were all marked by the war,' said John Huston. 'All of us who lived through it. Those of us who made films were the lucky ones. We could find a release for it through our work. We could reflect it in our work. That makes us privileged. I don't know if the soldier who becomes a bus driver or a bank manager can do the same – but I know that in the movie business we could.'

The common soldier, the man who was not privileged and who had seen the very worst of combat, can be epitomized perhaps by Lee Marvin. After he was wounded during the Marianas campaign, he spent thirteen months in different hospitals. Many nights he had a recurring nightmare.

I'd see Japanese soldiers moving swiftly from tree to tree, coming towards me. But I'm lying paralysed; I can't move my legs. I raise my rifle and take aim; I can see their faces getting closer. I'd pull the trigger and *click!* No ammunition. Then come the shells screaming overhead, and floating on the wind I'd hear *Moonlight Serenade*. Then I'd wake up in a sweat, scared to death. One night, when I was in hospital in Hawaii I woke up from this dream, only it ended with the wail of air-raid sirens, and when I woke up, the siren really was wailing. It made the nightmare so much more real. I thought we were all for it, but it was just a dummy run on the island for some visiting brass.

He said that when he received his discharge papers he was 'as depressed as hell. I didn't want to leave the Marines. I didn't want to *fight* any more, but I didn't want to leave the Marines; I missed the cameraderie. I'd been through all that with those guys and we used to sit around, and I really missed all that. It was just an emotional thing that you don't leave behind. Sometimes the memories hit me like an exploding shell in my head.'

Bibliography

Bach, Steven, *Marlene Dietrich*, HarperCollins, 1992.

Behan, Stephen, *Milligan: The Life and Times of Spike Milligan*, Methuen, 1988.

Bentine, Michael, *The Door Marks Summer*, Granada Publishing, 1981.

Bogarde, Dirk, *Backcloth*, Viking Penguin, 1986.

Bogarde, Dirk *Snakes and Ladders*, Chatto & Windus, 1978.

Dietrich, Marlene, *My Life*, Weidenfeld & Nicolson, 1989.

Faulkner, Trader, *Peter Finch*, Angus & Robertson, 1979.

Hastings, Max, *Victory in Europe*, Weidenfeld & Nicolson, 1985.

Hawkins, Jack, *Anything For a Quiet Life*, Elm Tree Books, 1973.

Howerd, Frankie, *On the Way I Lost It*, W H Allen, 1976.

Johnstone, Iain, *The Arnhem Report*, W H Allen, 1977.

Kiernan, Thomas, *Repulsion; The Life and Times of Roman Polanski*, New English Library, 1980.

Korda, Michael, *Charmed Lives*, Random House, 1979.

Lasky Jr, Jesse, with Pat Silver, *Love Scene*, Angus & Robertson, 1978.

Loren, Sophia, *Sophia: Living and Loving*, Michael Joseph, 1979.

Madsen, Axel, *William Wyler*, W H Allen, 1975.

Mills, John, *Up in the Clouds, Gentlemen Please*, Weidenfeld & Nicolson, 1980.

More, Kenneth, *More or Less*, Hodder & Stoughton, 1978.

Moseley, Roy, with Philip and Martin Masheter, *Rex Harrison*, New English Library, 1987.

Niven, David, *The Moon's a Balloon*, Hamish Hamilton, 1972.

Nolan, William F, *John Huston, King Rebel*, Sherbourne Press (US), 1965.

O'Connor, Garry, *Ralph Richardson; An Actor's Life*, Hodder & Stoughton, 1982.

Olivier, Laurence, *Confessions of an Actor*, Weidenfeld & Nicolson, 1982.

Pertwee, Bill, *Stars in Battledress*, Hodder & Stoughton, 1992.

Quayle, Anthony, *A Time To Speak*, Sphere, 1992.

Ramsey, William G, *After the Battle* Number 3, 1973.

Ramsey, William G, *After the Battle* Number 5, 1974.

Ramsey, William G, *After the Battle* Number 6, 1974.

Ramsey, William G, *After the Battle* Number 11, 1976.

Ramsey, William G, *After the Battle* Number 69, 1990.

Sinclair, Andrew, *John Ford*, Allen & Unwin, 1979.

Taylor, Eric, *Women Who Went to War*, Collins, 1988.

Whiting, Charles, *The Battle of Hurtgen Forest*, Leo Cooper, 1989.

Index